PRAISE FOR EXCELLENT ESSEX

'A delightful new biography of Essex... akin to barrelling through Essex lanes in an open-topped sports car while Darley swigs from a hip flask yelling "Ask me anything"'
Observer

'A sparkling progress of personal anecdote, witty commentary and discreetly footnoted history... Even if you've never been there, you may find yourself reading passages out loud and dreaming of Epping Forest – or even Butlin's'
Country Life

'A loving treatment of a slice of England made schizophrenic by the "pull and push" of London... [Essex] will now be a little less misunderstood' *Literary Review*

'Darley has a fine sense of history and an appreciation of architecture and landscape... all this comes through in her fact-packed and often entertaining book, which succeeds in making one believe that Essex really is a special and unusual place' *Spectator*

'Gillian Darley illuminates the landscape and its inhabitants, revealing how generations of people wanting to escape social conventions and limitations have been drawn to those vast, open horizons. The book is as thrillingly eclectic as Essex itself.'
FRANCIS WHEEN

EXCELLENT ESSEX

First published in hardback in 2019 by Old Street Publishing Ltd.
Notaries House, Exeter EX1 1AJ

This paperback edition published in 2021

www.oldstreetpublishing.co.uk

ISBN 978-1-913083-02-1

10 9 8 7 6 5 4 3 2 1

A CIP catalogue record for this title is available from the British
Library.

Typeset by JaM

Printed and bound in Great Britain.

EXCELLENT ESSEX

In praise of England's most misunderstood county

Gillian Darley

ORDER OF PLAY

INTRODUCTION

Why Essex?

Could the country be at war again, so soon? Newspaper readers in early 1953 must have thought so for a moment, scanning the grim front-page images of piled sandbags, columns of refugees pushing belongings in prams, and flimsy houses knocked sideways. But what they were seeing was the aftermath of an unprecedented natural disaster which struck the Essex coast overnight on Saturday January 31st, entirely out of the blue.[1]

The combination of high spring tides and a severe storm in the North Sea had brought devastation and mass loss of life to the Netherlands, as well as hitting the east coast counties as far north as Yorkshire. Essex paid more dearly than anywhere else in England, with 32,000 people evacuated, and 114 dead in the seaside communities of Canvey Island and Jaywick, many of whom died from exposure, sitting on their roofs through the night, waiting for the help that didn't arrive. It fell to locals to save as many lives as they could, to retrieve bodies and to salvage valuable items: there was no formal flood response plan but the war had nurtured an informal civil defence structure, and people were ready and willing to act.

Many of the victims were recent arrivals into the county's traditional, close-linked worlds of farmers and fishermen. During and after the war large numbers of East Londoners had been forced to settle permanently in their little summer holiday shacks and it was these, roughly built and single-storeyed, that proved the most vulnerable when the waters came pouring in, coming in a deadly pincer movement from both directions. But among the misery, the loss of lives and livelihoods, there was also huge generosity of spirit, exemplified by the army of women, volunteers from all walks of life, who mopped out the flooded houses so that their residents could return, and lit fires to dry out the rooms. The catastrophe spawned its own legends too; none more celebrated than the so-called 'miracle baby', eight-month-old Linda Foster who was found safe and dry in her pram outside the house, many hours after her parents

Eight week-old Linda, the miracle of Canvey, in the arms of her grandparents

had drowned nearby. Her grandparents, fortunately survivors, would bring her up.

On the fiftieth anniversary of the disaster, the then Director-General of the BBC, Greg Dyke, recalled his Granny Cooper, who had refused to be evacuated at first, heaping up a mountain of chicken food on her kitchen table and putting the birds there before she agreed to get into the proffered boat. On her return, several days later, they were alive and well, still eating their emergency rations. These happier stories, however embellished, can stand for the resilience of Essex as a whole, a county well used to being battered, literally or figuratively, while never going under, and always willing and able to find a way forward.

As the North Sea hit from one side, London was crashing through the other. The sheer scale of the mid-20th-century working-class migration from the city into Essex might have drowned the other, essentially rural county, but it didn't. In physical terms, planning came to the rescue, while attitude, forbearance laced by a dash of puritanism, took care of the rest. In writing this book, I've been continually struck by the literal steadfastness – 'sted' meaning place – of the Essex landscape and people. This is a yeoman countryside, in which staying put has always been the norm, come what may.

This is an upbeat book about Essex, somewhere many people would prefer to overlook, or demean with a handful of tired clichés, TOWIE, the bad news from Romford (no longer in Essex) or the downside of Harlow New Town. An acute friend pointed out that my title, *Excellent Essex* was, at first glance, an oxymoron – when 'apparently contradictory terms appear in conjunction.' When I began telling people that I was writing a positive book on the county I got plenty of flak, accompanied by a lot of muttering about white vans, fake tans and white stilettoes. I also met Essex-born people who admitted shame at their place of birth, others defiantly proud of their home county. Essex is a place of enormous, divisive contrasts, one where the electrifying elements of capital and country create intense energy, a mood of dynamism and optimism that I capture in these pages.

And there have always been at least two versions of Essex. In 2014, the area centred on charming Saffron Walden, Uttlesford District Council, beat 118 fellow non-metropolitan regions for its excellent quality of life. The *Daily Mail* dusted down quotes from Sir John Betjeman and raided its files for glowing images of bucolic village greens and pastel-hued cottage fronts from small towns like Great Dunmow, Newport and Thaxted all, the paper pointed out with a total lack of irony, 'in the shadow of Stansted airport.' The inevitable 'pastoral idyll' was evoked alongside mentions of the average weekly earnings (£819 a week, compared to the £608 national average of the time) and the intriguing claim that 'eight out of ten people in Uttlesford think what they do in life is worthwhile.'

Not thirty-five miles away from this cosy fireside image, the journalist could have also pointed out that Southend offered the lowest average pay rates of anywhere of comparable size while the town was birthplace of the Access (later Mastercard) credit card, 'your flexible friend', a marker on the potholed road to household debt since 1972. Nearby is Jaywick which has twice topped the deprivation league tables, while becoming the fly-tipping capital of the eastern counties and catching the eye of reality TV-makers, for whom the slide into desperation is a unique selling point.

But perhaps geography is fate. Perched on the eastern edge of the nation, Essex people have long felt marginalised; a sense of being out of step which has sometimes led to extremes. At the start of the 17th century, in a state of both high dudgeon and heightened expectation, East Anglian Puritans began leaving for the colonies[2]. They took home with them: first there was Essex County, Virginia, then Essex County, Massachusetts. That shredded coastline of islands and estuaries, which turns out to be several hundred miles long if you take a piece of string to the map, points its numerous stubby promontories to Europe and beyond.

Simultaneously and continuously, newcomers arrived in Essex[3]. Dutch engineers helped drain the fetid marshes and reclaim (and defend) good agricultural land. Then came the Huguenots, fleeing persecution on the Continent for their religious beliefs, astute in business and philanthropic in their communities. Activists and campaigners, many of them women, found Essex a convenient and, sometimes, fruitful launch-pad for changing society as well as a discreet place to live in alternative fashion. Admirable and unusual individuals travelled in both directions: out to the hitherto closed world of Japan, in from Russia bearing radical ideas and literature. An Irish-Italian physicist and a Swiss engineer chose Chelmsford in which to build up huge, world-transforming industries on the back of canny inventions. Thanks to an earthquake in Colchester, a small Victorian hardware store in Braintree evolved into the company that drove architecture towards the twentieth century, while the most heroic and far-sighted battle in 19th-century Essex took place in an ancient forest, dotted with Iron Age forts, began over firewood, and became a fight for the rights of the poor over the rich. The county saw front-line engagement in WW1 when uniformed Germans were encountered quietly walking towards Colchester. Meanwhile, Essex has consistently offered Londoners, from an early 17th-century Lord Chief Justice to 20th-century plotlanders and independent-minded women, both temporary and permanent escape, whether they came for fun, fresh air or freedom from convention. It has long combined ostensible remoteness with ease of access to the city – the best of both worlds.

The county, so conveniently poised between Europe and the capital, has been welcoming to those in need of refuge, whether they were fleeing the pogroms of eastern Europe (via the East End), or the blitzed East End itself. Others disembarked from ships or planes: at Harwich, Tilbury or Stansted. These fruitful comings and goings continue to this day, and the county's liberal tradition, early established by exceptional humanitarians, lives on, despite chilling episodes of prejudice and racism.

More than most English counties, Essex has shifted and actually changed shape. Boundaries retreated as London grew, advanced as man and the elements did their work. Until recently, barges passed the Palace of Westminster at dawn, heading for a landfill site (in a location happily named Mucking) to deposit their unsavoury cargo into the great pits of disused gravel works, before heading back for more. The decontaminated detritus of an entire London borough now underlies Thurrock Thameside Nature Park. Yet beneath that, in turn, is extensive evidence of prehistoric, Roman and Anglo-Saxon settlement.

Some 5,000 professionals, students and volunteers took part in the speedy excavation of this site between 1965 and 1978, directed from a caravan by the archaeologist Margaret Jones, who became known to her many admirers, perhaps unsurprisingly, as Boadicea[4]. In 360 hand-written notebooks, the uncrowned queen of Mucking detailed the finding of some 110 Anglo-Saxon round houses, 170 Roman burials, numerous Bronze Age barrows and a massive Iron Age ceremonial complex bearing strong resemblances to those in northern Gaul. When Jones died in 2001, a generation of eminent archaeologists recalled their rites of passage at Mucking, surviving on crates of bruised bananas discarded from Tilbury Docks. Where the diggers toiled and before that, Bronze Age peoples buried their dead, there are now playgrounds, cycling trails and nature walks. As the immense vessels ply to and fro the rest of the world and the new deep-water port, the cumbersomely titled DP World London Gateway, visitors can take their pick between ship-watching, bird-watching or tucking into a nice shepherd's pie in the café. Essex does not just regenerate but repurposes itself, again and again, of necessity.

My credentials for writing this book are long familiarity spiked with curiosity. My passport says I was born in Sudbury, on the Stour. Before postcodes were introduced, my childhood home address was 'Sudbury, Suffolk' but later we were devolved to Essex, via a Colchester (CO etc.) designation. Essex was to the south, Suffolk to the north. It's where I caught the train to Colchester and later on, to London, the train tracks following the river bank. In 1966 the draconian Beeching Report inexplicably spared our railway line to Marks Tey. It's the kind of luck Essex people count on.

I went to the Technical College in Colchester, possibly the

first modern building I ever knew, a 1950s curtain-walled block, designed by the County Architect, in which I learned Italian. A couple of times a year we went to the repertory theatre, in the handsome, arcaded former Corn Exchange, to see forgotten favourites such as 'The Ghost Train'. In my memory, the town is dominated by these twin institutions, modern and Victorian, 'Tech and Rep'.

I knew the county town, Chelmsford, much less well, though on family trips we used to drive straight through (long before it sprang an inner ring-road) on the way to the Tilbury-Gravesend ferry over the Thames. From there we went on St Margaret's Bay, the shortest crossing point of the English

The author, picnicking among the stooks, c. 1956

Channel between Kent and northern France. Somewhere near Grays there was, surprisingly, a steep hill and on one occasion the car battery, which lived under the back seat of the ancient Vauxhall, quietly fell out on the way down. We free-wheeled a considerable distance before juddering to a halt. (Someone kindly picked it up and brought it back). Otherwise I remember an entirely horizontal landscape, which I felt obliged to defend while friends harped on about how flat and dry Essex was, as if neighbouring Suffolk and Norfolk were full of hills and lakes.

Now I spend a lot of time in an unambiguous Essex postcode, CM for Chelmsford, albeit with an Ongar telephone number and the recycling bins and rates collected by Epping Forest

Council. Across the gentle roll of the seemingly unexceptional countryside, roamed by innumerable surprised deer, watered by seasonal streams and peppered with old moats, I am still surprised by the distant glimpse of Chelmsford's only tower block across the fields. What lies under the distant city is perhaps even more surprising: the Romans left behind a sizeable civic *mansio* building and an octagonal temple complex, now buried by a pedestrianised shopping precinct and busy roundabout, respectively.

When I first wrote this Introduction, 'Why Essex?' seemed a very good question. Eighteen months later, the answer seems all too clear. For much of 2020, Essex has offered respite, open country, quiet delight and unsung pleasures to a population that cannot travel, socialise or do the hundred and one things with which it normally passes the time. The county has come into its own, and when we are once again free to do as we please, I'm convinced many people will realise they've recently found a new and unexpected favourite place. To that end, this edition includes a selection of 'Walks and Wanders', with links to (hopefully) helpful online maps via the QR code on the back cover or at **tinyurl.com/excellentessex**.

If this book helps readers make discoveries of their own, then I shall have done what I set out to do. People and buildings and landscape jostle in these pages: achievements are marked and celebrated, while idiosyncrasy and incongruity are left free to roam. It is a personal and very partial account, offered with affection and admiration for what is, on balance, a most excellent Essex.

Gillian Darley, December 2020

1   FATT, FRUTEFUL AND FULL
OF PROFITTABLE THINGES

Finding Essex

It was Daniel Defoe, best known for his depictions of a desert island he'd never visited, who brought Essex to life on the page. In his *A Tour thro the whole island of Great Britain*[1], he describes no part with anything like the immediacy – or for that matter, accuracy – that he applies to Essex. Whether he is telling us about the creeping fogs and marshy afflictions, or listing the splendors of Tilbury Fort, guarding the Thames ('the Key of the City of London'), he takes us with him. Essex is his destination in the first letter of the Tour, and as it turns out, he is going home.

The celebrated author had bought a tile and brick works near Tilbury in the 1690s, and probably lived nearby on Chadwell Marsh for some years. By 1722, the year he began the tour, he'd resolved to live in Essex again, leasing a farm in Colchester until his death in 1731, securing the timber rights on the land, and taking steps towards establishing another tile and brick works.

Defoe, as he assures us, can afford to be perfectly relaxed about matters of history or antiquity, since the 'excellent' William Camden, antiquarian and author of *Britannia* (1586) together with 'his learned continuator', the early 18th-century Bishop of London, Edmund Gibson, had already 'ransacked this country'. Even so, Defoe can't resist adding to their existing tally since 'lately had been found out, in the bottom of the marshes (generally called Hackney-Marsh, and beginning near about the place now called the Wyck)… the remains of a great stone causeway, which as it is supposed, was the highway, or great road from London into Essex.' Reading his words, I wonder if Defoe ever considered the reality of that ancient road, the noise of Roman traffic thundering over those huge, irregular blocks?

But as he left town on April 3, 1722, Defoe's attention was largely on the present. He certainly crossed ancient Bow Bridge – the first stone arched bridge in Britain, and created, so legend has it, after Henry II's wife Queen Maud fell in the Thames while trying to ford the river. Since then, the essential bridge marked a clear boundary for Defoe and his contemporaries, 'where the county of Essex begins', and he headed due east to Barking, thriving fishing port and ship-building centre. From there, fleets of cargo-laden smacks headed back along the Thames to Billingsgate fish market, while on every side quays and docks supported a huge civilian complex of boat yards, almost dwarfing the royal naval dockyards across the river in Kent, at Deptford and beyond.

Beyond Barking, on the road to Dagenham, there stood (and still stands, girdled by neat 1920s council housing) Elizabethan Eastbury Manor, by Defoe's time 'almost fallen down' but still worthy of note since, it was then said, the Gunpowder Plot was hatched there. Owned by London-based graziers, it was ideally placed for shipping livestock straight to the capital while the house was left to deteriorate around their tenants. From there on, Defoe pointed out how the Thames coastal landscape suddenly emptied, now becoming thinly populated salt marshes, 'rich in land rather than inhabitants' since the (reclaimed) marshy land proved deadly for those unused to its unhealthy air, even if it was a goldmine for farmers fattening their sheep and cattle there. The graziers themselves may have become immune but in this 'damp part of the world' local men lost their wives at an alarming rate from the ague, carried by mosquitoes off stagnant water.

The grand manor – just a riverside entrepot for Whitbread & Co, c. 1860s

As Defoe wrote, life there was little more than a tragic lottery, in which women were brought down from 'the wholesome and fresh air' of the uplands into 'the fogs and damps'. When they succumbed, the widowed farmer went back, collected a healthy wife and the cycle began again. Defoe cannot resist mentioning a farmer said to have been left a widower twenty-four times. Modern residents of polluted London might note the irony of a countryside unhealthier than the city.

If young women and the elderly fared badly, sheep did well. The Essex saltings fed animals bought at Smithfield in the autumn and grazed there until Christmas, when the butchers sold them back to London at 'very good advantage' as 'marsh-mutton'. The sheep were also dairy animals, providing fine cheese as well as milk and butter. Of the sole, codling, flounder, whiting and 'middling turbet' that Defoe listed as he nipped in and out of the creeks on his route north, the best hauls went straight to London. For optimum speed and freshness they were carried on horseback, night and day, along with barrel-loads of Colchester oysters. *Iter V*, the Roman road (*iter* means 'path') continued to prove its worth, and in all these ways, Essex fed the capital.

The dependence upon London of which Defoe makes so much, and which the National Trust-owned Eastbury Manor still illustrates, that mercantile pull and push of the capital, can, with a little licence, be traced right back to the Romans. They had adapted and consolidated an ancient Iceni – Celtic – route, crossing the then fast-flowing Lea at Old Ford, and drawn a new line, a well-paved and efficient road, including the excavated section that Defoe celebrated, between London and their first capital, Camulodunum (Colchester).

Having built themselves the largest complex outside Rome itself, complete with temples and an immense arcade, Claudius' invasion force finally drew down the fury of the repressed and heavily taxed Iceni tribe and their semi-fictional queen Boudicca[2]. There are strong grounds for assuming that she existed, and on this point the Roman historians Tacitus and Cassius Dio are in agreement. However, writing from the perspective of the winning side, a century after the facts, they have shed more doubt than light and that has only been exacerbated by all the poets and novelists who have felt inspired to tell and re-tell the story ever since, often in the interests of nationalist hubris.

No one gilded the slim evidence with greater brio and imagination than Henrietta Marshall in *Our Island Story: a History of Britain for Boys and Girls* written in 1905 and as she put it in her introduction, 'not a history lesson, but a story-book'. In these pages Boadicea (more usually Boudicca today), 'her blue eyes flashing, and her golden hair blowing round her in the wind' was a magnificent, vengeful figure who had inspired her people to hate their Roman conquerors and enact their 'fierce desires for revenge'. As she prepared for battle her daughters knelt beside her, 'sobbing with hope and fear'. It could almost have been the Boer War.

Created half a century before Marshall's book, this engraving presents the same tableau: Boadicea harangues, daughters sob to the rear

We can, however, assume that some of the Roman accounts, especially those of Tactitus, whose father-in-law had served as a military tribune in Britain at the time of the revolt, include elements of truth. It seems likely that Boudicca's husband Prasutagus was among the tribal chiefs who'd been paid to remain neutral, if not loyal, to Rome and that when he died leaving a wife and two daughters, the Roman overlords felt the Iceni leadership was now sufficiently toothless for them to demand this money back. It is also feasible that in Colchester, a town where retired Roman army veterans had a visibly better standard of living than heavily-taxed locals, relations were already strained.

Whatever the cause, retribution for the treatment meted out to Boudicca and her daughters (flogged and raped by centurions, respectively) or the insult posed by the territorial (and material) success of the strutting Romans, Camulodunum was decisively razed and torched, and those within its walls killed. After the 9th legion lost almost a third of its men whilst trying to relieve the city, Rome retreated to London where, in time, Boudicca's armies followed them and attacked again. As school children still learn, wherever pits and tunnels are dug in London today, a thin layer of red marks the city set ablaze by the Iceni.

Here, however, the fortunes of Colchester and London parted. After further victories in St. Albans, Boudicca's army was defeated, possibly near Milton Keynes. For Henrietta Marshall that moment drew upon her deep well of Edwardian sentimentality, as well as adjectival overload. For her daughters:

> 'she was no longer a queen of fury but a loving mother. The end was upon them. Now taking a golden cup in her hands, "Drink," she said gently. The eldest daughter obeyed proudly and gladly, but the younger one was afraid. "Must I, mother?" she asked timidly. "Yes, dear one," said Boadicea gently. "I too will drink, and we shall meet again." The Romans bursting in upon them soon after found 'the great queen dead, with her daughters in her arms.'

Surrounded by fertile farmland and bisected by a great tidal waterway, London could hardly fail to renew itself. Colchester, however, remained something of a service town, dependent on the needs of Rome. It was rebuilt, on a larger scale than before, with a magnificent arcade surrounding the plinth of the destroyed temple. The full extent of this later arcade only became clear in 2016, after preparatory works for a new block of flats unearthed an archaeological site of enormous extent and value. The town, renamed 'Colonia Claudia Victricensis' (the City of Claudius' Victory) had thrived again for a couple of centuries, before the Empire began to crumble, marauding Saxon pirates appeared on eastern shores and the shrinking city edged back to agriculture. Colchester could never have become a capital, its options for trade curtailed by the feeble Colne river, but it is interesting to imagine what Britain and indeed the whole of Europe might look like today if it had.

The one constant, it seems, has been the oyster, nourished

by the mineral rich waters of the Pyefleet Creek which almost, but not entirely, turns Mersea into a proper island instead of a peninsula with ambitions. According to the Roman historian Juvenal, Colchester oysters were gulped down on the banks of the Tiber, and their distinctive shells have been found in settlements as far north as Hadrian's Wall. Romans had found ways to preserve fresh oysters, packed in snow, ice or seaweed, so that they could be transported over long distances; a volume of choice Roman recipes (named after the imperial cook Apicius) shared this advice, but even so the major part of the cargo must have arrived dead, and pungent. Closer to home, and our own day, every year a party of Colchester's great and good declares the harvesting season open at the start of September, starting the morning by going out in an oyster dredger and ending it with a fine lunch, it being the Mayor's privilege to taste the first oyster. In 2010, the incumbent became seasick and the waterborne part of the event had to be cut short. In late October, a civic Oyster Feast takes place in the town with guests, dignitaries and celebrities, invited from near and far to an 'historic' ceremony that was reinstated in the mid-19th century. No doubt the modern menu is more balanced but in 1898, when the Duke of Cumberland was one of the guests of honour, it was pointed out that a menu consisting only of 'unlimited oysters and brown bread and butter, all of primest quality' tended to dampen the diners' pleasure, despite the 'usual hilarity' provoked by feeble oyster jokes.[3]

From 1566 Colchester's ecologically-minded town council had declared a moratorium on dredging oysters during the April to mid-September 'breeding season'. Previously there had been a panic caused by over-fishing (perhaps fuelled by rumours of the aphrodisiac properties of the mollusc). All that changed, however, in 1741, when a scandal of the 'rotten borough' genus led to Colchester losing the ancient rights it had held over the fishing of the creeks and waters down to the sea. Control of the oyster beds was handed, via Act of Parliament, to an independent panel composed of Justices of the Peace and dredgermen from nearby Mersea. These men formed their own trading company, sharing profits and paying Colchester a fixed rent, at the same time as adjudicating on the proper price of their silver-shelled cargo, which unsurprisingly rose steadily. Eventually, the city fathers and the newly-wealthy dredgermen agreed to form a joint company and share the booty. That was when the 'quality' in Colchester began to show their renewed, and sustained, interest in the quality of the first-fished oysters.

COLCHESTER OYSTER FEAST.

Another lively feast in 1916

So lucrative was the market around 1850 that one of several coastguard watch ships – habitually anchored in the rivers Crouch and Roach to keep an eye out for smugglers – was moved closer to Paglesham Hard, specifically to protect oystermen from theft. The little ship in question was HMS *Beagle*, the ten-gun brig that had sailed away from Devonport in late December 1831 with twenty-two-year old Charles Darwin aboard. For him and his survey colleagues, the boat was to be their mobile base camp for the next five years, during which he made the observations and notes that would later crystallise into radical evolutionary theory. That *Beagle*, the nursery of these ideas, should have ended up on the fringes of puritan Essex, where the Bible was considered the very literal word of God, is surely the happiest of paradoxes[4].

As Darwin published his *The Origin of Species* in 1859, the ageing vessel, all its significance long forgotten and with civil status renamed Watch Vessel no 7, was now home to two coastguard officials and their families. Taken onto the saltings in the 1860s, it was partially broken up and then quite forgotten. In 2002, encouraged by occasional finds of ballast and timber and driven by tenacious, knowledgeable locals – as well as a gratifying filip from the late Professor Colin Pillinger, who had decided to call his Mars spacecraft *Beagle 2* – a scientific team began to investigate around Paglesham. They found evidence of a ship fitting the description of the *Beagle* there, albeit some seven metres down in the mud. *Beagle 1* seemed to have been located at last. Unlike *Beagle 2*…

Today's Colchester is reminiscent of that tantalizing mud at Paglesham, disguising and consuming everything that went before. To reach Colchester Town, as the little station in the centre is called (the larger one, on the mainline to Ipswich, is in the north of the city), the train takes a looping alternative route, going over a level crossing that rudely scissors through a stretch of medieval town only to arrive back quite near to where it had branched off in the first place.

Once on foot, you head into town past the 1980s brick Magistrates Court, perhaps diverting through the denuded remnants of St. Botolph's Priory, where Roman tile bricks have been inserted like little tell-tales in the rubble-built walls and columns. Even its most telling feature, the west front, with its tiers of arches knitted over one another like an Arran pullover, is shorn of the romance that John Constable found when he sketched it in 1809, half-buried and sprouting random vegetation. Since then, the railway line and the road system have between them carved up this part of town, while the council endlessly messes with the bus station and cars are parked against the finest stretch of Roman bastion and wall, bumpers nudging the antique world from their bound gravel parking slots.

St Botolph's Priory: Roman tile bricks and later material knitted into the arches

Signs point on to the castle, the park, the canalized section of the Colne, the Roman Road, the Minories and Firstsite. Tiptree, local jam makers known around the world, operate the tearoom behind the Minories Galleries. From there, you look out over a garden and a now-incongruous Gothic summerhouse. A little further off, custard-coloured cladding and a black-glazed prow nudge into view. This is Firstsite, a prominent Lottery-funded arts centre designed by Uruguayan 'starchitect' Rafael Vinoly. The 'golden banana', as it has been nicknamed, became a major bone of contention between the town's two MPs as the years passed, contractors came and went, and the budget soared. Today it survives, commendably energetic, on a slender thread of goodwill.

Structures as solid as Colchester Castle, on the other hand, do not depend on public approval. Built on the foundations of the sacked Roman temple, which is quite visible once the guide points out its footprint, and gleefully repurposing Roman bricks and clay tiles, this thousand-year-old fortress is still largely intact. King John besieged the place, Matthew Hopkins interrogated his prized suspected witches in its dungeons, and a 17th-century ironmonger made such a mess of demolishing it with gunpowder that the project was abandoned and much of the premises given over to grain storage. Looking at the castle today, flags flying and grounds close mowed, it's hard to square that sturdy and proud image with the true historical picture: a classical temple first, an 11th-century castle next, fashioned from salvage like a stony bird's nest, half-blown-up and then forgotten.

But Essex is rarely exactly where or what people think it is or was – that is, if they consider it at all. As Colchester Castle was nearing completion, a quick-witted 11th-century *apparatchik* by the name of Hamon Dapifer, William the Conqueror's Sheriff of Kent, had eagerly spotted the potential for collecting a sizeable slab of taxes and tolls from traffic criss-crossing the Thames[5]. He cared little whether it came from the Kent or Essex bank. By his sleight of hand, or purse, the area in question became known as 'Woolwich in the parts of Essex' and remains so to this day. Modern north Woolwich lies, embarrassed, in the London Borough of Newham, much as North Ockendon now finds itself the only London village to lie outside the M25.

To begin with, maps of Essex were sketchy, its towns and villages scattered like birdseed across the countryside[6]. Essex was shown as a homely, cushion-shaped, bulwark against the eastward spread of London. In 1594 the lawyer and surveyor John Norden included the county in his ambitious, if uncompleted, *Mirror of Britain*. The River Lea cinched in the countryside tightly from the advancing city – much as the M25 does now – while signs of life progressively thinned towards the estuarial coast. Norden gave Essex a special encomium: 'this shire is moste fatt, frutefull, and full of profitable thinges, exceeding (as farr as I can finde) anie other shire'. His outpouring had hidden motives: he was buttering up the Earl of Essex – too late as it turned out, since the queen's favourite was shortly thereafter disgraced and executed. The sycophantic Norden rapidly engaged reverse gear, claiming that another man with the same name had written the words.

Equally chunky and impressionistic is the map tucked into the bottom left corner of Grayson Perry's tapestry, 'In its familiarity, golden' (2015).

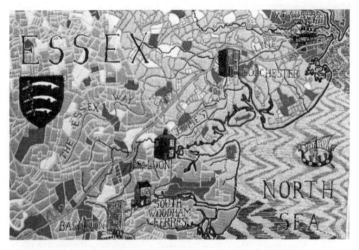

The haptic and the cartographic meet in Grayson Perry's tapestry.

The map includes the three seaxes, the short thick Saxon swords that from the 17th century became the armorial bearing and emblem of Essex, and concentrates on the southern half of the county, including the Essex Way and a handful of identifiable landmarks such as Brooke House, the tower block at the heart of Basildon, and Colchester Castle. Julie Cope is the fictional creation of Grayson Perry, around whose short life A House for Essex was designed a few years earlier. This remarkable building-cum-exhibit overlooks the River Stour in the village of Wrabness, and marks the Turner Prize winning artist's wish to build a chapel to his home county, with which he has an inspiringly ambivalent relationship. Referencing wayside chapels and pilgrim sites, including Julie's 'grave' nearby, it's also a bright and comfortable two-bedroom house available for short stays, and crammed with original, sometimes disconcerting, works by Perry (see Chapter 11).

Maps are more often created out of necessity than in tribute, of course, and in the case of Essex, vulnerability drove the engine of cartography. Whether exposing its flank to the North Sea or offering the Thames estuary for covert assault, Essex has always been open to invasion and memories of the brazen Dutch sailing up the

Medway in June 1667 were still raw more than a century later. In March 1799, in the face of the Napoleonic threat, William Mudge, director of the Ordnance Survey, was ordered to shift his team's effort away from the south coast and begin mapping Essex with all the speed and accuracy he could muster[7].

His initial points of reference were to be from triangulation points on Hampstead Heath (north) and Shooter's Hill (south) facing eastwards towards Brentwood church spire, Langdon Hill and Tiptree Heath. But the heavy smog over central London soon meant he had to find a better, more central, vantage point. The obvious choice was the 365-foot dome of St Paul's Cathedral. Heaving his heavy brass theodolite up a long succession of stairs and ladders to the very highest point of all, the top of the cross and ball, Mudge settled down aloft, balanced on a rickety platform, to take the essential measurements.

Triangulation complete, the team mapped the interior of the county, showing 'the Towns, Villages, Woods, Rivers, Hills, omitting only the [boundaries] of the Fields.' The accuracy and ambition of the project were unprecedented. By 1803 all the information gathered had been collated and engraved in outline, ready for printing. Although Kent was also being mapped over the same period (and for the same reason), that publication was private and so Essex beat it into public print. Napoleon became the unwitting godfather of the first authoritative map of an English county: published in April 1805, it was printed on four sheets, each measuring almost four feet (1195 mm) by six feet (1810 mm), at the scale of one inch to one mile. To consult it must have required an extremely large dining table.

A passion for maps gained me my only 'A' at Advanced level, in Geography. Crack the code of fonts and symbols on a modern Ordnance Survey map and you enter an intriguing maelstrom of history, geology, topography, economics and more – all nowadays laid out on a single sheet. A recent addition to the O.S. symbols is what looks like a pinch of ground pepper, and which on examination turns out to represent landfill sites;

there are surely whole social, cultural and economic histories to be written in amongst the changing ideograms of these much-loved maps.

What's certain is that, even in an age guided and ruled by GPS (to the extent where disorientated people drive into rivers because their onscreen device has ordered them to…), our map-reading muscles are still active. When, in 2015, the BBC's early evening news magazine programme, *The One Show*, ran a design competition for new symbols, there were seven thousand entries. The six winners included one for electric car charging points, another for solar farms. One has to wonder what gems were contained within the rejected 6,994.

The nature writer J. A. Baker, while himself maintaining a studied invisibility, added his own set of markings to his heavily-used Ordnance Survey maps: 'SH' for sparrowhawk, 'LO' for little owl, and 'P' for peregrine[8]. He pencilled and red-crayoned the terrain he traversed in pursuit of his quarry, particularly the Blackwater Estuary and around Danbury Hill, giving himself continuous *aides memoire*. In his years as an active birder, Baker never left home in suburban Chelmsford without packing his bicycle saddlebag with sandwiches and thermos flask, binoculars and notebooks, and those invaluable maps.

Maps, telling as they are, only go so far. They are informative rather than intuitive, rarely suggesting those aspects of the scene that endure longest in the memory. They cannot evoke the mewing of buzzards over meadows or the clatter of geese flying above you, the rich, yeasty smell of late harvest or the musty effusion of a muddy estuary or a disturbed pond. But Baker brought something personal to his precious bundle of maps with their initialled notations, especially of the elusive peregrine falcon about which he would come to write with such devastating force and insight. During the migratory season (several months of rich harvest for raptors) Baker quartered the lanes and waterways in an area bounded by the rivers Chelmer and Blackwater. He ranged far afield until a cruel arthritic condition progressively curtailed his mobility. More than an ornithologist in a narrow sense, Baker was an acute observer of the wider environment, reeling at the terrible damage inflicted by new agricultural chemicals on the land and its bird population. He took pleasure in grey plovers feeding in the muddy ooze, seeming to listen before 'leaning forward like Pointers on a leash.' But only the cheerful absurdity of the little owl with its 'furry eyebrows' made him smile.

Interest in the elusive Baker grew once the *New York Review of Books* reprinted *The Peregrine* (1967) in 2005, with an introduction by the environmentalist and author Robert MacFarlane. The rich cache of diaries and miscellaneous papers which turned up in 2013 revealed Baker to have been an employee of the Automobile Association in Chelmsford in the 1950s and 60s. The working life of this non-driver must have been an endless immersion in road numbers and mapping. Perhaps he worked on those detailed, *à la carte* route finders, made for AA members only, their meticulous mile-by-mile directions typed out, guillotined into pamphlet size and leavened, where possible, by interesting snippets and headmasterly exhortations, such as 'Courtesy *creates* courtesy' and 'Take a pride in your driving'. Could Baker even have helped to write the *vade mecum* on which my parents depended for our interminable annual drive from Sudbury to Helmsley in North Yorkshire, via Scunthorpe and Selby – a time-consuming but necessary deviation since they intended to avoid dual-carriageways? I like to think he might have been our anonymous guide. I also can't help wondering if Baker could have produced such luminously intense prose about the land and its life if he'd been able to drive, instead of experiencing Essex through all of his senses as he pedaled around the lanes.

I've a suspicion Baker was a natural hermit, part of a longer county tradition. *The Tatler* of July 1902 published a lengthy item on Hainault Forest's 'Doctor' William Bell, who spent some twenty years tending his vegetable patch and peddling herbal cures, whilst officialdom sought in vain to remove him. Bell was made of sterner stuff, perhaps, than the Cluniac monk appointed by Henry II for Writtle Forest in the 12th century. A second hermit was soon added, the first being unable to endure the solitude.

Ecclesiastical and mercantile, the ancient routes still offer a better way to explore Essex than the car. As bridle-ways or designated footpaths for long-distance walkers, shown by festoons of red (or occasionally green) dots and diamonds, they offer precious leafy tunnels through the wide, hedgeless, arable landscape. The Essex Way (thus named in 1972), runs from Epping to Harwich, follows intermittent watercourses and even takes in ancient fishponds, while in the west of the county it skirts innumerable moats. On the OS map, these spring off the sheet, loudly marked with the bold old Gothic script shared by remnants of Saxon settlements or Norman forts; in reality many are wholly or half-gone, dry or only seasonally full of water. (For many decades, OS maps had used blue to indicate whether moats were full or partially full; only dry moats were indicated in black.) Experts continue to argue about them. Were they for drainage or defence, or merely areas where animals or crops were safe from predators? One view is that they were essentially status symbols, like the crenellations on a house that no longer needed to defend itself but wanted to show the world that it could if it so chose. The late Oliver Rackham, historian and supreme observer of the East Anglian countryside, allowed that 'moats are still rather a mystery... a warning against trying to write history from documents alone.'[9]

In the mid-20th century, the Essex agricultural landscape was ironed into compliance, sweetened by subsidies for the farmers. The awkward old field shapes didn't suit the new and ever more enormous machines and were quickly run together to allow ease of access. By unhappy coincidence, that most prolific of East Anglian hedge trees, the elm, was decimated by deadly beetles at much the same time, during the 1950s and 60s[10]. With the hedges went many of the insects and then most of the birds; the paths still run across fields along the old lines, but now looking unalluring, like zips on super king-size duvet covers of plough or spring crops.

Maps show all the hamlets, villages and towns to be meshed, laced by lanes and byways, intersecting, bifurcating and occasionally making a dash for it, straight from point to point. Close examination reveals many 'dead ends', a promising sign for those, like me, in search of an unruffled rural scene with unsung architectural pleasures to share. When church attendance was obligatory for tenants and farm workers, unless chapel-going, the latter confined to the pews at the back, the track to the church was the most important, whether in life or death. Today it is often the road least taken. At Matching, the metalled lane leads nowhere except to a group consisting of the church, a jettied-out medieval 'marriage feast room', a former vicarage and a handsome yeoman farmhouse surrounded by an as-yet unconverted tithe barn and a cluster of traditional farm buildings. Another dead end lane leads to Norton Mandeville, where a small, flint-built church, rescued by a redoubtable band of parishioners in the 1980s, is wrapped by a mid-Victorian model farmstead with huge, low barns (all still in working use) adjoined by a sizeable Gothic Revival farmhouse and a couple of quirky pairs of cottages.

For some, of course, that combination of rural remoteness and relative proximity to the capital was ideal, whatever a mixed blessing it might turn out to be in practice. Just over a mile from Matching is the village of Matching Green, its shape dictated by the enormous common at its heart. Here, from Christmas 1903, the rising young artist Augustus John installed his wife Ida and their two babies, soon to be joined by his muse, model and mistress Dorelia McNeil in a complex, bohemian domestic arrangement. They were renting, Ida wrote, one of the only two ugly houses in the village, but the sizeable Green itself gave her immense pleasure, as did a burgeoning friendship with Dorelia, once she'd fallen pregnant herself. That winter the village was hosting 'heaps and heaps of geese', their cackling as dogs chased them almost the only sound to be heard, and a continually shifting series of gypsy encampments. No landscape painter, but a huge admirer of Romany life, John judged the village 'curiously beautiful in a humble way – the Green… full of ponds' although he headed back to London at the first opportunity, a connection via Harlow being just four miles away. Ida, her mood soon turning to acute depression ('I am surrounded by cows and vulgarity') had been left 'a lady slavey' by her husband. Short of money, without electricity and too exhausted by another pregnancy even to tend her garden, her rural fastness, for all its great skies, handsome elm trees and cricket on the well-mown grass pitch, was testing her to the limit: she had decided that Matching Green was 'a foreign land'.

Yet as she recovered her spirits again, following the birth of another son, she showed incredible mettle. Now Dorelia was nearing her due date, and Ida decided that the family dog Bob should go to guard her husband's mistress, so she set off on a bicycle, the dog running alongside, to catch a train from North Weald. She missed the train but pedaled gallantly on to Epping where the pair headed into London to deliver the amenable Bob. Her only complaint, after her return that evening, was of the effort of pushing the bike through the mud. By September 1905 the Essex experiment was over and both women and their many infants were in France. In March 1907 Ida died giving birth to her fifth son.

Parish boundaries, long fixed by manorial custom like common rights over village greens, bring their own anomalies, on and off the map. In *What is Coming: a European Forecast* (1916) H.G. Wells illustrated the difficulties of forging a new world order through the microcosm of the neighbouring Essex parishes of Braintree and Bocking, which were divided by a single road. Bureaucracy had determined that the south side be the responsibility of Braintree, an urban district, the north that of rural Bocking. Thus, for some 13,000 people, many of whom worked for the same employer (textile manufacturer Courtaulds) there were two water supplies, two sets of schools, two cemeteries, two administrations, involving two boards, two clerks, two series of jobs and contracts. Bocking, paying lower rates with a smaller population, had no rubbish collection. Wells took his tins to the Braintree side of the road and dropped them into the ditch there. If Braintree and Bocking could not begin to agree on shared services and amenities, what hope was there for a World State, let alone World Peace?

In late autumn 1915, the poet Edward Thomas, approaching forty but newly signed up for the Artists' Rifles, found himself in a grim, chilly shed in High Beech (often spelled Beach), an area of Epping Forest that had, he observed through gritted teeth, once passed for 'a pleasure resort'. Now requisitioned by the army, the building had formerly been in use for 'Sunday school treats' – a kind of bivouac for beanfeasters. Then as now, the place offered a viewpoint over the entire area. With Thomas' eye for landscape – in 1913 he had published a book on the Icknield Way, slightly to the west – and his lifelong passion for maps, it was clear that he had a useful role to play in preparing troops for the battlefield. Lance Corporal Thomas (promoted from Private) was set to work, helping a group of around a dozen men learn to demarcate, with compass and protractor, the features of the local topography[11].

It's a little surprising that the task had not been delegated to some company of enlisted geography teachers, explorers or cartographers, as the specialisms of the 'pals' battalions' had become many and various by 1915, including separate detachments of stockbrokers, footballers, golfers, London Welshmen and wool textile workers. The Artists' Rifles were themselves relocated from the forest to a better fitted-out camp just outside Romford, at Hare Street, Gidea Park where, for the next eight months Thomas shared his new quarters with the much younger Wilfred Owen, though neither knew that the other was a poet. As one of his biographers, the poet Matthew Hollis, surmises, Thomas may well have instructed Owen in map-reading. He is known to have made firm friends with the painter Paul Nash (whose younger brother John would later settle in Essex) and John Wheatley, an artist who would become the director of

Sheffield City Art Galleries. Over the long months, the particular quiet qualities of the Essex landscape must have, little by little, made inroads on each of the artists as they awaited call-up.

Considerably more comfortable in the new camp, Thomas was also able to visit an old friend, Edna Clarke Hall, who lived at the Great House, Upminster Common. The pair took the opportunity to renew their intimacy, taking long walks together, presumably plotted in advance by poring over local maps. It was during this time that Thomas wrote the four so-called *Household Poems* for his children. The first two, dedicated to his eldest daughter Bronwen and his only son Merfyn, were entirely embedded in the local landscape, knitted together by the place names of Essex, delicious concoctions from which he extracted rhythm and resonance, polyphony and playfulness, while finding rhymes that played with his children's names. Bronwen's poem, 'If I should ever by chance grow rich', runs through a list of places near Brentwoood – 'Codham, Cockridden and Childerditch, Roses, Pyrgo and Lapwater' – for which her father asks her to pay annual rent in early white violets, primroses or orchids – though if she found blossom on 'furze' (gorse) she would be absolved of any debt. The poem ends: 'Roses, Pyrgo and Lapwater – I shall give them all to my elder daughter.'

Perhaps when out cycling or walking, or when instructing his fellows in map-reading, he had been collecting the curious place names, with their whiff of local dialect, their hint of other tongues, often Norman French. In Merfyn's poem he plays out, line by line, the once familiar names of ancient fields, quirky as well as descriptive, alongside the odd words which designate the hamlets, parishes or farms. 'Margaretting or Wingle Tye, Skreens, Gooshays and Cockerells' then 'Shellow, Rochetts, Bandish and Pickerells, Lillyputs, / Their copses, ponds, roads, and ruts'. He evokes fields in which the steaming plough-horses laboured, as well as a more domestic setting, gardens with their hedges and shrubberies, harbouring blackbirds that sing at dawn. Echoing the theme of the previous poem, he would give all this to his son 'if he would let me any one / For a song ...'

Essex had taken Thomas by the throat. His role as a map instructor gave him a rich source for his own writing while consolidating his skill as a cartographer. By the spring, now a full Corporal, he was one of those instructing a hundred-strong company in the science of reading and making maps. In August he decided to become an Officer Cadet in the Royal Artillery where, on receiving his commission in November, he joined the Royal Garrison Artillery (Special Reserve) and prepared himself for overseas posting. In the meantime, his wife Helen and the children had moved to join him and they celebrated Christmas 1916 together in High Beech. He and Merfyn spent their last companionable hours together over a weekend in January 1917, studying maps.

In France, he was stationed near Arras and given the daily task of finding an observation post from which the German lines could be located. Yet in this landscape, hardly anything remained standing, not even chimneys or the ubiquitous poplars. He had to learn to relate aerial reconnaissance photographs to the near featureless ground; only maps offered clues now.

It has recently come to light that an unexploded shell fell close to Thomas the very day before he was killed by a direct hit. His poems, with their quiet landscapes sketched from small and telling details, seem the very antithesis of the featureless, grim war to which he was heading by his own choice. Even as he wrote, the fragile rural scene in Essex was being drastically depopulated on the battlefields of Northern France and Flanders, a trend exacerbated by the regional nature of regiments and the likelihood that the men in pals' regiments from single workplaces or walks of life, were heading for their deaths together.

In Essex, as everywhere across Britain, the wartime losses were later marked by village war memorials and the official Imperial (now Commonwealth) War Grave Commission graves scattered in village churchyards and town cemeteries. In the churchyard of now redundant St. Peter and Paul, Shellow Bowells, three graves, all commemorating members of the Root family, sit in a row. On one side is a cheap wooden cross, the writing only legible late in the year when the sun is angled low; on the other, a solid stone memorial from 1938. Between the two, a war grave remembers Air Mechanic 2nd Class, P.S. Root, Royal Flying Corps, 1915 who had in fact died in Chelmsford; once conscripted every fatality, even if from flu, was given an official burial. The three offer a graphic illustration of a country family, lifted out of poverty but over-shadowed by tragedy.

Over the fields, the parish church of St. Christopher, Willingale Doe (the name derived from a 14th-century grandee, Count D'Ou) houses a memorial on an entirely different scale and ambition. According to the *Illustrated London News*, it was the first stained glass window ever to represent a fallen soldier in khaki. The uniformed man in the two-light window on the south wall – supported by two angels, one to his head, one to his feet – was Major Arthur T. Saulez, middle son of the rector, the Rev Robert Travers Saulez, who had been the incumbent since 1906. Major Saulez was a thirty-three-year old officer in the Royal Field Artillery killed at the Battle of Arras on 22 April 1917. The window was unveiled exactly a year later. In the churchyard, now shared with the adjoining and earlier, St. Andrew and All Saints, the parish church of Willingale Spain, (this manorial name derived from a 12th-century grandee, Hervey d'Espagne), is another official war grave, marking a gunner, Edward James Tyler, who died in 1940. The second church, cheek by jowl with its neighbour, was judged surplus to requirements in the early 20th century and was assigned to the USAF during WW2. It is now cared for by the Churches Conservation Trust. On this spot, the strands stretch almost eight hundred years linking medieval landlords with professional men and modest farm workers, now on a level within a single Essex churchyard.

Like those oddly derived parish names, Edward Thomas' place names mostly still exist, some miraculously preserved by the Green Belt. They suggest something of the poet's months in the Essex countryside, offering, like Baker's markings, clues on an intensely personal word map. Though the field names may be lost, along with the field margins themselves, many still remain in farmers' memories. Typical of his day, when no such folk detail went unrecorded, a Victorian historian from Loughton, William Chapman Waller published an exhaustive list of Essex field names, perhaps now best enjoyed as Thomas would have done, for their poetry alone: Adams Beard, Bamberry Hoppet, Biggotts, Upper and Lower and Break Egg Field…

Equally individual were the cheeky, anarchic offerings of Ian Dury, a former Walthamstow College of Art student and frontman of the Blockheads. His lyrics were often based around limber wordplay, the most famous of which, 'I'm not a blinking thicky/I'm Billericay Dickie/And I'm doing very well' were constructed from Essex place names dusted with witty innuendo.

Dury claimed to hail from Upminster, which wasn't true, but he had spent part of his boyhood living with an aunt in Cranham not far away and for whatever reason, the chauffeur's son identified with subtopian Essex more than the north-west London suburbs he'd actually grown up in[12]. Perhaps it was some recognition of the marginal outsider in himself – he had pronounced physical difficulties after contracting polio at the age of seven – and within the county. At any rate, much like his 'Harold Hill from Harold Hill', Dury's name became so merged with that of Essex, and his own cheerful neo-cockney rhyming slang built out of perky place names, that not a single national newspaper fact-checked his true origins when publishing his obituaries in 2000.

In the early 1960s, the truculent, polemical and inspired architectural journalist Ian Nairn – the man who had coined the term 'subtopia' ten years earlier – paid a visit to Cranham. He had chosen the straggly village to exemplify the clash between the outer suburbs and the inner countryside, a moment of high tension now held in check by the imposition, unmarked on either OS maps or the ground but embedded in legislation, of the Metropolitan Green Belt. He surveyed the disappointing Victorian church and its roomy churchyard, the handful of unexceptional older buildings that were all that remained to signal the centre of the village.

Nairn, the only child of a draughtsman on the R101 airship, had been brought up in suburban sterility in Frimley (Surrey) after his father was relocated to Farnborough following the airship's crash en route to India in October 1930. 'Of all the ways London meets its countryside, this is the least credible,' he wrote of Cranham in *Nairn's London*, reflecting on how, only two fields from where he stood, the 'outward swell of building stopped dead.' Even so, against all the odds, the 1930s dream of a Green Belt had worked in practice, leaving Nairn to feel 'as Canute might have on the beach, but unexpectedly successful.'

Despite the verdict Nairn reached, the whole notion of a Green Belt remains controversial and politicized, pitting idealists against pragmatists, conservationists against developers and the haves against the have-nots. And, as a notion, it has a long history stretching back at least to John Evelyn's 1660 idea of a scented cordon sanitaire between the city and its riverside industries downstream, as proposed in his pamphlet *Fumifugium, or, The inconveniencie of the aer and smoak of London dissipated together with some remedies humbly proposed by J.E. esq. to His Sacred Majestie, and to the Parliament now assembled* editions of which were still in print, thanks to the National Smoke Abatement Society, as recently as the 1960s.

In modern outer London these tensions over restrictive planning, as it is now viewed, were epitomised when a handful of particularly right wing councillors in the London Borough of Havering proposed a 'Hexit', back to Essex. They were eager to evade the planning criteria and politics of Greater London and arrive back in laisser-faire, rural Essex County Council, the authority for the area until London boundary changes in 1965. As the borough artist in residence Verity-Jane Keefe says, the London Borough of Barking and Dagenham is continually 'gazing longingly towards Essex.' Back in Havering, the whole thing turned out to be illusory nonsense but demonstrated the rising tensions in which Green Belt legislation can often hold a precarious balance. Essex now fences the capital, instead of feeding it.

Where Ian Nairn had stood in Cranham, fifty something years on, I find that a small domestic development, tucked behind an electronic gate, has replaced the farmyard of his day[13]. A motley collection of converted barns and newer buildings considered to be 'in keeping', are nosed at by a herd of parked cars and vans. Otherwise, Cranham, with its scruffy little crowd of buildings gathered round All Saints church, appears hardly altered. It is still slightly down-at-heel, still remote, somewhat insular – with one of the lowest figures for ethnic diversity of any London ward.

The main alteration half a century has brought to the landscape falls on the ear, in the pounding dissonance of traffic on the eight-lane motorway a couple of hundred yards east. Seen from the M25, the open country around Cranham is distinctly lunar, dominated by the ranked photovoltaic panels of solar farms, and random sandy bunkers peppered across rather unfancy golf courses, no membership needed. Cranham is a typically confused beneficiary of 20th-century Metropolitan Green Belt designation, beset by growing 21st-century pressures, pushed and pulled between London and Essex, the urban and the rural.

Interestingly, the most famous historical resident of Cranham, James, Baron Oglethorpe, who is buried in All Saints churchyard, campaigned strongly against unregulated urbanization and the depletion of the countryside. A philanthropist and politician, opposed to slavery and to the brutal conditions in England's jails and armed forces, the resident of nearby Cranham Hall founded the colony (now the U.S. state) of Georgia in 1732, with the intention of settling the land with family-run cotton farms, staffed by the deserving poor of England. His view was that the pull of major cities like London at once made the countryside unproductive and drew morally sound people into spirals of debt and lives of crime. Carrying a packet of seeds from the Chelsea Physic Garden in his luggage, Oglethorpe was instrumental in establishing the cotton industry in Georgia and he forged strong links with the local Creek Indian tribes, later on bringing a number of members back with him to meet King George II. In some ways, today's Cranham seems to strain against its parochial character and be reaching out towards the wider world. The primary school is named after Oglethorpe, as is a university in Atlanta, and two otherwise ordinary Cranham streets bear the names of Georgian towns – Macon and Moultrie. And perhaps that tells us something important about the county as a whole: those who want to see the world must first get past Essex.

2 THE GOLDEN PATH

Getting to Essex

At the height of the spring fashion season in the mid-18th century, a successful Colchester milliner – of whom there were many – could leave town in a coach for London in the small hours of the morning, reach Aldgate with enough time to do business locally, bring her stock bang up to date and return the same day. At an average speed of around 10 mph, with time built in for essential stops, it was a long, tiring journey. From Chelmsford or Maldon, the journey was less arduous. In 1754 the enterprising Deborah Gooding advertised the Chelmsford Machine Fly (certainly no flying machine) departing from the Coach and Horses at 7 am to arrive at the Spread Eagle in Grace-church Street at midday, leaving again at 2 pm. The only delay came with a change of horses in Romford. A stage coach covered the same ground, heading west on Mondays, Wednesdays and Fridays, returning on Tuesdays, Thursdays and Saturdays. The fare depended on whether you travelled inside or out. Among the many alternatives on offer, Mrs Gooding included hearses[1].

In 1821 the body of George IV's estranged wife Caroline, the woman so recently debarred from entering Westminster

Abbey for the Coronation, was heading to Harwich so that she could be buried at home in Germany. Only nine months earlier, during a trial on charges of sexual misconduct levelled at her so that the king could gain a divorce (regardless of his own serial bad behaviour) she had gained the support of an unlikely alliance of radicals, non-conformists and feminists alongside 'the respectable middle-ranks'. When the case was dropped, the principled Essex silk manufacturer Samuel Courtauld arranged celebration illuminations and a procession, while an evangelical Essex clergyman at a pro-Caroline demonstration in London found himself alongside the French woman of letters and political thinker, Mme de Staël. Caroline's cause united unlikely fellow-supporters and now her cortege travelled out of London provoking serious rioting and unrest. When the procession of carriages and hearse arrived in Colchester, it was heralded by a crowd of two hundred on foot and twenty on horseback. Church bells tolled, businesses closed and a dinner for a hundred was laid on at the Three Bells. The High Street was lined with crowds.[2] As she lay overnight in St Martin's church, members of Caroline's household screwed a plate into the wooden coffin. It read 'Caroline of Brunswick, the injured Queen of England.'

Funeral processions apart, the great prize, assisted by well-maintained turnpikes and gentle gradients, was speed. In 1823 the *Chelmsford Gazette* recorded that two new Colchester coaches had been fined £3 7s each for 'furiously driving'. They were spotted, as bad luck would have it, by the magistrate himself, 'going at the extraordinary rate of from 14 to 15 miles an hour' (presumably his estimate was based on a comparison with law-abiding traffic). In the 1820s some forty coaches ran between south-east Essex and London daily. Just twenty years later, it was all over, despite the new dawn promised by the as-yet untested Essex Steam Coach. People found the idea of being conveyed on top of a boiler unappealing and there was, in any case, a far better way of harnessing steam power for travelling, and that was on rails with the engine and passenger wagons well separated. The opening of the Stockton to Darlington Railway in 1825 pointed to a revolution. In November 1843 the Colchester to London coach, the 'Golden Path', took to the road for the last time. Despite the loss of many jobs and a heavy drop in demand for hay, there would now be 'no other public conveyance between this town and the metropolis than the railroad trains.'[3]

The architectural historian Professor Nikolaus Pevsner began his epochal series of county volumes, *The Buildings of England*, with Cornwall. Three years afterwards, and having toured and written up several more counties, he arrived at Essex. He did not warm to it, noting that it was 'not as popular a touring and sight-seeing county as it deserve[d] to be' because people were revolted by 'the squalor of Liverpool Street Station', with its 'suicidal waiting-room' and 'cavernous left-luggage counters'. Pevsner's solution was to avoid the station altogether and to stick to the roads, having borrowed a caravan which his long-suffering wife Lola towed, as it swung alarmingly to left and right, through the winding lanes. They stayed in accredited campsites, thanks to their temporarily acquired membership of the Caravan Club[4].

In the postwar years, increasing numbers of people came to share Pevsner's view of the main railway terminus to eastern England. Its depressingly dank interior was matched by the confusion of its awkward layout, driven by rapid expansion in the 1890s, which had left two separate concourses linked by narrow and easily blocked walkways and only half of the platforms able to accommodate 12-carriage trains. A plaque within the station precincts pointed out that it had been the location of the 13th-century Priory of St Mary of Bethlehem – the original Bedlam. For the crowds of hurtling commuters on a winter evening, it was a distinctly hollow joke.

Rackety Tom Driberg MP – a furious champion of the county and its constituents – agreed, branding the station a 'hell-hole'. Driberg was as vociferous in the House on the unsung virtues of Essex as on the deficiencies of its public transport. 'Once you get away from the arterial roads and the shanty towns – the worst defilement of England since the heyday of the industrial revolution – you find a peaceful countryside, within 30 or 40 miles of London, almost entirely free from the inter-war speculative jerry-building and the "stockbroker's Tudor" which have largely ruined the once-beautiful counties of Surrey and Sussex and even Buckinghamshire.' But the unsullied countryside came at a cost, in a paradox Driberg was quick to point out: 'Rural Essex is largely unspoiled because rural Essex has always had the worst communications, certainly the worst train service, of any comparable area near London…'[5]

Fenchurch Street station – the original point of departure for a train journey into Essex – was charming, but it only served the south-east of the county. Everyone else was dependent on lugubrious Liverpool Street. Even in the late 1960s, when steam had given way to diesel and the LCC to the GLC, my journey back into London from Essex offered a grim introduction to the capital. The first phase of the journey ran cheerfully alongside the River Stour in a rattling small train with just two carriages. Then, at Marks Tey, we changed trains and platforms, transferring to the main line which passed through amorphous Shenfield, Romford and the City of London cemetery, before the crammed slate roofs of Bethnal Green and Whitechapel marked the still smoky approach to what the architectural campaigner John Betjeman called a 'dark cathedral'.

Betjeman was a fan: in his 'Men and Buildings' column for the *Daily Telegraph*, the future poet laureate argued that urban spaces like railway stations were just as worthy of conservation as country churches and medieval barns. With its structures of wrought iron and glass, Liverpool Street was, he wrote, 'the most picturesque and interesting of all the London termini' and, whatever their disagreements in detail and style, the apparently avuncular Betjeman and the still Teutonic Pevsner stood staunchly shoulder to shoulder when the Victorian Society formed in 1958 to battle with officialdom over buildings of that period and quality.

The railways had arrived early in Essex. The Eastern Counties Railway company opened its line from Mile End (later, Bishopsgate) to Romford in 1839. This was extended in increments towards Brentwood, then to Colchester, and was fully open by 1843. Only a year later, the entire line had to be expensively readjusted: the company had paid the price for early adoption, having chosen the wrong gauge[6]. And there were famous fights, as the main line through Ingatestone still shows, town to one side, entirely open country to the other. A landmark High Court case in 1843, *Lord Petre v Eastern Counties Railway Company*, hinged on the underhand behaviour of the railway company and so the Petre estate (still there) literally turned its back on the railway. Everywhere, fears and feverish excitement surrounded the new mode of transport, exemplified by the career of 'Railway King' George Hudson, who purchased the Eastern Counties line in 1854.

Hudson was a Yorkshireman, son of a tenant farmer, who'd begun his working life as apprentice to a linen draper. With a small inheritance from a great-uncle, Hudson had started out as an investor in the York and North Midlands Railway, and as he acquired a small empire of lines throughout the east of England, he also kept options open with a career in politics, taking one of two seats in Sunderland. With hefty dividends being paid out to investors, it took a couple of decades before people realized that Hudson's web of railway lines was more of a pyramid, wherein newly-hooked punters provided the funds that were dressed up as the profits for those who'd invested earlier. None of this necessarily mattered, until Hudson failed to secure a seat in the 1859 general election at which point, with creditors gathering and his immunity gone, he was forced to flee to France.[7]

Hudson's more fortunate customers, however, were benefitting from first class saloons on the Eastern Counties line, including plate-glass windows and mahogany tables and lamps. Soon afterwards, they introduced first-class compartments: bankers and stock-brokers, it seemed, neither wanted to tangle with the *hoi polloi* nor have their business conversations overheard. By 1862 some of the more troublesome East Anglian lines had been consolidated into the more resonant Great Eastern Railway. The line was crowned in 1884 with a luxury hotel at the terminus, so lavish that a train was brought up from the coast each day, bearing nothing but fresh sea water for the hotel's bathing pool. But the mass of the travelling public were commuters, so-called since their fares were reduced (commuted) by buying a season ticket. They were a staple crop of the Essex railways, enduring their twice daily purgatory to get out from the City of London. Even in 1919 the suburban lines from Essex, the busiest in the country, carried in excess of 107 million people annually. During World War Two, a wit observed that the best punishment for Goering and Himmler would be to ride, perpetually, between Liverpool Street and Romford.

Grand as this portal to the east had once been, few commuters had much affection for it until, in 1975, British Railways announced their plans to demolish and redevelop Liverpool Street and the smaller Broad Street station next door. Betjeman presided over a tenacious campaign with a cohort of high profile, outspoken, allies such as the comedian Spike Milligan and actor-politician Andrew Faulds, whose voice alone could drown out the opposition.

British Railways tried to deflect attention by announcing a prodigiously expensive upgrade of their carriage design on this route. In the autumn of 1981, ITV news splashed the story, the luminaries competing against the forlorn notes of a jazz band, itself impeding the exhausted commuters as they dashed as they had to every evening for their familiar dingy and compartmented trains.[8] Behind the scenes, the fate of the building was soon placed in the hands of a public enquiry, leading to a far more cautious and protracted phase of redevelopment that did not finish until 1991.

The end result, most agree, is a great success, with original features preserved and light and air brought into the station's luminous white-floored central concourse and its upper galleries.

At 11.00 am on 15 January 2009 three hundred and fifty dancers erupted throughout the station, as the tones of gritty Glaswegian Lulu ('you make me wanna SHOUT') pounded out and briefly drowned the whistles and public announcements. The travelling public seemed bemused and delighted in equal measure – caught in footage for a prize-winning advertisement, flash mob style, for a mobile phone company. You can still enjoy it on You-Tube. Meanwhile hardly anyone bothers to look at the station any more, heads bent over the little screens in their hands.

And nothing stands still. Broadgate, bearing the name of the station that was demolished and then becoming a sophisticated office development in the 1980s, is being redeveloped – again for offices but this time taking name of Broadgate Campus, giving it a belated touch of Silicon Valley. By the time you read these words, Crossrail (the Elizabeth Line) may have come tunneling in, a bit late, far below Moorgate, Broadgate and Liverpool Street, linking Essex with central London and Reading in the west. Shenfield, a town effectively brought into being by the opening of its railway station in 1886, is the matching bookend in the east.

In microcosm, Shenfield's development from village to the 'affluent commuter suburb of Brentwood' that Wikipedia describes it as, epitomises the railway-fuelled boom in Victorian Britain. A register of Shenfield men with voting rights from 1826 lists only seven: a pair of labourers, a gardener, an ostler, a carpenter and just one outrider of the middle classes, in the form of a land surveyor. By 1895, the rolls included solicitors and vicars with letters after their names, corn merchants, gentlemen and retired generals. And it's obvious what had drawn them there, the convenience of that essential railway link west, keeping them in touch with the male world of Pall Mall clubs, livery companies and learned societies, as well as a more familial social life with friends in town and even shopping in the new department stores and luxury goods shops of the West End.

Shenfield's changing face is also reflected in its crimes. Around 1820, poaching was the most common misdemeanor but by the 1870s one Alfred Walter Cammell was in court on charges of theft from the Great Eastern Railway Company itself, though whether the swag in question was coal, cash or cargo went unrecorded.[9]

A recent outrage marks the zenith of that journey from hamlet to affluent satellite of the capital. In 2014, Robin Clark, who was known in City circles as the Wolf of Shenfield (alluding to the film, *The Wolf of Wall Street*) was shot in the leg in Shenfield station car park at 5.45 am by a masked assailant. A man was soon arrested on suspicion of conspiracy to commit murder: according to some newspaper reports, this was a work colleague to whose daughter Clark had allegedly made suggestive comments. Described in the *Daily Mail* as a 'high octane city boy' the euro derivatives trader with the three Porsches and the two divorces then moved to Spain, to work in Madrid and, possibly, begin to solve his rumoured pressing financial problems. Meanwhile, rising affluence creates rising temptations for some in Shenfield: one recent burglary was foiled when the intruders were disturbed. They left fast, running away – as the local paper carefully noted – across the victim's 'bark garden'. However, the villains returned later, taking away thousands of pounds' worth of jewels and electronic equipment. Presumably the bark now usefully disguised their footprints… unless it was just a typographic error in the *Essex Chronicle*.

Chelmsford's changes have happened similarly suddenly but very recently. It is scarcely the same place that inspired the writers of the satirical *Framley Examiner*, who met at school in the town in the 1980s (see Chapter 11). In 2012, the Queen's Diamond Jubilee gave Chelmsford city status, alongside Perth and St. Asaph (population 3,500), almost a century after it had upgraded its chunky, pleasing parish church into a cathedral in 1914. The proud new city has acquired a Bond Street (the name taken from an earlier department store) and a John Lewis, as well as a vast bicycle park that could be in the Netherlands. Some old industrial and civic buildings are at a loss for purpose, such as the elegant Shire Hall, formerly the Magistrates' Court, a neo-classical building by the best architect in Georgian Essex, John Johnson. Until it became a loud bar, the Quaker Meeting House commemorated the heroic Anne Knight, abolitionist, suffragist and leading light in the Chelmsford Ladies' Anti-Slavery Society of the 1830s. But the County Hall is more recent, built between 1909 and 1939 with undistinguished newer additions. Despite the off-putting exterior, the interiors (a feast for the eye funded by another member of the generous Courtauld family) are lavishly fitted out with marble, fine stone, leather doors, oak and stained glass. On the walls hang a series of history paintings by various hands, showing in faithful detail a series of highly imaginative scenes from the county's past as seen in the late 1930s, in which women play a gratifyingly important role – Queen Victoria handing Epping Forest to the people, Queen Elizabeth I rallying her troops at Tilbury and Boudicca destroying Roman Colchester.

County Hall apart, the city core is no more than a symbolic hub to an expanding wheel, which includes an immense recent housing development dignified with the name Henry VIII gave to his Essex palace, Beaulieu.

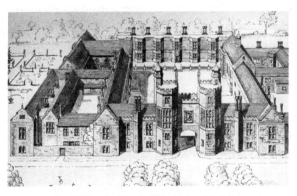

New Hall/Beaulieu/New Hall School in its original glory

Originally called New Hall, the crown took the estate from the Canons of Waltham Abbey in 1450, passing it to the immensely rich Earl of Ormond by way of recompense for his having been declared a traitor during the preceding Wars of the Roses.

The Earl's grandson, Thomas Boleyn ended up selling it to Henry VIII for £1,000, whereupon around 1520 the Tudor king spent a further £17,000 on fixtures and fittings, the chapel and gardens, whilst attempting to divorce his first wife and ensnare and marry Boleyn's daughter, Anne. This achieved, Henry evicted his own daughter, Mary, from Beaulieu although she was allowed back again after Henry had matched and dispatched a couple more of her stepmothers. In 1547, an inventory of the palace included 29 'great beds' with four bathing rooms and a royal library with 37 books, ancient manuscripts of immense value demonstrating a more reflective side to the notorious king. One of them, *Ruralia Commoda* was a Latin manual concerning agriculture and country pursuits written c. 1300, although Henry's own edition dated from around 1490.

After reverting to the old, pedestrian name of New Hall, it passed into the hands of the Duke of Buckingham, who sent his gardener abroad for plants and ideas, and commissioned a handsome avenue of limes, a favourite tree with Dutch gardeners. Visiting in 1656, the diarist and expert in arboriculture John Evelyn called New Hall a 'fair old house', greatly exceeded in beauty by its tree-lined southern approach. By now it was nominally in the possession of Lord Protector Oliver Cromwell, who had acquired the estate for the paltry sum of five shillings.

New Hall finally became home to the Canonesses of the Holy Sepulchre, a Catholic religious order fleeing war-torn Belgium. How the wheels of history turn: the Canonesses had set up their order on the continent to provide English girls with a Catholic education that was forbidden to them at home, following the Reformation sparked – in England, at least – by Henry VIII's desire to wed New Hall's erstwhile owner's daughter. Although Essex in 1798 was a more tolerant milieu, the nuns preserved a certain air of vigilance and secrecy, referring to their pupils as 'fishes', a name now proudly borne by New Hall alumni such as the designer

Anya Hindmarch and the ascendant Conservative Cabinet minister, Amber Rudd. Earlier pupils included Adele Domecq, daughter of the sherry magnate, who was visited at the school by an infatuated John Ruskin in 1838.

The Canonesses have now sold the surplus land, presumably ensuring the school's future in perpetuity, and what now remains of house and grounds are shrouded in the new Beaulieu: a development planned to comprise 3,600 homes. Not far off, the line of the avenue so admired by John Evelyn remains, the lime trees replanted several times since. From those new front doors, thousands of commuters will sally forth – and the betting is that most will be heading towards London, by train.

One of only two underground routes to venture beyond the borders of Greater London, the Central Line, from Epping onwards, is the second-most frequent service in rush hour, a statistic underscoring how just much human traffic enters from the Essex direction. Travelling back out east, along this longest of all tube lines, you are progressively peeling off the onion skins of outer London, those parts formerly in Essex and those parts remaining there. It surfaces beyond Stratford slicing through layer upon layer, offering an entire chronology of suburban housing for those with the eyes to see it – Victorian, Edwardian, interwar and, finally, postwar. An easterly loop, taking in Newbury Park – home to an underground aircraft factory in World War Two – to Chigwell, rejoins the main stretch and presses on, as one again, to Loughton and Debden, one of the first so-called 'out-county' garden estates to be built in the surrounding counties after World War Two by the London County Council. Then, quite suddenly, on the approach to Theydon Bois comes the countryside. The clue is in the name. Modest fields and hedges and old oaks – to one side of the track – serve as reminders of what postwar planning achieved, a line marked on a document to denote the end of permissible development, in theory engraved there far into the future. When the

Greater London Council (GLC) replaced the London County Council (LCC) in 1965, it took in the former Essex boroughs of Barking and Dagenham, Havering, Newham, Redbridge and Waltham Forest. The area now referred to as 'historic Essex' only survives, tellingly, in certain institutions, the Diocese of Chelmsford, the Brentwood Catholic Diocese and the Essex County Cricket Club.

This enormous bureaucratic change gave rise to all manner of adjustments and difficulties, some ostensibly no more time-consuming than changing the lettering over the entrance to a Town Hall from Romford to Havering, others very human and involving a strong sense of severed identity, even personal injury. Most people were, understandably, extremely confused. Historian Margaret Willes found that responsibility for her educational future had been handed on overnight, on 1 April 1965, from Essex County Council to the London Borough of Redbridge, yet without agreement as to which council would honour the grant for the place she had been offered at Lady Margaret Hall, Oxford. There was an awkward meeting with her bank manager after her (first ever) cheque bounced, before justice and persistence finally prevailed and Willes was able to take up the first Oxbridge place ever offered to a pupil from her school.

From 1965, the Essex county boundary no longer followed the dependable path of the River Lea. (The two lines didn't reconcile again until much further north, around Waltham Abbey). The Lea Valley, its industries having grown up where nursery gardens once flourished, is border country still. In *The Great Caper,* his biography of the Barking-born, radical actor-director Ken Campbell, Michael Coveney describes this area, where the fringes of London encountered the outer edge of Essex, as 'an experimental compromise between the town and the country, the expanding city and the defiant swamp-lands.' Provisional in many senses, the new boundaries threw up an 'edge city'. In the south, near the Thames, old gravel pits became a series of unlovely lakes, and on their shores arose Thurrock Lakeside Shopping Centre, at the time of building the largest retail park in Europe. Essex was filling up fast – and not only with water.

The Queen Elizabeth II road bridge opened for business in 1991 to alleviate pressure on the two existing tunnels under the Thames between Dartford and Thurrock.

Queen of bridges, the QEII

The handsome bridge soars over the Thames and is the back-drop to an archetypical volume housebuilders' town, Chafford Hundred, built from the late 1980s onwards on six hundred acres of reclaimed former industrial land adjoining the Essex marshes[10]. Seen from the approach, the cable-stayed bridge makes a dramatic approach to Kent, its four towers reaching almost 450 feet. The underground return journey – for traffic is one-way over the bridge, except when tunnels are being repaired – is more than a little bathetic, the cars, vans and lorries funnelled into Essex like moles incessantly travelling in single file. Before this, the cross-river journey had always been on the ferry, from Tilbury to Gravesend, a childish treat for those, like me, who did not have to do it that often. Perhaps to compensate for its inescapably horizontal landscape, Essex has embraced the vertical in its built structures, from the hawsers of the bridge to the stems and blades of massed off-shore wind turbines. Like a weird municipal flower bed in the water, a vast and serious wind farm frames Clacton's sea view over the cheerful oriental cupolas of the pier. It is only from the air that its extent is clear. Inland, spindly electricity pylons and inventive versions of the gloriously solid (and once essential) water tank are dotted around the countryside. In many other parts of Britain, the eye is easily distracted from these reminders of modernity – by downland or hills, mountains or torrents. Here in the east, where the land shades into the sea with little to mark the moment, the geometric and the manmade has the last word.

Inland, at peak harvest time, with no time to waste, fearing either a change in the weather or a turn in the market, the drivers of an army of massive combine harvesters chew through the crops, grinding on late into the night, their headlights probing the sky and the land and warning off the occasional hare or dizzy herd of deer. There is a man in every one of the machines (though possibly not for much longer) although navigation is by GPS. As I experience it from the eyrie where I usually write, their steady thrumming pavanne, the limelight on hedge or crop drowning out the moon and stars, is like a passing cinematic illusion, sometimes coming from several sides at once, a moment of Tarkovsky lost by the morning. In another twelve months, the dance will begin again.

But there is plenty of static drama too. The lumpen, muted form of the old nuclear power station at Bradwell-on-Sea looms from a great distance, adding a dash of menace to the easterly horizon. The ubiquitous John Betjeman had been one of many objectors when its construction was proposed, on a pristine coast, a few hundred yards from the remains of seventh-century St Cedd's minster. He attended the public inquiry held in Maldon in 1956, later entertaining readers of his 'City and Suburban' column in the *Spectator* with a neat description of the bureaucratic cut and thrust of the hearing. The case was heard by an 'amiable inspector' in a Congregational Church hall. A posse of resolute, besuited men from the Central Electricity Generating Board argued in favour, supported by skilled lawyers whose objective, in Betjeman's words, was to 'lead a witness into a trap and pounce.' For those like himself, unused to such gladiatorial contests, 'the ordeal [was] terrifying.'

Betjeman had joined a loose opposition of somewhat equivocal locals, torn between the tempting prospect of new jobs versus the threat to the Dengie Peninsula and its immutable way of life. He spent his lunch break up on the tower of Maldon's Moot Hall, looking out over the tiled roofs of the elegant town, full of fine Georgian merchant houses, and over a 'mild pastoral landscape and the gleaming water.' He pondered how the electricity officials, enmeshed in jargon and technicalities, could remain so indifferent to their surroundings. 'Yet to mention beauty at that enquiry seemed rather like talking about religion at a canasta party, essentially bad form.'

In the 1950s, Michael Morpurgo spent school holidays at Bradwell, spotting skylarks and 'shouting into the sea wind', an idyll abruptly curtailed when the power station appeared, and the family moved[11]. His 2018 novel *Flamingo Boy* transports that sense, of something treasured in the shadow of a monster, to the Camargue salt-flats and invading Nazis.

Bradwell operated from 1962 until 2002, and the contaminated hulk continues to threaten the lansdcape while decommissioning continues with difficulty. Meanwhile plans are being drawn up for a so-called Bradwell B, a joint venture by the Chinese state nuclear power corporation (CGN) and a British spawn of EDF, the French state enterprise. Maldon District Council is back in the firing line again, this time faced by two global power giants and an environmental lobby of great sophistication and considerable powers of persuasion. So far, the council has only been required to give consent to initial exploratory works. Their job is only just beginning.

Welcome or not, the carcass of Bradwell A adds an extra eeriness to the Dengie peninsula, although its current treelessness is due to that plague of the mid-20th century, Dutch Elm disease. As a name, Dengie seems disturbing – until you disassociate it from the mosquito-borne fever of a similar spelling, which is Swahili in origin and nothing to do with the malarial infestations of the Essex marshes. (The *Oxford Dictionary of Place Names* applies its default Old English explanation to Dengie: 'island or well-watered land belonging to a man named Dene', which is more comfortable even if mere supposition.) The great slab of clay that makes the Dengie Peninsula is exceedingly fertile and well protected from the sea. Few people live here and there are rare survivals, such as some traces of dialect (discussed in Chapter 6) and telling physical features, such as the star-fish shaped decoy ponds that wildfowlers once used while out on the marshes. As John Hunter, the great authority on Essex landscape, made clear, farmers on the Dengie have been working to reclaim and secure their land since at least the 17th century[12]. Now an ambitious cooperative venture grows alfalfa and lucerne for animal foodstuffs and hardly grown elsewhere. The sharp green fields, far denser than hay or other feed crops, are highly distinctive; the Dengie is always a landscape apart.

21st-century Essex is becoming an ever-denser mesh of lines, road and rail, bridge and runway, all centred on the capital, thinning out towards the periphery. In 1963, Dr Beeching's report, cutting branch railway lines across the country by a third, let Essex off lightly. Rail tracks and trunk roads fan out as spokes from the central London hub, main line railways and fringes of the underground system nose up into the daylight as if desperate for fresh air. Only airport runways (and a canal or two) are short and defined, but there is a continuous descant of expansion plans involving further runways. Currently Southend has one runway, and there are two at Stansted. A succession of false alarms and government flannelling about airport expansion has nurtured local folklore, such as the classic taxi driver's claim that the third runway at Stansted is already there, hidden under the soil and vegetation, rather like the paved Roman road to Colchester, biding its time.

Also underfoot and largely out of sight are dozens of village airfields, almost all long disused. They are indelible reminders of the Second World War. Built in a jiffy, like munitions villages and ordnance factories, many 1940s runways boast indestructible six-inch deep concrete paving. They are dotted awkwardly in maps, marked over the OS contour lines, in actuality their heavy-duty surfaces still doing duty as all-weather practice tracks, a boon for off-road learner drivers but also the kind of places that attract illicit comings and goings, from fly-tipping to drug-dealing.

It is an over-used trope, of course, that designation of the remote spaces of Essex as a conveniently accessible hiding place or dumping ground for the London underworld, but it nonetheless possesses a grain or two of truth. In 1949, the carpet-wrapped torso of used-car dealer Stanley Shetty was consigned to a light aircraft and disposed of well out to sea after his business partner, Brian Donald Hume, had decided to do away with him in revenge, so his later confession claimed, for kicking his terrier. The grisly bundle was found on the Dengie shore by a local man out hunting ducks. The history and habitual dealings of both victim and killer suggest the episode had had more complicated roots – much like the airfields themselves.

More recently, Brentwood smuggler Andrew Wright, known as 'Biggles' since he flew his own Cessna, was apprehended as he prepared to hop over to Germany with a sizeable cocaine delivery. Possibly to keep the law off his scent, he had avoided flying from an airfield in his home county and chose one in Yorkshire, a decision which was to land him a 19-year prison sentence.

Chipping Ongar's airfield was constructed between 1942 and 1943 for the USAAF. For a while hefty Marauders flew off runways constructed from rubble salvaged from the London Blitz and in the 1970s, locals were amused when some of it was recycled again as hardcore for road building around Brentwood. (A case of Essex, in a very real and solid sense, being formed out of the bomb-damaged

East End). That tiny air-
field, just outside the village of Willingale and
some distance from
Ongar, was briefly twice
on the shortlist to be
London's third airport
and I remember hearing
the announcement on
the car radio, so unlikely
on the grounds of its
obscure location that I
nearly drove into the ditch.

*Recycling of the starkest kind at Chipping Ongar, in 1944
bombers on a runway built of bombed houses*

By then the Labour government's Roskill Commission,
reporting in January 1971, had already identified Cublington in
Buckinghamshire as their preferred location. When the Con-
servatives gained power, they switched to support the minority
report submitted by the eminent environmental planner Colin
Buchanan (best known for his *Traffic in Towns*) suggesting
an Essex location, Maplin Sands (off Foulness). Long used as
a defence establishment (in the 1950s for the Atomic Energy
Authority), its remoteness and its importance as an over-win-
tering stop for migrating birds made it a long shot. Another
change of government, followed by the 1973 oil crisis, and
Maplin Sands disappeared off the agenda.

Today, it remains an unsettling spot, even the staid referencing system of the Ordnance Survey maps signalling, in red
Gothic lettering, that rights of way across the sands can be dangerous, and that local advice should be sought. One particular
route, known as the Broomway, is so apt to be swathed in fogs
and overcome by tides that it has claimed over 100 lives, 66 of
those interred in Foulness' churchyard. Edwardian newspapers
seized on its reputation with lurid glee, christening it 'the Doom-
way'. Walkers today are still warned of the path's dangers, which
include unexploded ordnance from the army testing ranges on
Foulness. It would take an extremely big leap of the imagination

to see that landscape crowned by the swooping steel and glass wings of a major modern airport, itself the portal to a world of intoxicating duty-free goods and destinations beyond.

The great airport location debate, meanwhile, passed from the macabre Maplin Sands back to self-effacing little Willingale. In May 1979, *Flight International* declared that this village was the site now favoured both by British Airways Authority and the Air Transport Users Committee. In shock, the Willingale Anti-Aircraft Group was founded in the summer of 1979 and held several meetings, the urgent agenda relating to the siting of London's third airport in the village listed alongside more quotidian matters relating to playing fields and allotments. It is indeed, hard to picture those meetings without casting it as an Ealing Comedy in which Stanley Holloway, Alastair Sim and a crowd of plucky schoolchildren see off the men from Whitehall. At any rate, the Willingale resistance group and the need for it, were short-lived. Stansted, the former RAF Stansted Mountfitchet, moved onto centre stage, being available, already in limited use for holiday traffic, and with planning permission for expansion granted in 1984. Dunmow, one of the most unassuming and delightful Essex market towns, was unwittingly caught in the slipstream.

The new terminal by Norman Foster Associates, opened in 1991, is a flagship of late 20th-century architectural modernism, the style sometimes referred to as High Tech due to its highly visible structure. One of the practice's very best buildings, it is a tough, yet slight, steel-and-glass pavilion within which natural light and clear functionality work to its advan-

Stansted in 1967: a far cry from Foster

tage, until, that is, you arrive at the recently inserted cash cow, a serpentine duty-free mall that leads passengers an unpleasant, disorientating, dance towards the departure gates.

Set against this clean vision of modernity, designed by an architect besotted by the imagery and technology of aircraft (asked to choose a favourite building for the BBC tv series 'Building Sights', Foster came up with the Boeing 747) are those ghostly wartime airfields, constant reminders that the eastern counties were the first line in aerial defence in both world wars. Along with the runway remnants, there are even occasional remnants of planes. An eccentric Fyfield farmer has a collection of several wings and tail fins, left poking out of sheds bordering a footpath across low-lying water meadows, the rest of which were once occupied by an enormous collection of K6 red phone boxes, now mostly sold on, and the remnants faded. There, not far from the local airfield, conventional agriculture was not the only option for a lucrative crop.

Another airfield, North Weald, still operational, has taken on a new life – used by hobby pilots, for car boot sales, vast outdoor markets and anything else that can make use, below or above the legal radar, of a huge hard-standing easily reached from the motorway. In this shifting arena on a Saturday, come stall-holders and shoppers in their thousands, bringing with them the jostle and buzz, raucous as an old East End market such as Petticoat Lane, their stock as multifarious and cheap as it can possibly be – globally made and sold to peo-

Every Saturday and Bank Holiday Monday: deep discounts and a dash of drama at North Weald airfield.

ple from everywhere and anywhere. This old airfield, built to keep the nation secure from invasion, is now a writhing melting pot of products, people and styles of salesmanship. Top of the heap are multi-tiered butchers' wagons, towering over the awnings of the stalls below and around them, and worked by a miked-up salesforce, those in the gods shouting out the bargains of the moment and making terrible puns about sausages, those down below bagging up the cheap cuts and shovelling them out to the customers in exchange for cash. It's an astonishing, vital, kind of pop-up carnivore theatre.

Here the Green Belt and the M25 pull in opposite directions, aiming both to keep development at arm's length and to bring it in. Yet Essex and the City of London still line up as before, however contrived the connection more than fifty years after the divorce settlement which took the outer boroughs back into London. An early 18th-century bird's eye view linked the second, opulently neo-Palladian incarnation of Wanstead Hall, renamed House, to the distant newly built dome of St. Paul's Cathedral, much as Renzo Piano's Shard, a tapering finger of glass, now fights for your attention as you drive into London on the M11 link road.

This joins up with the hard-fought A12 extension, built in the late 1990s after a series of bitter environmental battles, in particular fought over Wanstead's old village green and its ancient sweet chestnut tree, which echoed so many of the currents of radicalism in the county's history.

Causes are magnetic, and can be sociable affairs, people drawn to them often as much by the energy, the sheer opportunity to protest and join others in doing so, as the issues at stake. Looking back at media coverage from the mid-1990s, or 'You've Got To Be Choking', the award-winning documentary produced by some of the key activists, it seems clear that more than traffic and trees were on the agenda. People were angry, and Wanstead was a handy way of expressing it.

Plans to construct a link road out through East London (and the future M11) had been in the offing since the 1960s when

Wanstead had still been in Essex. By 1976, when Wanstead had been given to the Conservative-run GLC, they were sufficiently formed to give rise to an action group which began a vigorous campaign. By the time compulsory purchase orders were issued for a number of streets in Leyton and Wanstead in March 1993, the response was not quite as expected. With the threat of demolition and major road building hanging over the area, many properties had fallen vacant and into disrepair. Communities of squatters, artists, activists and students had moved in, many of them with strong views about the environment and the evils of the oil-based economy, many of them eloquent, educated and skilled in the arts of direct action.

As bailiffs and burly construction workers moved in on the streets, trying either to demolish properties or render them uninhabitable, the protestors put on a counter-display, deploying enormous courage and ingenuity. Aware that every day of delay was an expense, and that there would be a tipping point where costs outweighed benefits, they focused on thwarting the demolition project in every way they could. They reinforced inner walls with concrete and created hidden trapdoors and tunnels between houses, they built special tubes within partition walls so that two people could securely handcuff themselves either side, and they used bicycle D-locks to attach themselves, often by the neck, to chimneys and roofs.

This anti-motorway maquis was media-savvy, too: using early desktop publishing packages to create newsletters and press releases and send out faxes. The press, for their part, loved the activists with their piercings and dreadlocks and, on occasion, their well-to-do backgrounds – what journalist wouldn't when there was this continual and colourful display of copy-ready conflict going on, a short hop from Canary Wharf?

It was not a charismatic campaign, though – a clutch of ugly streets on the unloved London/Essex borders would never pull many heartstrings. What changed things was a tree. Many of the longer-established locals had had time to make their peace with the road, not least because they'd been promised that their

much-loved 200-year old sweet chestnut tree would be preserved, with the A12 running under it in a tunnel. When this
plan was declared to be unviable, people felt they'd been lied to
and when bailiffs attempted to prevent the locals from holding a tree-dressing ceremony by erecting tall wooden fencing
around it, extraordinary scenes ensued.

There's a very striking photograph from the time, summing
up the contrasts. Men in balaclavas and camouflage gear are
scaling the wooden panels like a rebel army. On the ground,
a respectable-looking grandmotherly figure gazes coolly into
the lens, holding a very carefully-written placard that reads:
Long Live The Spirit of Wanstead. She could almost be Queen
Elizabeth down at Tilbury in her suit of armour.[13]

With an aptness bordering on the sublime, a local lollipop
lady joined the groups of locals and activists in trampling the
fences, and as a result was suspended from her job. Women who
might easily have been the backbone of the local Women's Institute linked arms with anarchist eco-warriors in nightly vigils
around the tree, and if they didn't share much in common, they
certainly shared a justified outrage at the levels of force used
against them by police and bailiffs.

The letter of the law, meanwhile, was turned against itself,
as people posted hundreds of 'Dear Tree' letters from around
the British Isles, conferring upon it (as the High Court at one
point agreed) the status of a legal dwelling. Echoing the chutzpah of the utopian and radical communities set up in Essex
in the 19th century (see Chapter 6), missives were sent to the
United Nations declaring that the last few squatted houses had
now become sovereign micro-nations, with names like Eupho-
ria, Wanstonia and Munstonia – a nod back to west London's
Republic of Frestonia of the 1970s.

None of which made a jot of difference in the end. The last
houses were turned to rubble, the A12 now heads north along
a deep-cut gulley and through a tunnel – the whole stretch
potentially a piggybank for the local authority to extract
speeding fines on a four-lane dual carriageway that looks

Protecting the tree: the protest on George Green, Wanstead in 1994

tempting for fast vehicles. That lost chestnut tree was an echo of the equally emblematic Fairlop Oak of Hainault Forest, around which tens of thousands of 18th-century Londoners gathered annually for their summer Fair until, sadly depleted except for its immense trunk, it blew down. The end of the oak, in the 1820s, came just before the start of the clearance and enclosure of almost the entire forest. At Wanstead as at Fairlop, people came together in a common cause, whether for pleasure or protest. There had proved to be a tangible thing, society, whatever Mrs. Thatcher might have said to the contrary. In that less strident, if still Conservative era under Prime Minister John Major, the Battle of George Green, Wanstead was a necessary wake-up call, if hardly the Battle of Orgreave.

Circling Essex via the M25 is one way to see the county. You might choose to be guided by Roy Phippen, a likeable and absurdly well-informed taxi driver, previously a primary school teacher and before that antiquities buyer for a well-known London saleroom. However, it was Phippen's continual circumnavigation of the M25 in a cab that led, forty years later, to his book *Travelling Clockwise* (2005). He describes, with admirable accuracy and concision, the highlights of that chunk of inner Essex between junctions 26 and 31, from Copped Hall to the Mar Dyke and the river crossing, combining nuggets of history with some of the engineering feats that the motorway represents. Since, on the return journey, he was often travelling alone, Phippen began to go off the motorway to feed his curiosity about nearby places. One was Waltham Abbey, an unlikely beneficiary of the motorway, having been a harassed little island swamped by traffic pre-M25, and now returned to a state of monastic calm, with water meadows and medieval ruins offering a prelude to the interior splendours of the Norman abbey.

After a repeated visits to each location, Phippen found himself well placed to offer 'rapid, though faithful sketches', and he began relaying them to a voice recorder on his dashboard, those lonely monologues forming the basis for a splendid little book.

By contrast, Iain Sinclair's expressionistic musings on the Essex sector of the circuit, as told in *London Orbital,* are characteristically uncomfortable, as the writer and his cronies duck and weave under the shadow of the motorway, and then on a bit. He lingers at anodyne Claybury (the former Victorian asylum now a cleansed upmarket housing development) and

Unlikely neighbours: St. Clement's Church and the Procter and Gamble works, West Thurrock.

Chafford Hundred (another conglomeration of recent housing, but less toney), seeks out the 'blighted townscape' around the A13, following Bram Stoker's lead to Purfleet, the location of Carfax Abbey in *Dracula*, and West Thurrock where stands what is destined to be known forever as 'that church' from *Four Weddings and a Funeral* – St. Clement's, kept in tip-top order due to the good offices of its belching industrial neighbour, the Procter and Gamble works. Then, after sketching estuarine junkies, Sinclair settles for a gallery of grotesques from the film *Essex Boys,* the story of a drug-related triple killing at Rettendon in 1995, before heading back to Hackney on the – inevitably – alarming dawn of the Millennium.

Elsewhere, the shape of Essex is changing at breakneck speed. Managed retreat is the order of the day: sea water now enters where sea walls have given up the unequal struggle. New archipelagos for birds emerge, while agricultural land and remnants of settlements and outlying houses have disappeared, including an entire village, Walton-le-Thorpe. On the list of vanished pre-Domesday settlements in Essex at least one, Scilcheham, appears to have been on the coast. The erosion of the coastline dogs the collective psyche of East Anglians, its most easterly exposed sections suffer unforeseeable but continuous depredation by tide and current as well as extremes of climate. On his tour Defoe had pressed on to the Nase (Naze), the 'nose' of land beyond Walton. There, he was told, 'the sea gains so much on the land here, by the continual winds at S.W. that within the memory of some of the inhabitants there, they have lost above 30 acres of land in one place.' A very tall octagonal tower had just been built there by Trinity House as a navigation aid, later used as a military lookout. Today it faces no worse menace than the sea itself. In the words of Ursula Bloom, writing in *Rosemary for Frinton* about the crumbling cliffs of Walton-on-the-Naze: 'Too much land has slipped into the sea in this part of the world… it is a thieving sea.'

I was taken to Frinton for bracing sea air after my tonsils were removed. As the tides washed gently in and out, my father tried, fruitlessly, to teach me to swim. My mother, sitting by a breakwater high up the beach, was convinced it wasn't necessary. No one could possibly drown on those gently graded acres of sand, and since she had never learned, why did I need to? Yet the 1953 disaster was still very recent and one of my earliest memories is hearing that the giant hangars on our village airfield, officially known as RAF Sudbury, had been used to store and disperse sandbags, part of that immense East Anglian chain of response. As Hilda Grieve notes in her gripping, Pepysian account of the flood story *The Great Tide*, the logistical exercise of getting millions of sandbags to innumerable breaches in sea defences along the east coast was one of the most extraordinary feats of administration ever seen in peacetime. It all took place within a flood relief exercise originally conceived in 1949 between the RAF and the Essex Rivers catchment board, codenamed, perhaps rashly Operation King Canute.

The storm surge of 2013, during which a couple of hundred terrified Clacton residents sought shelter against the predicted extreme tide levels, was a reminder, yet again, of how fast things change and the dangers of complacency. Wind speeds between 70 and 80 miles an hour were recorded across south-eastern England, after a rising area of low pressure in the North Sea created a tidal 'bulge' that was then funnelled towards the land. That, at least, was how the BBC's weather presenter Matt Taylor broke down the meteorological science behind the biggest storm surge to hit Essex since 1953. Elsewhere within the BBC there was a considerable struggle to describe and explain, to the international audience of the World Service, the purpose of the most heavily storm-damaged building in Clacton, its helter-skelter.

Walton-le–Thorpe disappeared long ago, along with Walton-on-the-Naze's medieval parish church – lost to the North Sea in 1796. But safely away from the thieving waters, old Essex buildings are an enduring and endearing amalgam of materials, skills and vernacular traditions.

3 TURNING THE VIEW
UPSIDE DOWN

Shaping Essex

William Morris was the oldest boy in his family. A cosseted child, fed on calves-foot jelly for his health, he quietly noted and stored away details from his solitary local explorations and observations. In *News From Nowhere* (1889), his novel which fused utopian and socialist strands within a freeze-framed medievalist view of England, the most memorable visions were on the upper reaches of the infant Thames. Yet Morris' starting points were the estuarial, tidal Thames in Essex ('all flat pasture, once marsh, except for a few gardens… very few permanent dwellings there; scarcely anything but a few sheds and cots for the men who come to look after the great herds of cattle pasturing there…') and Epping Forest, the place he knew 'yard by yard', particularly the form, texture and history of the pollarded hornbeams. In Morris' utopian return, his childhood territory in Woodford was again thickly wooded following 'the great clearing of houses in 1955.'

Morris, who combined the roles of designer, writer and political and social activist in adult life, had been thrilled as a child to discover Queen Elizabeth's Hunting Lodge still standing in Epping Forest. It had been built from forest timber, felled and dried and stored on the spot before Tudor royal carpenters skilfully sawed and spliced it together into an intricate, lofty, tower that broke through and over the tree canopy. Morris couldn't have known what modern tree ring dating tells us so precisely, that those oaks had been cut down in the year 1542.

Once complete, it was one of two grandstands (the other was at Loughton) to offer a 360-degree view over the progress of the hunt in the forest far below. The panorama was the point and had the Lodge survived in that form, it is hardly fanciful to imagine it high on the list of local attractions, a kind of Essex Eye. But things turned out otherwise. By the 1840s, the upper storey loggia had been altered beyond all recognition, the open sided balcony fully enclosed, to lose and obscure its original function.

But even so heavily altered, the Epping hunting lodge became a benchmark for Morris, as his biographer Fiona MacCarthy puts it, representing 'the things he always hoped to find in buildings; solid structure; quirky detail; the sense of the organic, the accretion of past history; and a certain loneliness.'[1] That spirit infused his poetry and thinking, his aesthetic and design approach, for the rest of his life. In *News from Nowhere* he celebrated 'that exhilarating sense of space and freedom which satisfactory architecture always gives to an unanxious man who is in the habit of using his eyes.' He loved the grandiose tapestry-hung upper room, writing of it with a sense of rapture undimmed by the years: 'I remember as a boy my first acquaintance with a room hung with faded greenery at Queen Elizabeth's Lodge... *and the impression of romance* that it had upon me!... Yes, that was more than upholstery, believe me...'

Morris was, surely, torn between his admiration for the detail of the Tudor interiors, his appetite for a semi-fictional past and even the lodge's contemporary function. For in spite of commissioning the lodge, the increasingly frail Henry VIII was unlikely to have visited it by the 1540s, much less tackled its steep stairs. It's similarly unlikely that his daughter, Elizabeth I spent any time there, and nobody, even in Morris' time, can have believed that she rode her horse upstairs to celebrate the victory over the Spanish Armada. But the very survival of the Hunting Lodge made it a resonant stage for historical fantasy.

In fact, when the young Morris first visited, it was still in use as the Manorial court and this link to customs and traditions with roots reaching much further back than the Tudors must have appealed to him. Every 40 days since the year 1250, the Verderers of the forest, a body of notables, had been gathering in Epping to pronounce their arcane judgements, spiced up with Norman French, such as issuing fines for 'offences against the vert', or breaches of forest law like allowing your pigs to forage for acorns without paying a fee. By the time Morris would have witnessed court proceedings at the Lodge, the strains between the impoverished locals and those imposing and enforcing out-dated manorial rights were growing and presaged much trouble ahead. Later on, Morris would sharpen his political teeth in the long and fraught battle over public access to Epping Forest.

An expert campaigner on many fronts, Morris provided architectural conservation, as opposed to antiquarianism, with a clear philosophy. Alongside Philip Webb, the modest but accomplished architect who had helped Morris design the Pre-Raphaelite Brotherhood's Red House in Bexleyheath, he founded the Society for the Protection of Ancient Buildings (SPAB) in 1877 – the second-oldest such body in the world. The fight against the relentless march of the 'restorers', those heavy-handed architects (and clerics) who removed (scraped) anything from a building that looked even slightly worn, how-ever original, had been inspired by John Ruskin, and hence their campaign soon became known as 'Anti-Scrape'.

The mid-19th-century work on the Hunting Lodge epito-mised the kind of fight that the SPAB would have on its hands from the beginning. Ever less authentic, its open loggia had long gone but now folksy leaded windows and extra close stud-ded timbers were added to give the 16th-century building a 15th-century effect. With every step, the Victorian restorers made it more *ersatz*. It was not until around 1990 that 'a judicious compromise' was achieved, given urgency by the need to deal with an outbreak of deathwatch beetle.[2]

Queen Elizabeth's Hunting Lodge, Epping Forest, with Victorian encumbrances (top), and today, happily without.

Despite a sophisticated system of protection for listed buildings being in place, the late Teresa Gorman, Conservative MP for Billericay from 1987 to 2001, decided to confront the rules head-on when she and her husband bought their listed, though partially derelict house in Orsett in 1990. Her battle was more libertarian than architectural, and the wretched building was the victim of her extreme views. A good deal of Old Hall Farm dates from the mid-15th century but Mrs Gorman, daughter of a demolition contractor as well as director of the Aphrodite chain of HRT clinics, had little time for the valuable evidence of history[3]. She and her husband Jim embarked on a substantial 'restoration' programme without seeking any consent whatsoever. Original features, such as open fireplaces and 18th-century brickwork, disappeared while a modern porch in 'period' style, false beams and pastiche rendered panels appeared, to beef up the house's 'medieval' claims.

Thurrock Borough Council took the couple to court, showing admirable resolve, given Mrs. Gorman's high profile as a redoubtable, if maverick, figure on the populist hard-right of her party, fiercely Eurosceptic and a stalwart of the Freedom Association. She claimed that Thurrock's case was a political manoeuvre by the Labour council, choosing to overlook that they were solidly supported in the case by Essex County Council, who were themselves firmly Conservative. She played the press along, discussing her case on BBC 'Newsnight' with Chris Smith MP (at that time Shadow Secretary of State for National Heritage) who rebutted her claims clearly and effectively, before she invited readers of the *Daily Mail* (11 December 1995) to see her brand-new inglenook fireplace and faux exposed beams under the headline 'How the taste police destroy our dreams'. In *Private Eye* Piloti (aka Gavin Stamp, John Betjeman's successor in the role) bluntly pointed out: 'Mrs. Gorman has buggered up a decent old listed building *entirely without listed building consent*'.

But characteristically, she warmed to the chase, inviting interested parties to breakfast in the Jubilee Room at the House of Commons in April 1996 'to discuss problems caused by current planning legislation.' As she wrote, 'my own well publicized experience… indicates that current legislation is far from satisfactory and needs to be addressed by people with hands-on experience'. Unfortunately, she miscalculated; most of her guests that morning were principled conservationists, including the SPAB who had offered the local authority whole-hearted support throughout, and she had omitted those parliamentarians with any interest in, or knowledge of, the matter. Sir Patrick Cormack MP (since 2010 Lord Cormack), her fellow Conservative and Chairman of the All-Party Parliamentary Arts and Heritage Group, had received no invitation to the event and knew 'absolutely nothing about it' as he wrote to the then Secretary of SPAB, Philip Venning who himself recalls the eventual meeting as entirely pointless.

After three years, judgement in the case, involving some twenty-nine separate infringements of planning law, came down on the council's side. The legal costs for the Gormans, who had continued to appeal the decision, were considerable, even if the maximum penalties were paltry. They were ordered to remove the porch and pay a fine of £6,000; small change compared to the alleged £60,000 solicitors' bill. But for once legislation had trounced libertarianism.

For a few, such as the arch-contrarian critic Martin Pawley, there were troubling paradoxes in this. In *Terminal Architecture* he mentioned the Gorman case whilst arguing that architectural conservation was akin to the farce of keeping elderly people artificially alive, 'propped up' in hospital.

But for Morris and Webb, whose stirring call to arms became and remains the basis of the SPAB Manifesto, the issue was clearly not about preventing change, but keeping it visible. They argued that this 'strange and most fatal idea… Restoration' posed a threat to architectural heritage because of its inauthenticity, its champions mistakenly believing it 'possible to strip from a building this, that, and the other part of its history – of its life that is – and then to stay the hand at some arbitrary point.' Instead of buildings 'alive with the spirit' of all the changes made to them over the centuries, the restorers' agenda, guided by individual whims as to what was desirable and contemporary, sought to take architecture back to some randomly chosen fixed point, creating a 'dull and lifeless forgery'.

Fortunately, while the Gormans were fighting the conservation officers through the courts, a more thoughtful and careful repair work, in line with the SPAB's principles, was taking place at the Hunting Lodge in Epping Forest. The outlook tower was carefully nudged back closer to its 16th-century form, while inside visitors can read an honest and unvarnished account of the subsequent building history. Most importantly, the unlimited prospect of Epping Forest from above was reinstated, albeit through glass and with no hunting in view.

Due to its largely horizontal topography, Essex has always been an excellent landscape against which to make an impact. Take Layer Marney, some ten miles south of Colchester, a florid red brick Tudor tower which looms improbably, guarding orderly troughs of plough, set against distant glinting inlets and matte salt marsh. In a single glimpse, you see the confluence of geology with economics, of social and political history with technology and aesthetics.

When Henry Marney commissioned this lofty, intricate, gatehouse, prettily iced with four towers, the peaceable structure dominated everything in sight, whether seen over Layer Brook towards the River Blackwater and the sea beyond, or from further inland. The form reflected the man: Marney was a confident individual of wealth and good fortune who, combining the role of Privy Councilor to Henry VII and VIII along with those of Captain of the King's Bodyguard, Keeper of the Privy Seal and Sheriff of Essex, was doing nothing more than trumpeting his own considerable status in bricks and mortar. The effort to surpass expectations has paid off in more recent times, allowing modern Layer Marney to advertise itself for weddings and special events as 'England's tallest Tudor Gatehouse.'

Layer Marney is a sophisticated conglomeration of fine brickwork and terracotta ornament – the kind of exquisite decoration that had only been introduced to England recently by Italian craftsmen versed in Renaissance workmanship. Alongside the house stood Henry's own church, his proprietorship underlined since it was built and crafted of the same brick and terracotta. It had a fine tower of its own, to vie with that of the great house. Yet by 1523, not ten years after embarking on this eye-catching and extravagant venture, Henry was dead. In the will he had made just

Layer Marney Tower, photographed in the 1880s

two days beforehand, Lord Marney specified the funeral arrangements. His black velvet draped carriage, embroidered with a
white satin cross, was to be attended by mourners on horseback,
friars, priests and torch-bearing poor men on foot[4]. The procession, departing from the City of London wended its way onwards
east, via Chingford and Maldon, pausing for Requiem Masses (or
food or sleep) at appropriate points until they eventually reached
his intended burial place, St Mary the Virgin at Layer Marney.
Even by the standards of the time it was a remarkable performance, and one which bred familial disapproval. His son John,
the second Lord Marney, died just two years later, leaving terse
instructions that his remains 'be buried with as little pomp as
they can.' The family line had ground to a halt, the grand house
now the sole bearer of the surname.

In a neat paradox, Walter de Zoete, former Chairman of
the Stock Exchange, who bought the house in 1904, carried
out extensive and expensive works both on it and the church,
but also added a modest little garden pavilion to help set it all
off. Doubtless the first Lord Marney had often climbed up to
his eyrie to admire and congratulate himself on the full extent
of his lands, but his Edwardian successors, their money coming from the City rather than the land, happily pottered down

the garden path to enjoy a cup of tea and gaze back up at the resplendent house they had brought back to life. They had, as it were, turned the view upside down.

An Essex water tower triptych: Colchester's brick 'Jumbo', High Easter and Church Langley

That emphasis on height was given practical architectural expression in the glazed Georgian *belvedere* (the Italian word means beautiful view) that many a merchant added to his house in Maldon, a useful look-out as he waited anxiously on the return (both physical and financial) of valuable cargo back to port. Across the county, all shapes and sizes of church tower and spire, topped by finials, turrets or a cupola, break through the trees or onto the horizon. The telecoms companies circle them now, seeing perfect installation points for masts and dishes for better reception, but are (usually) beaten off by the protection they enjoy on the grounds of historic fabric. Then came unapologetic concrete water tanks on stilts, in recent years cheekily barnacled with communication devices. One, at Church Langley, has its own website, proudly set up by one of the original builders (it dates from 1990). No longer a source of water, the tower is now a big draw for Harlow New Town's fearless band of abseilers, and a cherished beacon signalling the home stretch for Essex residents returning from long motorway journeys.

The beadily observant Tudor historian William Harrison, though London-born, moved east and became the rector of Radwinter and later also the vicar of nearby Wimbish. He is one of the earliest, and most acute, observers of the countryside, in his *Description of England* (1577) picking up details that convey both the immediate landscape and the wider social and economic context. The text was his own contribution to the multi-authored *Holinshed's Chronicle*, in which many aspects of wider British history were explored. In Essex, Harrison's adoptive county, 'the houses... stand scattered abroad, each one dwelling in the midst of his own occupying.' The yeoman farming landscape evoked in that telling phrase, continuing much as before the Dissolution, the tenancies transferred to those like Thomas Cromwell's canny right-hand man Sir William Petre who bought the lands of Barking Abbey, was not very different from the one observed by the poet Edward Thomas at the start of the Great War (see Chapter 1). Both men conjure up a patchwork quilt of small pastures, water meadows (often seasonally flooded) and odd-shaped arable fields – many with remembered names, even if the meanings might be long lost – stitched together by habitual footpaths and lanes, the lines in the landscape.

However unremitting the new agriculture is compared to that traditional scene, the seasonal rituals of seeding, early growth, maturity and harvest, bring a shifting swatch of colours to the farm landscape, not all (step forward, oilseed rape...) pleasant but always changeable. Sometimes there's a wash of blue linseed, or the soft blue-mauve of borage. Here and there pioneer spirits, such as the Fairs family at Great Tey, grow the

A traditional mid-Essex farmstead in the early 1930s

crops of a vegan future, quinoa and chia seeds. Nearer the water, away from cultivation, the shades become quieter, the bleached natural linen tone of reeds, picking up the duns and near-mauves shading to maroon of winter marshland. A while ago I went to Tollesbury Wick, at the head of the River Black-water, to tread out the locations used in a television adaptation of *Great Expectations* in order to produce a leaflet for those who enjoy walking in the footsteps of period dramatisations.

On a short, brilliant December day we passed the encampment of ghostly trees, stripped bare and left for dead after a sudden inundation of salt water, where Magwitch, played to great effect by Ray Winstone, loomed up out of a thick brown soup to encounter Pip. On our outward journey along the sea-wall path, the water hardly touched the trees; on the way back, scarcely two hours later, the trunks were submerged and water had reached their upper branches. With a rough map, marked up by the director, we explored the close-cropped, sheep nib-bled grassland and, beyond, the lusher cattle pastures, all vari-ants upon the estuary landscape. But it is a tidal calendar that walkers need here, not a tourist pamphlet, for the rate at which the sea pours back over the land, even on the quietest days, is startling, not to say terrifying. Dickens set his novel across the Thames in Kent, but today the remote Essex saltings convey the necessary dramatic impact best. Yet, turn around and you see the inelegant hulk of the Bradwell nuclear power station where, to the delight of many, peregrines moved in for a while to nest on its late 1950s brick cliffs, indifferent observers of the dangerous decommissioning process below.

Essex landscapes are resourceful and resilient. Old gravel and sand pits have been returned to nature, landfill sites regained, delicate habitats secured. A number of national and local bodies provide impressive and under-appreciated levels of landscape protection and stewardship, matched by public access. As well as the Corporation of London's Epping Forest, these include the 8,000 acres managed by the Essex Wildlife Trust, small pockets of National Trust land, and numerous RSPB reserves. In a county often associated (by outsiders) with arterial ring roads and featureless postwar housing, the keen-eyed visitor can see buzzards, fallow deer, seal colonies and vast flocks of Brent geese. These managed bits of wilderness all offer alternatives to the conventional agricultural landscape, and the attractions aren't even solely natural. At Thurrock Thameside Nature Park (not so long ago the Mucking landfill site and archaeological treasure trove) the pleasures extend to 'ship-watching' as the great vessels come and go from Tilbury or the Dubai-financed London Gateway deepwater port. 'Best time to visit,' they say, 'January to December.'

Take a day in mid-February, when temperatures have soared and the spirits with them. Trains run out of Fenchurch Street to Benfleet (and onwards) all the time but we three mid-week walkers, my old friend-from-university, the birder, and my newer friend, the Essex sage, have the place almost to ourselves. On arrival we walk east, past an unchic marina where the boats tend to have women's names, *Beryl*, *Elsie* or *Nancy*, themselves memories of an earlier generation, like plotland houses. The boatyards on the opposite bank are at work. We take the gate into the unassuming lower reaches of Hadleigh Country Park and follow a grassy path along the broad sea wall, unscrolling gently to reveal distant Leigh-on-Sea and beyond it, Southend, boasting a tower apiece. Below us, to the right, is salt marsh clad in dense, fashionably taupe-coloured sea lavender and then the glossy mudbanks newly revealed by the low tide. To the left, much further away, beyond the busy little railway line, several rolling hills – on one of which the Olympic cycle speed trials took place – are overlooked by the spreading Salvation Army farm (much of the land here is theirs). Then come the remnants of Hadleigh Castle, a gable end and a drum-shaped tower which come together and then part as you walk along. Constable, recently widowed, saw it in a very different, troubled light.

But today is a miraculous one for birds (and for city-sized container ships as shifting backdrop, too). As the tide turns, innumerable flocks unravel in the estuary, distant skeins of duck and goose, drifts of dunlin and more, but, truly extraordinary, a flypast which even I can easily identify, perhaps as many as a hundred curlew. Soon, I am told, they will be far away on the moors but today they form an astonishing overhead phalanx of curved beaks and broad spreading mid-brown wings. Given the worries about their falling numbers, it is an exhilarating sight. Inky-black cormorants follow them overhead, fewer but with no ambitions to go on anywhere, momentarily clumsy as they come in to land on random stakes in the mud, their splayed feet suddenly dropping in preparation like webbed aircraft wheels. The colour notes come from the redshanks and the oyster catchers, working along the fringes of muddy tongues out in the water before all is lost again. Their sounds are everywhere but nearer to town, radio-controlled model planes and drones buzz around and make the birds jittery. The avocets are about to arrive and breed on Two Tree Island, and human guardians are preparing to mount their annual watch, overnight. Co-existence is difficult but worthwhile.

Arriving in Leigh, the waterside sheds belonging to the fishermen have been recently smartened up, evidence of the healthy trade in local produce and the growing attraction of the pretty riverside town itself, while the heavy work of packing and stacking, the coming and going of boats according to tide, goes on at its own irresistible pace. There is a marker on the wall in Leigh, showing the height of the tide that day in 1953 when the water and the sewage poured in. But today it's easy to move on from that, partaking of seafood and local beer in the sun as the tide rushes in, and stops, blessedly, at the quayside.

Go deeper into Essex, as the year progresses, and you find cornfields shading from soft chalky green to pale ash blonde. Add a harvest moon and the world turns upside down, the ground paler by far than the sky. After the combine harvester has done its work (the cheerful old red machines now monsters of yellow or green, often working by night), the Swiss rolls of compacted straw add their own geometry to razor cut fields of stubble before being packed into teetering, chunky, cliffs back in the farmyard or under lofty Dutch barn roofs. Until recently bales were rectilinear blocks, temptingly built into children's fortresses, slab by slab; in the 1990s, my daughter and her small friends made do by clambering, illicitly, up prickly climbing frames of straw blocks seemingly erected for their delight. Longer ago, in my own childhood, the harvested fields were dotted with little temples, three or four corn stooks at a time, leaned tip-to-tip to offer a sweet and secret, if scratchy, tent for a picnic. The scene caught by 19th-century painters was still in view, even if the corn was no longer harvested by men with scythes and heavy horses were no longer the engines of it all – as they had been until the 1930s.

Countryside like this, so familiar to me as a child, might seem dull yet, as the former Poet Laureate Andrew Motion, brought up in mid-Essex, told his interviewer in the Ramblers Association magazine *Walk*, the area around his home at Stisted offered 'all the riches of the universe bundled up together. It felt quite a hairy, ramshackle place then. But it was there that my senses started to function and I did all my growing up... that's the generic landscape in my mind.'

For Motion, whose commuting brewer father settled in Essex

because it was 'proper country', the terrain remains disconcertingly intense, its pull enduring, however mundane its features and contours. He described his feelings about it as deeply contradictory, not least because it was while galloping across the countryside on horseback that his mother suffered a life-changing accident. 'The earth rose up and hit her.' Yet Motion's second memoir, *Essex Clay*, is testament to the enduring hold of plain, slow-burning, Essex images on the eye, in that landscape of the 'rabbity ditch', the phrase which summons up my home turf as much as his[5].

Long before, in sketches as in finished oil paintings, John Constable captured the water meadows, rough tracks and ancient oaks that formed his own childhood memories, and the emotions evoked by that landscape. As he famously wrote in 1821 to his friend, the Rev. John Fisher, 'I should paint my own places best; painting is with me but another word for feeling… these scenes made me a painter, and I am grateful.' He also took care to note the homely construction details of the farmhouse in the *Hay-wain*, nudging into view on our left, just by the ford. Constable often looked at buildings that way, incidentally instead of head on, as they tend to appear in life. He liked a telling corner or oblique angle, a sighting of chimneys and tiled or thatched roofs emerging through the trees or no more than the distant prospect and vague mass of a building. Humble domestic or functional farm buildings were built from whatever materials came to hand (clay, straw, timber, even sand for glass) while their builders, the local labourers and artisans, inevitably lived no further away than the day's cart ride, there and back. The absence of railways and machine-made brick ensured that the language of buildings was the true vernacular.

Constable included a typical open-sided wooden cart, the wain or wagon, taking tradesmen and their materials, especially timber, to sites in and around Dedham once they had disposed of the seasonal crops. It was, to exaggerate only a little, the white van of its day, possibly stopping a while in the waters of the Stour to cool the horses' hooves, or to prevent the wheels from expanding out of shape in the summer heat, as well as taking the shortest route from Suffolk into Essex at that point.

The corner of Willy Lott's 'cottage' that nudges in quietly, the plastered wall bulging a little over a substantial brick base and revealing a hefty brick chimney on the gable end, housing both the bread oven and the flues, was topped with a reassuring hat of plain tiles above. That stolen glimpse of a modest 16th-century house, later extended, is a neat introduction to local traditional building, as essential an ingredient in the landscape as the water, and the trees and meadows beyond. When Constable painted the scene in 1821, Willy Lott was still a tenant farmer, but four years later he could buy the house and the thirty-nine acres that went with it[6]. Lott died there in 1849, unmarried, at the age of 88. Now it is a Grade I listed building, owned by the National Trust. Meanwhile, the soaring market value of Constable's homespun images mirrors the absurdity of modern property prices in desirable, highly protected, Dedham Vale.

The introduction of brick chimneys in the late 16th century had been a great step forward and transformed domestic living. Carpentry detail can be misleading, but chimneys never. The crucial clue to the age (or ages) of a house, they are prone to appear unexpectedly, like uninvited guests, from behind the rooftop, arguing with a more recent (Georgian) 'polite' facelift in which symmetry and fashion dictated the result, so neat and obedient. Tudor or Jacobean chimneystacks, unlike symmetrical 18th-century versions, are surprisingly massive, shouldering a bundle of flues, confected from brick that has been precisely cut and fitted. High quality masonry was, by then, being produced by local men who, in turn, had probably learned their skills from those who built the region's 'prodigy' houses such as Layer Marney, Leez Priory and New Hall, among them consummate craftsmen brought from mainland Europe, men from Italy or the Low Countries, whose names went unrecorded.

William Harrison saw and recorded the scale of change

during his own lifetime, and in relatively modest circumstances, as corroborated by the locals, 'old men yet dwelling in the village where I remain… have noted three things to be marvellously altered in England within their sound remembrance.' These were the introduction of chimneys and the improvement of domestic furnishing and household implements. Where building was concerned, Essex was learning fast from neighbouring Europe, and since Harrison's wife was the daughter of Flemish immigrants, he was particularly aware of the material improvements that had flowed from over the North Sea. In the houses of 'inferior artificers and many farmers' those newly subdivided, smaller rooms now well warmed by fireplaces and flues were also better furnished. The same old men who had told him about the chimneys commented on 'the amendment of lodging' – from straw pallet to feather mattress, from wooden tableware to pewter, from bare floors to 'covers and carpets of tapestry.'

The monks of Coggeshall Abbey, in the dead centre of Essex, began producing bricks and tiles for the market in 1200 – the earliest brickyard recorded since the Roman period – proof, if needed, that the absence of stone was the mother of invention. But quality imported materials were also playing their part. Flemish bricks first appear, mixed with other local materials such as flint, chalk and clay lump, in 14th-century churches in coastal Essex, for example at Purleigh, Dengie and Maldon. Brick and, more often, tiles may have arrived as cargo, in exchange for wool on the return trip. Otherwise, having no local source of quarried stone, dun-coloured septaria was the only option, lumpy and crude and extracted from the river banks – but nevertheless handy. Timber framing, plaster and weatherboarding were, in the absence of alternatives, ubiquitous.

In 1957, the American novelist John Updike settled in Essex County, on Boston North Shore, Massachusetts. In the town of Ipswich, Mass. he found himself close to a wilderness of salt marsh and sand dunes scoured bone-clean by sea winds, a climate and conditions which at last offered him a measure of relief for his psoriasis. Recalling his house and those of his neighbours a little over three decades later, Updike wrote that they were in tune with a modernist aesthetic. 'It was Puritan; it was back-to-nature, it was less is more.' His life in a 17th-century house 'felt like an honor, a privileged access to the elemental clarity of the spirit that created the first Puritan settlements in the New World.'[7] He seemed to have forgotten that devout Essex County had also witnessed one of the most terrible episodes in early colonial history, the persecution of the Salem 'witches'.

Though his own forebears were Dutch, Updike found himself in what seemed almost a province of eastern England. Curiously enough, not just the surviving oldest houses but the very topography looks like an off-cut from the estuarial shores of Essex, UK. To this day the Winthrop family, whose puritan ancestor John Winthrop Sr. had spent his early married life looking out over Foulness before becoming Governor of Massachusetts Bay Colony in 1630, are still there. Now they are housed in a svelte 1920s-pillared classical villa, set off by glossy horses grazing behind immaculate paling fences.

Ties to the old country, generation after generation, continued to represent a kind of umbilical cord, essential connective tissue. Essex donated many place names to the new colony, as well as something distinct on the ear. In New England early settlers clung to anything familiar, resulting in the clapboard clad, timber-framed houses so familiar in 17th-century colonial America and after. John Whipple, whose house stands (although moved to a different site) in Updike's then home town, Ipswich, MA., was a carpenter by trade and he came from Bocking, a prosperous textile town, its main street a succession of gabled, timber-framed houses[8]. The rather different conditions prevailing in the colonies had to be taken into account: some clapboard houses were externally clad with lathe and plaster, seemingly to avoid their timbers being torched by disaffected natives – not such a problem for the builders at home in Bocking,

It is striking, looking from Essex to Essex across that distance almost four hundred years later, how closely the proud New Englanders of the 17th century stayed to their original points of arrival. The plain old Massachusetts houses, John Whipple's or John Updike's, are the pure-blooded ancestors of solid timber-framed yeoman farmhouses and weather-board cottages ('clapboard' in the USA) of agricultural Essex, seen here and there to this day.

In Essex, major building timbers, of good length and diameter, often have a history more complex than anything that could be imagined. After a spell at Chelmsford School of Art and two decades teaching in Essex schools, Cecil Hewett joined Essex County Council's historic buildings team. His seemingly wild conjectures of impossibly early dates for wooden structures were often dismissed out of hand by academics, despite the clear evidence that these buildings fabrics offered of extensive reuse or of what Hewett – a carpenter's son from Laindon – saw as 'archaic carpentry'. The ease and regularity with which such buildings were dismantled and their materials reused, with old mortise and tenon marks as evidence, stirred up scholarly confusion and dissent among experts, and was particularly intense over the early date Hewett had suggested for the barns at Cressing Temple.

The 14-acre site at Cressing had been given to the military-cum-monastic Knights Templar in 1136 by King Stephen's wife, Matilda of Boulogne, and its community of millers, bakers and farming tenants would have been busily engaged, from the outset, in the cultivation and storage of crops. In spite of that, scholars were reluctant to apply a date earlier than the 14th or 15th centuries to any structure without obvious historical context, and that included Cressing's immense wheat and barley barns.

Based on his analysis of the timber joints, Hewett suggested a date between the 11th and 13th centuries, and eventually, advances in tree-ring and carbon dating techniques proved him correct. Equally, Hewett established that the substantial but apparently unexceptional 17th-century Falconer's Barn at Good Easter incorporated timber posts, with capitals, dating from the 11th century, pointing to their origins within an important prebendal hall.

The story of Hewett, successfully deploying his native wit, observation and truculence against the lofty disdain of the learned, is a kind of Aesop fable from Essex – another win for the tortoise – and he achieved academic recognition only just in time. In April 1998, Anglia Polytechnic University awarded him an Honorary Doctorate, three months before his death[9].

Hewett believed in the evidence of the eye, applied to a thorough chronological knowledge of technique. Old roof ridges wriggle along, reflecting the hand-cleaved chestnut or elm lathes and rafters lying below: today a rigid roof ridge is an immediate giveaway to an insensitive restoration or conversion. Indoors, the walls and ceilings had the irregularities of woven lathe and plaster – no right angles, no sharp corners – all smoothed over with puddled mixtures of horsehair and lime plaster, and perhaps a scant pinch of earth pigment added, like turmeric in curry, to the mix – inside and out. In the handsome small towns of north-west Essex, like Saffron Walden, Thaxted and Dunmow, the palette of colour used on exterior plaster has exploded in recent decades. The strong, bright tones are a postmodern addition to the scene, as garish as aniline dye, but at least impermanent. Organic ochre and oxblood have ceded to chemical holly green and ultramarine, lilac and buttercup yellow, but only for now.

Externally, the lime plaster was often impressed with a stencilled ornament in a process known as pargetting, geometric like woodblock prints, packed into neat panels or compartments. The work must be done fast, the block pressed swiftly into the pliant damp material (nothing like the harsh sand and cement renders now used), urgently seizing the moment as in fresco painting. In the early 1980s I worked as a researcher (and wrote the tie-in book) for 'Built in Britain', a Channel 4 television series that aimed to show the vernacular roots of rural buildings in eight British regions, and rightly so, one programme was largely devoted to Essex. We filmed an experienced pargetter at work on a modest street-front house in Saffron Walden, and it was nail-biting to watch him, lest his hand slip or the drying process happen too quickly. He was, of course, consummately practised and calm and no expensive film stock, in that nervy pre-digital era, was wasted.

The good clay of Essex, the same that furnished Daniel Defoe's early 18th-century brick and tile works, and that no doubt periodically filled his purse before plunging him into debt, encouraged arable farmers, in the off-season, to use their time, labour and opportunity to develop modest local brick-yards. In the same episode of 'Built in Britain' we filmed the family firm of Peter Minter, still operating to this day in the midst of an arable farm outside Sudbury, at Bulmer (officially in Suffolk but originally in Essex). A thriving concern, it's the kind of business that would once have been a regular sight all over the county. The Minters had bought it, merely part of the farmyard along with the barns, in the 1930s. The kilns, including one rebuilt in the 21st century, sit in the midst of the farm-yard, as they did everywhere before local brick was overtaken by the standard issue machine-made product, brought in by the railways. Time has brought rewards to Minter's: increasingly sophisticated conservation practice, available funds for heritage and a far deeper understanding of conservative repair has given artisan brick-makers a niche market, trusted by professionals around the country to produce the 'specials' that match their historic counterparts, specified on an astonishing range of high quality repair projects. Layer Marney Tower now incorporates Minter bricks, as does St. Pancras station[10].

The 'Great English Earthquake' occurred on April 22 1884 and had the man from the *Manchester Guardian* reaching for his (modest) superlatives, 'a real earthquake, though it may be neces-sary to confess it a very small one, is something to be proud of in this country' before returning to the bathos of reality, describing how 'it asserted itself by shaking walls, breaking crockery, ringing bells, and toppling down chimneypots.'

The seismic event, fortunately leading to no loss of life, was the biggest ever recorded in Britain, shaking Colchester and a wide

Damage from the Essex Earthquake; this one hung onto its windows

swathe of villages to its east. Measuring 4.6 on the Richter scale, some 1,200 buildings were affected. The timing, at 9.18 am in the morning, when most people were at work or about their daily tasks, may have helped to prevent any fatalities. The same newspaper article goes on to place the event in the same category as the British weather: frustrating and typically idiosyncratic, musing as to whether future days will bring news of some grander geological catastrophes abroad, for the Colchester quake could hardly be placed on the dramatic register alongside an eruption of Vesuvius, which was continually active throughout the 1880s and 1890s.

The Essex Field Club, a body of amateur scientists (who would soon make their home in the Hunting Lodge in Epping Forest) took an admirably thorough approach, providing in their 1895 report of the earthquake an international chronology of seismic events, going back to the third century AD, and most recently, the collapsed 'minarets of mosques' in the Turkish city of Kastamonu and the loss of houses in Djakovar in Hungary, both episodes from the year before.

If they seemed over-keen to place events in Essex in a global context, the denizens of the Essex Field Club were highly organized in their pursuit of data, carrying out precise surveys and interviews in the months after the earthquake and making careful note of details, such as the direction in which a clock pendulum swung, or the behaviour of the clouds. At the same time, they treated anecdotal accounts with healthy scepticism, disregarding the Tillingham man who claimed to have smelt a sulfurous vapour moments after the tremors, and the account from Wivenhoe, of a bright steel corkscrew that had changed colour due to some imagined traces of infernal gas.

Whilst patiently recording dozens of eye witness statements, they also created a rich and very human testimony of the day's events, with moments of language that border on beauty. 'A man hoeing in the field near the White Hart (West Mersea) felt the twisting motion of the earth and had the hoe jerked up in his hand' – we can all imagine how frightening that must have felt, to a man on his own, in a field, who had probably never experienced anything remotely like it. More luminous still are the words of Mr W. Blatch, station-master of Colchester North who heard 'a rumbling noise resembling distant thunder and directly the platform seemed to give a gentle heave, like the motion of a wave' [11].

For Frank Crittall, a chapel man, the earthquake was an Act of God, but one that perhaps had creative elements, as well as destructive ones. Until then employed in the 'back shop' of a small family hardware store in Braintree, young Frank (F.H.) Crittall had been tinkering with machinery and metal, 'more interested in making than selling'. Now he seized his opportunity. Shattered window frames needed urgent replacement. Metal took the place of wood; casement the place of sash; and soon, as he wrote drily, 'several useful orders came our way and for a few months we enjoyed a brief boom'. In 1889, launched on the back of its rapid response to this unprecedented natural disaster, the Crittall Manufacturing Company Ltd was born. Looking back in 1934, Frank wrote, with justifiable and almost evangelistic pride, that it was then that he first 'took up a task destined to create at least one entire town of its own, to employ thousands of people here and abroad, and to stretch its tentacles to almost every corner of the globe.'

It wasn't long before the firm garnered several plum government contracts, including the kitchens of the House of Commons. The private residential market proved harder to crack, since Crittall windows were still relatively expensive and somewhat cumbersome. But there were no limits to Frank Crittall's ambitions. In 1907 he took a berth on the *Lusitania* (its second voyage) across the Atlantic to establish production in Detroit. Like the Puritans who made the crossing almost three centuries before, Crittall was a man of faith, with a vision of bringing light to the darkness, albeit in a rather more practical fashion. When the *Titanic* set sail, it was fitted with Crittall windows and, more importantly in the event, another remarkable Essex product, the Marconi

CHARACTER SKETCH BY MR. A. J. MUNNINGS, R.A.
DINNER AT THE GREAT EASTERN HOTEL ON DERBY NIGHT, 1919.

Frank Crittall, captured enjoying Derby Night at the Great Eastern hotel, 1919, by Alfred Munnings

wireless telegraph system which, with its skilled onshore operators, proved invaluable as the ship began to sink.

Continuous research into lighter steel, new corner welding and, above all, the 1909 patent for the slender 'Fenestra' joint which gave improved levels of light, suggested that the firm was near to cracking the residential market, when the war brought their plans to a sudden halt. But their innovations pointed far ahead, to new ventures and invaluable experience.

Energetic Frank Crittall was central in a cooperative of East Anglian engineering firms (largely agricultural engineers, notably Ransomes of Ipswich) who turned their businesses over to the manufacture of shells. He served on a government Reconstruction Committee, gave evidence to the Tudor Walters committee on housing standards and, crucially, offered to build a pair of demonstration 'Unit System' houses. Frank Crittall had always wanted to be a builder. Now came his opportunity; postwar he was centre stage in British housing reconstruction, advising Dr Christopher Addison, Minister of Health and the architect of the crucial 1919 Housing, Town Planning &c. Act which took his name. In 1920, Crittall's eldest son Valentine (later to be Labour MP for Maldon) successfully persuaded the Ministry of Health to include a standard Crittall 'cottage window' in government specifications. It was to be the standard window in British public housing schemes for the next fifty years. To meet the anticipated high demand, Walter 'Pink' Crittall, another brother, was radically changing the company's factory processes, including a shift from skilled artisan workers to semi-skilled men, lowering costs and raising productivity.

The Unit System experiment was carried out in Crittall's customarily fearless fashion. Off Cressing Road, Braintree, in less than apple-pie order these days, sits a clutch of semi-detached houses. Most of the Clockhouse Way cottages have been much altered but, despite appearances, these were the first flat-roofed concrete houses to be built in Britain. Modernist more by accident than design, Crittall told the professional press that the flat roofs were 'an attempt to overcome the prejudice with which this method is generally regarded' while the metric system allowed for standardisation and didn't need skilled labour. Designed by Walter Crittall and architect C. H. B. Quennell, they were published widely and appear under construction in a Pathé Newsreel feature[12]. A well-dressed group of onlookers, both men and women (presumably members of the Crittall family) watch the proceedings from below. On completion in May 1919, Crittalls claimed that the first pair of Unit System cottages had halved pre-war construction costs. But the Unit System did not sweep the country due to circumstances beyond their control or even that of the coalition government. Crittalls had sold their Unit System to Alfred Booth & Co. soon after the end of the war; and as so often, a miracle solution to an urgent problem had proved of limited practicality

Before long the Crittall company, ever more commercially successful, its factories ever larger, had gone public. Now Frank

Crittall embarked on what he variously called the 'Great Adventure' or the 'Great Idea' since now 'with every justification, we could launch into building on a large scale.' As he sipped his nightly whisky and soda, the imaginary new town had spread out before him, he 'saw a pleasant village of a new order, planted amid fields and trees and streams; I saw its quiet thoroughfares, its fine open spaces, its modern dwellings with ample gardens, its playing fields, recreations and amusements, and above all... a contented community of Crittall families enjoying the amenities of town life in a lovely rural setting.' The words could have been Thomas More's, describing Utopia in

Still looking Modern: Silver End housing in 2016.

1516, or Essex Puritans, envisaging a Promised Land across the Atlantic. From then on, Crittall spent every spare moment combing the countryside of mid-Essex for a site somewhere between Witham, Braintree and Maldon – the triangular limit set by their factories – in which to set his New Town. Silver End was to be it.

In his disarming if frustratingly incomplete account, *Fifty Years of Work and Play,* by 'Mr and Mrs. F. H. Crittall' (his wife provided the latter section but died before publication), he is engagingly proud of the planning and building of Silver End, the Crittall company town set out in the fields near Witham for their ever-growing workforce. But the streets of flat-roofed 'white modern' houses, which would have looked startling even in a city, were not despite appearances, built of metric concrete blocks. Every house, whether flat or pitched roofed, its walls rendered or not, was built of brick, while the church was weatherboarded with a thatched roof. By the late 1920s a judicious mix of tradition and innovation seemed a more suitable backdrop for that all-important product, Crittall metal windows for the home.

As it prospered, the company, with factories in Braintree, Witham and, before long, in Silver End village itself, remained exceptionally generous in providing facilities and amenities for their resident workforce. One factory was built expressly to give suitable employment to injured ex-servicemen. Yet Silver End mixed whole-hearted philanthropy with considerable expediency, for all the houses, traditional or not, were fitted with the firm's metal windows. In fact 20th-century Britons looked out through little else, whether at home or at work, in industrial villages or fashionable resorts, in garden suburb or, later, New Towns. They answered a practical need: dealing with the discomfort of draughts as well as the financial drain of endless redecoration, for suburban owner-occupiers or tenants on council estates. The latter, fleeing London for the green towns of Essex, may have seen them as modern and 'swish', a symbol of their upward and forward mobility, but they probably appreciated the insulation and the durable frames even more. The same mix is visible throughout much of the county's history: dreams, visions, ambitions... and sheer expediency.

4 OVER GROWNE & SUDAINLY MONEYED

Spending it in Essex

The successful Londoner moving to the Essex countryside in search of new beginnings and fresh air, a larger house with a garden, is a stereotype, but one stretching back centuries. The annual Rich List published each year by *Essex Life* offers a mixture of cliché and intriguing life choices. The billionaire Amstrad founder and star of the original (British) TV show, *The Apprentice*, Lord Sugar of Chigwell frequently tops it, while in 2016 pharmaceutical entrepreneurs Vijay and Bhikhu Patel ran him close, along with the property magnate, Regus founder Mark Dixon. They came, respectively, from Hackney (via Russia and Poland), Kenya (via Gujarati India) and Dagenham (via employment at the Ford factory). Of the fifty names on the list, only four had inherited money. In 2017 Sugar ceded his position to a new entrant, a man who offered a snapshot of another, more questionable, route to great wealth, a privately educated London estate agent from an army background in Colchester: Jon Hunt of Foxton's. Two years on, the list featured most of the same names, often in similar running order, despite some big financial losses. Property, construction and care homes would seem to be the perpetual trades of choice for Essex oligarchs, but reality-tv is also represented (Romford's Mark Burnett), along with metal recycling and gambling. It's a list that always offers surprises, like Chingford-born industrial designer supreme, Sir Jonathan (Jony) Ive of Apple, and holiday park supremo Alfie Best, who befitting both his business and his Romany roots, was born by the roadside in a caravan.

Those impregnable high hedges of cypress *leylandii* and gilded iron gates surmounted by electronic eyes, activated security lighting and swivelling CCTV lenses are the modern moat, and, like many an old moat, more for show than defence. Behind them are the people whom others aspire to be, particularly those who came from the poor boroughs of East London (where they had often been propelled by 19th-century pogroms and persecution in Eastern Europe or by harsh regimes and despots on other continents).

The sudden death of John 'Goldfinger' Palmer in 2015 on the lawn at his well-gated home at South Weald outside Brentwood was a reminder of the enduring existence of the old Essex underworld – its wealth, menace and chutzpah. Palmer, in his late sixties, was at first assumed to have died from natural causes. He had recently had open-heart surgery, and the six neat wounds on his chest were mistaken as surgical in origin until an eagle-eyed paramedic realised that bullets rather than a scalpel were the cause. Palmer's demise quickly became a murder enquiry. His past included strong links to the 1987 Brinks-MAT robbery – a crime of which he was acquitted on the grounds that, as a simple scrap metal dealer, he could not possibly have known the source of the gold bullion he was busy melting down in his garden, as well as time spent at Her Majesty's pleasure due to his part in a massive time-share fraud. Nevertheless, he had survived longer than many of his friends and workmates and had a splendid second home in Tenerife[1].

Different and more legitimate stereotypes are presented, only slightly tongue in cheek, by the media-savvy, and self-evidently highly lucrative, creations of reality TV, in particular 'The Only Way is Essex'. TOWIE follows the life style of a group of twenty-somethings in and around Brentwood, nudging them into contrived televised encounters dramatized against 'the backdrop of cars, bars and designer gear.' When TOWIE was announced in 2010 there was a swell of anger in Essex. Why should 'Britain's most maligned county' be traduced again?

Twenty years earlier the political journalist Simon Heffer (an Essex resident writing anonymously but soon outed) had coined the term 'Essex Man' in a *Sunday Telegraph* article. Heffer's character, 'young, industrious, mildly brutish and culturally barren' was the human embodiment of Mrs. Thatcher's notorious remark (to an interviewer for *Woman's Own*) in 1987, that 'there is no such thing as society... people must look to themselves first.'

Heffer's dashed-off caricature had resonance; conjuring up the brash son of a working-class East Ender, a docker or market trader who had got ahead thanks to his wits rather than his old school tie or parental connections. But when TOWIE appeared on British television screens, Heffer's gentler colleague from the *Daily Telegraph*, William Langley, wondered if Essex deserved 'to be duffed up all over again?' Six years before the extremities of eastern England voted so enthusiastically for Brexit, Langley collected outraged reaction to TOWIE from many quarters, including Essex County Council's head of heritage and culture, Jeremy Lucas, who considered that it 'undermines everything we've tried to do.' [2]

The sociologist and historian, Dr Pam Cox from the University of Essex also weighed in, arguing

But who's laughing? One of several Essex-themed 'humour' publications

that the county was an all-too convenient destination for those in the media or politics who wanted a quick snapshot of what was going on outside London, but couldn't be bothered to travel too far, or look too closely. Once in Essex, they tended to find what they wanted, political isolationism and crude materialism.

Comedy treatments of Essex vary from the crude to the fond. Harry Enfield's foul-mouthed plasterer character, *Loadsamoney* ('I've got Piles'), was from Essex, while his *Tim Nice but Dim* was SW-postcode London; both rich, but only one of them offensive. The hugely popular sit-com 'Birds of a Feather', from 1989 onwards, is a more nuanced affair, featuring two sisters, Sharon and Tracey, one sensible and drab, the other spendthrift, thrown together in the latter's 'dream house' in Chigwell (their men being inside, after convictions for armed robbery). Life is made all the merrier with their man-mad, laugh-a-minute, Jewish neighbour, Dorien Green played with gusto by Lesley Joseph. Essex (or old cockney) pride is fondly evoked by a pair of script writers who know exactly who and what they are writing about.

TOWIE took shape when co-creator Tony Wood was asked to come up with a British equivalent of the US hit Laguna Beach, which places real people without scripts in structured situations. In an interview with *Drama Quarterly* in 2015, the former producer of soap operas 'Coronation Street' and 'Hollyoaks' made a case for the structured reality show as a new take on television drama. In the same way as the soaps - originally, at least – focused on distinct communities, such as working-class terraces in Salford, or new-build cul de sacs on the edge of Liverpool, structured reality shows home in on well-defined groups and social enclaves, and in that sense can be seen as modern celebrations of identity – often, in fact, playing to the advantage of the subjects. The people in question, whether twenty-somethings from Brentwood and Shenfield, Asians from suburban west London ('Desi Rascals') or traveller communities

('Big Fat Gypsy Weddings') do seem content to be placed under the spotlight, demonstrating their individual trials and triumphs, collective values and, by default, a certain shared sense of pride. But they are also left very exposed; the latter series, for example, provoked an unpleasant backlash against law-abiding travelling communities[3]. The line between fact and fiction, actuality and scripted reality, is blurry and it can, on occasion, seem closer to hunting with dogs.

In contrast, *Fish Tank*, the 2009 film made by young director Andrea Arnold and shot in locations around the fringes of south Essex and alongside the A13, was focused on a single parent family living in poor conditions. It is, for all that, a moving story of adolescence, fiction well rooted in sobering reality. Katie Jarvis was chosen to play the part of disappearing fifteen-year-old Mia, after being spotted arguing with her boyfriend in Tilbury, the bleakest outpost of the docks. Much like Vittorio de Sica's *Bicycle Thieves,* it tells a story of vulnerability and fading hope, personally and politically acute as well as socially telling.

However TOWIE is judged, celebratory of a distinct local culture, or insidiously harmful, it has produced a booming, if unlikely tourist industry around Brentwood. Several compa-

Reality-tv-tourism. Only in Essex…

nies, highly (and not so highly) rated on TripAdvisor, compete for custom from hen parties and groups of fans, offering luxury mini coach tours of up to four hours' duration, taking in the Sugar Hut, the nightclub within a 15th-century coaching inn, and various boutiques and beauty bars (for those tans and nails), in and around the town, ostensibly run by stars of TOWIE, and all proudly promoted by Brentwood Borough Council. Who loses, and who wins?

As 2020 ended, there was victory, certainly, for a campaign group who argue that the term 'Essex Girl' is derogatory and encourages sweeping judgements about women based on external details. Oxford University Press agreed with (or backed down to) the Essex Girls Liberation Front, and announced that the term would no longer feature in its Advanced Learners' English Dictionary.

Chelmsford-born writer Sarah Perry offers a more nuanced take in her book *Essex Girls*, which celebrates the county's 'remarkable women', from seventh-century Saxon Abbess Ethelburga and Rose Allin, martyred for her beliefs in 1557, to Quaker abolitionist Anne Knight. These are not so much 'alternative Essex Girls' as some more, whose presence dilutes the stereotypes to the point of rendering them meaningless. The difference, Perry argued in *The Guardian*[4], between the women in her book and the outspoken, provocative, irrepressible white-stiletto-wearers of myth and (partial) truth exists mainly in the eye of the beholder. Snobbery and sexism determine where the label lands; its most harmful aspects disproportionately felt by those already disadvantaged.

For centuries, the journey east from the capital was a flight rather than a choice, triggered by poverty, disease, uncomfortable associates or urban pressure. The enormous wave of those who came to be called the 'plotlanders' was the single largest influx from city to county, the confluence of untenable population densities (and atrocious slum housing conditions) in East

London with the desperate agricultural Depression of the late 19th century. As we shall see, enterprising families who were able to do so sought freedom, self-determination and a fresh start on the poor quality, cheap farmland that had become available for next to nothing.

From the 17th to the 21st century a snapshot of the exchange of population between London and Essex includes City bankers and financiers, East India Company merchants shading over the centuries into hedge fund executives, IT wizards and Premier League footballers, successful policemen and busy taxi drivers, and traders in innumerable commodities from precious metals and leveraged bonds to cocaine and fruit. The skills required on a market stall and those used on the foreign exchange floors in the City were pretty interchangeable, and from the 1970s, the old barriers of class and gender were starting to come down.

As the decade began, 1970 Valerie Thompson was a 15-year-old school leaver from Dagenham with a good head for figures, sharpened by all the hours she'd spent working alongside her father in his greengrocery business based at London's Billingsgate fish market. From a modest start as a telex operator, she soared to become a legendary Euromarket trader, the first female foreign exchange trader in the City, and by 1986, vice president of Salomon Brothers International. But, as she put it, disarmingly, 'If you're trading fruit and veg, they're perishable goods, and if you don't sell them today you could lose everything, that's how I learned to assess risk. Trading apples and oranges isn't very different from trading securities; the principles are the same as in the City. So I started. It's amazing what you can do if you have to. I made money. I learned how to do it and I made money.'

Valerie's was one of the many experiences of work laced together by historian Veronica Horwell into an audio performance called *City of Women* performed at Leadenhall Market in 2018. Thompson had already turned her experiences into a 'trading room bodice-ripper' novel, entitled *Laws of Contrition*.

In the past, the rich could strut from London into Essex and use their wealth to do as they pleased, on someone else's turf. Within a generation or two the newcomers would have settled down, learned respect for country ways and rural language and merged into the background. Or gone bankrupt and vanished. The picture is rich and varied. Daniel Defoe was positive about the growth of new houses on the eastern edges of London, far away from the pox-ridden marshes. The influx had, he noticed with the satisfaction of one who may himself have been a beneficiary, increased 'the value and rent of the houses formerly standing'. He cited Stratford, Leytonstone, Walthamstow, Woodford, Wanstead as well as 'the towns of' West Ham, Plaistow and Upton.' The new stock consisted of numerous handsome houses and the upswing had benefitted old houses too, 'now being repaired.' Some of these residents divided their time between the country and the city, others 'being rich, and having left off trade, live altogether in these neighbouring villages, for the pleasure and health of the latter part of their days.' He also noticed how city wealth 'spreads itself into the country, and plants families and fortunes, who in another age will equal the families of the ancient gentry who perhaps were bought out.' Defoe liked a bit of grit in the social mixture.

But Essex was not for everyone. It was never the county of choice for the Victorian manufacturer turned country gentleman. For those who sought an idealized country life, it seemed ever less attractive as London spilled over its boundaries with abandon. In his landmark account *The Victorian Country House* (1971), architectural historian Mark Girouard identifies just four grand homes from that era in the county. One, Down Hall, was a brave early venture in concrete, dating from the 1870s, and is now a spa hotel marketed as a wedding destination (tragic 'Big Brother' star Jade Goody was married there very shortly before her death). Another lumbering Victorian mansion, Berechurch Hall, was 'probably' – according to Girouard – the first house in the country to have electricity installed in 1882, and, fittingly for an owner who was in insurance, built with obsessive attention to fire-proofing. Unlike

For four centuries, the frescoes at St. Michael and All Angels Church, Copford were hidden by a layer of Tudor-era whitewash

Norfolk, Essex didn't offer proximity to royalty or the scions of the aristocracy, with blue chip hunts and shooting syndicates to help mix thrusting people together, but it was an excellent place to try out new things and to draw people's attention to the result.

Compared to other parts of the country, architectural grandeur is in short supply in Essex – almost all the monastic foundations were quickly eradicated after the Dissolution. But accidents of ownership sometimes lead to the unexpected, such as hidden

Sir Thomas Smith (d. 1577), at rest in St. Michael's Church, Theydon Mount.

Copford church, an exquisitely decorated chapel for the Bishops of London, whose manor it was since before the Norman Conquest. A series of 12th-century paintings originally lined the little church from floor to ceiling, the elongated figures almost Byzantine, and, even now, despite heavy-handed Victorian interference, you could be in the Carpathians or the Troodos Mountains, rather than a couple of miles off the A12 and its menacing spawn, in the shape of continual threats of 'Garden Village' developments in the area.

Further south, just off the M25 at Theydon Mount, an important early classical mansion, Hill Hall, gutted by fire after years as a women's prison (Christine Keeler served her sentence for perjury there) still boasts remnants from a set of wall paintings, of a sophistication rarely seen in Britain. They date from around 1570 and were commissioned by the erudite Sir Thomas Smith, a Privy Councillor and diplomat who, for all his refined tastes, is reputed to have drawn daggers during a dispute with his embassy superiors in France.

Palaces were thin on the ground in Essex, despite (or because of) proximity to London. It seems likely that Henry VIII chose New Hall, formerly the summer residence of the abbots of Waltham, in the belief that this was exceptionally healthy countryside – both for the air and the water. For Mary Tudor the principal appeal of the place was stability – she'd spent much of her childhood there – and proximity to Woodham Walter, where the Catholic Henry Radcliffe, 2nd Earl of Sussex, kept an escape boat always ready for her at Maldon.

Three centuries on, a disgruntled elderly Georgian landscape architect, Humphry Repton, was acerbically observing the habits and manners of rich incomers to Essex. Born in Suffolk in 1752, Repton had spent his professional life fulfilling the wishes of the landed classes but, more recently, found himself indulging the foibles of the new rich, their fortunes often built disreputably during the Napoleonic wars. A carriage accident in 1811 meant that he was often confined to a wheelchair, a factor in the depression he suffered in later life, living resentfully in his modest cottage in Hare Street, just outside the prosperous Essex market town of Romford.[5]

Repton had settled at Hare Street forty years earlier, considering the cottage to be a temporary measure. It was a convenient spot from which to launch his late choice of career, catching the eye of a clientele that tended to be London-based even if their estates were not. But, as his admiring memorialist, the gardener John Claudius Loudon, put it: 'this humble dwelling subsequently became so endeared to him, as the scene of some trials and many blessings, that he never afterwards sought any other home.'[6]

In person, Repton was proud of his flexible attitudes and sociability, both in the modest setting of his own home and elsewhere. He was, he claimed, entirely at ease with the grandees of Romford, the East India-enriched Benyons of Gidea Hall and the stone-merchants-made-good Wallinger dynasty of Hare Hall, since 'mixing with all mankind' was his stock in trade. He invited the families to his carefully presented house. 'A few drawings and musical instruments and birds, flowers in one small room and a few well-chosen books in the other, a garden judiciously stocked with shrubs and flowers and an air of home comfort, all supplied the place of costly magnificence...' and soon a monthly get-together was instigated, for dancing and cards, held at the village inn since the homely cottage had become too small for all of Repton's many acquaintances.

This rose-tinted period came to an end when the Benyons inherited a mansion in Berkshire around 1800 and sold Gidea Park to Alexander Black, a military contractor (albeit supplying tents and bedding rather than munitions). John Wallinger, who had insisted on Hare Hall facing north, instead of sun-catching south, so that everyone could see his grand pile from the road, died in 1792 and the estate was divided between his two sons, then vested in trustees and subject to years of legal wrangling. The old decencies owed to long-term tenants and village life were forgotten, with frequent evictions and properties left to rot, as Repton reported. The village emptied and Repton entered a long-running dispute over his own tenancy.

The proximity to London, and excellent transport on the high road, was attracting a new class of professional men, who viewed land as investment rather than responsibility. In

Repton's own view at Hare Street: unimproved (top) and improved

Repton's eyes, Romford, formerly the well-appointed apron-stage to the theatre that was London, had become the very reverse – a launch pad towards the city for newly rich men. The landscape was littered with vacant and abandoned properties – much like those houses in the hamlets around Stansted airport whose compulsory purchase for unfounded runway expansion plans in the 1990s left them empty, prey to almost inevitable arson and dereliction.

Yet in a brief moment of optimism in 1813, Repton scented a possible upturn in his fortunes – a site even nearer to London, but convenient from Hare Street: Wanstead. The Duke of Wellington's nephew, William Wellesley Pole had married Catherine Tylney Long, a descendent of Josiah Child, the late 17th-century East India Company chairman and banker and believed to be the richest woman in Essex. Repton's client now went by the extensive name of William Tylney Long Pole Wellesley, to match his windfall. Though suddenly wealthy, he could not be called *nouveau riche*, or so Repton persuaded himself. Even though, greatly to the architect's mortification, Wellesley had specifically asked him not to draw up one of his famous Red Books, he did so in any case. Correctly suspecting that payment would not be forthcoming, he added the designs, without a location, to his final excoriating book, *Fragments* (1816) – in which he also included a 'before' and 'after' of the view from the windows of his own modest home.

Well before, the diarist John Evelyn had echoed Repton's views of men with new money. The author of the (still) definitive study of trees and forestry, *Sylva* (1664) had heard about Josiah Child's extravagance 'in planting of Walnut trees, about his seate, & making fish-ponds, for many miles in Circuite… in a Cursed & barren spot.' The barren spot in question was Child's new Wanstead estate. With more than a hint of *schadenfreude*, Evelyn imagined that the parvenu would come unstuck through foolish over-spending, as often happened with 'these over growne & suddainly monied men'. As it turned out, Evelyn was wrong.

Josiah Child had been born in London in modest circumstances, starting out as a merchant's apprentice, later embarking on a string of unsavoury commercial ventures built upon slave labour in Africa and Jamaica, triumphantly buying the entire Wanstead estate in 1673. Ten years on, Evelyn believed him to be worth £200,000, a colossal fortune. Child died in

1699, having never rebuilt the Elizabethan manor he rented in 1667, when he was still a minor, if savvy, shareholder in the East India Company. His son Richard took the next step, in 1715 commissioning Colen Campbell to crown the park with the most perfect Palladian mansion ever built in England, Wanstead House.

Repton's idea was to cut back the overgrown plantation at Wanstead and open a direct vista, largely over water, between the windows of the great house and the City of London. The dome of St Paul's Cathedral, just eight miles away, would act as a distant eye-catcher, as do the towers of Canary Wharf, the City and the Shard to the modern motorist driving towards London. Wellesley pressed on with the scheme, forgetting only one thing – payment. He was spending money like water, on everything conceivable and inconceivable, such as a stag hunt complete with liveried hunt servants which he disbanded almost before they had a chance to don their uniforms.[7] He was profligate beyond even Repton's experience – by 1822 the great mansion had been seized by his creditors and in 1824, with no buyer in sight, it was demolished and sold as building material, little more than a century after its construction. Humphry Repton had died in 1818, broken, but Wellesley, still lord of the manor, styling himself the 4th Earl of Mornington and, briefly, sitting as MP for Essex in 1831-32, lived on until 1856. The perfect mansion he destroyed is now a slight dip at the first tee on the Wanstead golf course.

In the 18th and early 19th centuries, the villages to the east of London made ideal weekend country house locations for rising City men. Several of the young architect John Soane's early clients were Directors of the Bank of England. In 1788, their collective recommendation, based upon his proven professionalism and clear ability, gained him the stellar job of architect to the Bank of England, at the age of thirty-five, a post he would hold until 1833. The outskirts of the capital were the professional stepping-stones to the City as well as its lungs.

Well before Soane's ascent or Repton's descent, the Huguenot family of Houblon had travelled from Lille, via the dense yards of Spitalfields to a comfortable existence in bosky Leyton. Diarist Samuel Pepys' close friend Sir James was a merchant and MP for the City of London while his younger brother, Sir John, became the first Governor of the Bank of England in 1694. His Forest House was a typical small seat for a rising City man – a 'pretty villa', John Evelyn had thought. A century later Soane remodelled it for Samuel Bosanquet, another Huguenot Governor of the Bank. The next generation of Houblons added Hallingbury Place and nearby Hatfield Forest (not to be confused with Hatfield House in Hertfordshire, built by Queen Elizabeth I's favourite, Robert Cecil) to the family holdings, a substantial inheritance. The ascent to the landed gentry took hardly a couple of generations, but the return journey could be even swifter.

The Hallingbury estate was eventually auctioned off in 1923 (and the house demolished) but the future of the adjoining Hatfield Forest was secured in a – literally – last-minute effort by the Walthamstow MP and conservation campaigner Edward North Buxton. In his youth, Buxton had helped secure Epping Forest for the public and later almost single-handedly saved the final scraps of once great Hainault Forest, handing it to the LCC. Hatfield Forest was his swansong: he died the day after buying it for the young National Trust (founded 1895), to prevent the original purchaser, a Yorkshire timber merchant, from felling any more oaks in the ancient deer park. Edward's son Gerald and other family members, along with a surviving Houblon, then moved quickly to secure the rest of the entire post-enclosure Forest. By October 1924 they had bought more than 600 acres[8].

With the acquisition of Hatfield, a fragile and rare survival of a royal hunting forest, as well as the 18th-century parkland and lake, were added to the lengthening list of important (and inalienable) properties that the National Trust secured for the public; it opened that same year. Hatfield Forest remains one of the most precious of all the landscapes in its care, and however carefully managed, is more threatened by the sheer volume of visitors, almost all arriving by car given the lack of alternatives, than by any other factor – even the close proximity to Stansted Airport.

William Morris' father had been a typical commuter, living in a country village and taking the stagecoach to his London office daily. His son was born at Elm House, Walthamstow. The early 19th-century house had a large garden and commanded gentle views over the Lea Valley towards Epping Forest. As he became more successful as a City discount broker, the family moved up a rung to the considerably larger and more expensive Woodford Hall, a Georgian mansion on the very edge of the forest, rented for £600 per annum[9]. The full estate included a park and farmland and, importantly for the children, easy access to fishing in the River Roding.

But this steady climb in status and expenditure, reflected in the location and scale of the family homes, was cut short when Morris Sr. died in 1847 and his firm collapsed almost immediately afterwards. The family then moved to Water House, Walthamstow, a smaller version of the previous abode, now handsomely presented as the William Morris Museum. Each of these houses was a version of an ascendant City man's 'box', and perhaps the upheaval of down-sizing to one clouded young William's view of Walthamstow for good. In 1883, he described it as 'a suburban village on the edge of Epping Forest, and once a pleasant place enough... now terribly cocknified and choked up by the jerry-builder.'

Around 1820 an unknown client commissioned an extensive tea service, showing all the country seats scattered around Walthamstow – a rather cheeky provincial version of Catherine the Great of Russia's 1773 Wedgwood 'Frog Service' (which stretched to 1,244 views of the British Isles, especially its country seats). Soon after, the railways would tip the balance in this area of comfortable villages near the capital, dramatically telescoping distances and with time, driving the development of a region unrecognizable as either the country or the city: suburbia.

In his own time, Daniel Defoe had seen the advantages of new blood coming into Essex. The villages were 'much pleasanter and more sociable than formerly, for now people go to them, not for retirement into the country, but for good company' and, better still, they have become the haunt of good conversation, untainted by gaming or 'vice and debauchery'. One notable figure who came to Essex for the good of his precarious health was the elderly John Locke, suffering from severe asthma intensified by London's polluted air. In 1691 Sir Francis Masham and his wife, Damaris Cudworth, the latter Locke's particular friend and intellectual equal, suggested he join them in High Laver, a farming village in the Roding Valley. Their manor house, Otes, would be his home for the rest of his life. He paid rental for himself, his trusted amanuensis and a horse, and was given the use of two of the best rooms in the house, including the Drawing Room, where he installed his four-thousand-volume library, a desk and specially designed chair, his meteorological and botanical collections and his telescope. He also had a 'great porous stone through which all the water he drank – and he drank nothing else – was carefully filtered.' He was no ordinary lodger.[10]

Due to Locke, Otes became 'one of the really important addresses in the world of European letters' and attracted visitors such as Isaac Newton and that eminent philosopher-politician, the 3rd Earl of Shaftesbury. The man who formulated the founding principles of the American Declaration of Independence, penned many years after his death, collected his thoughts and found continuing health in the good air (and water) of Essex. He is buried in an anonymous-looking chest tomb against the south wall of the parish church, close to the graves of his patrons, though his self-composed Latin memorial is now inside the church, including lines translated as, 'What else there is about him, learn from his writing which will set this forth in a manner more worthy of your belief than the suspect eulogies of an epitaph.' Set into a cat's cradle of knotted tiny lanes, and a confusing clutch of Lavers, Locke's burial place is scarcely more disturbed now than his adopted home (demolished in the early 19th century) was then – even though Harlow is just four miles west.

During the Civil War, the depths of rural mid-Essex seemed reassuringly far from London. Sir John Bramston the Elder had held the position of King Charles I's Lord Chief Justice and by 1635 the situation was looking fragile. That year Bramston bought Skreens, a medieval house outside Roxwell near Chelmsford. Almost twenty years later he died there, well out of sight and mind of those who might have given him trouble, and was buried in the nearby village church. His son, John Bramston the Younger, had practised at the Bar until, as he put it so charmingly in his *Autobiography*, 'the drums and trumpets blew his gown over his ears.' With the outbreak of the Civil War, he too retreated to his father's house among the Essex hop-gardens and woods.

After the monarchy was restored under King Charles II, Bramston reemerged to become the 'Knight of the Shire', that is the county representative for Essex in both the Convention Parliament formed in 1660 and the Cavalier Parliament from 1661 onwards. He stood for Maldon and took on a number of roles in the county, before, as he recounted, King James II instituted a new town charter and swept away the old civic order, Bramston included. He was clear about the king's aims and 'the Roman religion he resolved to establish'. To achieve his ends, Bramston wrote, 'he garbled the corporations and sent emissaries amongst them to influence them for choice of members for Parliament, such as would take away the penal law and test; gave indulgences and dispenced by his owne authority with all the laws: but this furious hasty driving ruin'd him, and all his.' In October 1688, the sixth Lord Petre, head of the premier Catholic family of Essex, honourably petitioned on behalf of all the dismissed justices for the county, some 37 men, including Sir John Bramston, Knight of the Bath. They were restored, only to refuse to serve under a Catholic Lord Lieutenant and so were replaced.

Around Old Skreens Park, wild service trees and hornbeams

dot the hedges and scant woods, sufficiently rare species to mark the whereabouts and boundaries of forgotten grazing or former meadows. Those enduring trees are backed up by the field names marked in a rare set of very early estate maps, which reveal the crops grown, among them, hops and vines. Otherwise, nothing remains of Skreens, either the early, essentially medieval version or the house rebuilt in 1728. Now it vied with a City grandee's establishment, the relatively modest house and landscaped grounds laid out for Sir John Salter, Lord Mayor of London, at Warden's Hall, outside Willingale scarcely four miles away. Compared to the Bramstons, the Salters were merely passing through the area, although Sir John was buried here in 1744.

Meanwhile Skreens was altered again around 1770, enlarged in the style of the moment, possibly by the able county surveyor John Johnson whose classical architecture is scattered throughout the Chelmsford area, unfailingly seemly and pleasantly proportioned, if sometimes no more than a 'polite' symmetrical front added to a shambling Tudor house spilling out to the rear.

The eldest Bramston in each generation took his seat in parliament and lived in style at the remodelled Georgian Skreens, while his siblings fanned out nearby, mulching down among the middling, professional classes of Essex and occasionally marrying back up the social ladder. The Rev. John Bramston became rector of nearby Willingale from 1797 and built a solid white brick rectory there. He was a worthy man, with a surprising wife.

In 1832 the Rev. Bramston had married Clarissa Trant, whose lively diaries ran to twenty-eight volumes. The daughter of an Irish officer in the Portuguese army, Clarissa's memoirs combine an Austen-like dryness with a traveller's eye for detail, describing perilous sea crossings during which she hid from pirates, her father's fending off of a knife assault from 'an intoxicated Voiturier' with an unloaded pistol and the gossip of society balls with the same, breathless energy. She could be waspish: 'she is versed in horseflesh and agriculture…' went one description of an acquaintance, 'and more inclined to sit with the gentlemen than retire with the ladies...' and yet when it came to meeting the Reverend Bramston, on a steam packet from Ireland to Wales 'with several hundred pigs for our fellow passengers', she seemed to have been smitten.

Sadly, for later readers at least, marriage meant an end to Clarissa's chronicles, and if she had any sharp observations of Essex village life to record, she did not live long enough to do so, dying in 1844 after bearing three children. Nor, it seems, did she manage to transmit any of her own *joie de vivre* to her husband.

In 1837 Bramston unsuccessfully petitioned against the Whitsuntide Village Fair at Great Baddow, where he was now rector. His aim was to stop vulgar traditional amusements ('jiggling matches – jumping in sacks – grinning through collars – bobbing for oranges' as listed in a report in the *Colchester Gazette*). Since most working people around there would have been chapel- rather than church-going, and thus not even members of his congregation, he was adding insult to injury. Fortunately, the result was firmly in their favour.

Several Bramstons followed the original Sir John, being buried or memorialised in or near Roxwell church. The family built the neat red-brick village school in 1834. A connection with the area, begun with a grandee's retreat from the intense dangers of city and court two centuries before, was now perpetuated by a conscientious middling professional family.

By the end of the 19th century, and after plenty of attention to no good effect, Skreens was an unwieldy, unattractive house, overwhelming the Georgian core. It had become a drain on the Bramston resources, for like all their neighbours, they had seen farm income fall away and their tenants broken under the burden. Rents had dropped to nothing, and the second Royal Commission on Agriculture of 1894 particularly noted 'the ruinous state of Agriculture in the Ongar, Chelmsford, Maldon – Braintree districts'. Across Essex, agriculture only survived by the arrival of farmers from elsewhere, usually Scotland or Cornwall, a process continuing up to the First War.

In 1911 Joseph Heywood came from Cornwall to rent Elms Farm in Roxwell, spending his first nights sleeping on straw in the front room. Heywood's possessions and stock came by train and his sister followed on, to act as housekeeper. By 1914 he was in a position to buy the farm. But Heywood was a late-comer, Cornish dairy farmers began pouring into west Essex in the 1890s, while a decade earlier, Scottish newspapers encouraged rural readers southwards with advertisements such as: 'Essex farms within 25 miles of London, at low rents and with freedom of cultivation'. Restrictive farm leases, particularly in Ayrshire, were another factor. They brought their herds and their working animals, and their horses, allegedly, struggled to understand commands now given in Essex dialect. Many of those incoming farming families remain, though dairy farming, at its height when tankerloads of Essex milk went into the city by train, is just a memory.

Skreens was sold in 1906 and again in 1914, along with twenty-seven farms, as well as lodges, farmhouses and cottages. Next went the big house, demolished during the war – a remarkable erasure, since not a sign remained when local men returned from the trenches. Were the materials sold off to help build those 'Homes for Heroes' that every village so needed and deserved for their handful of returning servicemen? In any case, where on earth did Skreens go?

Only the lake and some venerable trees survive from Skreens Park. It is now the busy centre for Essex Scouts, and in 2007 gained wider fame as one of several bases for the 38,000 attendees of the 21st World Scout Jamboree, held at nearby Hylands Park to mark the centenary of the scout movement's foundation. That summer fortnight led to numerous surreal, though good-natured encounters as bemused scout leaders from countries as diverse as Croatia, Japan and Senegal were found wandering the Essex lanes in search of their campsite.

It is ironic that Finchingfield, the ultimate picturesque East Anglian village, illustrated in at least a hundred books about pretty places, would be the home, for almost half his long life, of the acerbic Norman Lewis, travel writer and surely the crabbiest ever resident of Essex. In an essay for the magazine *Granta*, balanced between offering a documentary account and a satirised version of reality, he launched into an attack on the county. 'Essex is the ugliest county...' began the opening sentence. Lewis had retreated to Essex for quiet but found it 'flat and untidy and full of water.' Even well inland, 'gulls drove the crows out of the fields.' He was proof against the mystery of the marsh, or the quiet pleasures of the farm landscape, but behind his antagonistic mask, he was fascinated by the changes taking place around him.

In 1957 and 1958 Lewis rented a farmhouse in a village which he calls Long Crendon (it was actually Wendens Ambo), noting that the farms and villages had 'odd and even poetic names... the more fanciful the name the more dismal the place.' Lewis relished it all, one paradox at a time, including the suicidal farmer whose house he was renting. The deep moat spawned a good crop of excellent oyster fungus, collected by an Italian from Chelmsford in return for a bottle of Asti Spumante. Then a new farmer took on the land, rooting up trees, planting 'horse-beans, the most hideous of all crops' and spraying chemicals on everything. In a single year he altered every detail in the landscape that Lewis had enjoyed until then. Yet as so-called Long Crendon found affluence in the 1960s and 70s, Lewis turned the idea of change on its head. He could see that village Essex was altering in front of his eyes, but being a contrarian, he quite liked what he saw and he recognised the benefits. The object of the stay in Wendens Ambo was to find a permanent home for him and his latest girlfriend, Lesley.

Returning after a stint abroad, Lewis stayed at the village pub, which had gone up in the world considerably. However readily he made things up when it suited the story, his portrait of the place was founded on acute observation. In 1959 they (or he) had chosen the Old Vicarage in Finchingfield because of its relative remoteness and its exceptionally high ceilings, Lewis being far too tall for an Essex cottage.

In general, Lewis considered, two influences were changing the villages. One was renewed activity and expansion
at the nearby American air base, Wethersfield, leading to a
nefarious trade in surplus supplies from the back of trucks,
after-dark activities which added a strand of the illicit very
much to Lewis' taste. The second was incomers, people like
himself, 'frontiersmen' as he called them. The new money on
occasion introduced elements of 'brutal modernisation' such
as knocking through fragile old walls indoors and installing
metal gates outdoors, and the locals had started emulating
these signs of modernity. Nor would he bow to the niceties
of village life, in particular those of his bugbear, the local
bourgeoisie. As his biographer and editor, Julian Evans puts
it, he fought 'boredom with mischief', ensuring a rich seam of
village gossip, for example, asking an impressionable female
guest at his dinner party whether Lesley had yet taken her
upstairs to see the mirror suspended over their bed. The
sprightly storyteller milked Essex mercilessly for its potential, tongue lodged firmly in cheek. Outdoors, the 'mute Essex
plain' stimulated Lewis' sardonic observation and when Evans
drove the old man through Braintree's suburbs, 'his travelling
eye was as enthusiastic and acute in disenchantment as in
pleasure.' The University of Essex awarded Lewis an honorary

Picture-postcard-perfect Finchingfield, sullied by only one vehicle

doctorate in 1987. The same year, he was on the BBC's Desert Island Discs, choosing Stravinsky's 'Petrushka' for its iconoclasm, 'being a bit of an iconoclast myself.'[11]

He drew a picture of Essex raw, its villagers becoming upwardly mobile but not necessarily mindful of what they were leaving behind or even destroying as they rose. He admired the 'real' villagers, 'silent as the Romans, although, unlike the Romans dragooned by memories of a past that had taught them to keep their opinions on all subjects strictly to themselves.' He sought the underside of what looked, at first glance and to the eager tourist, like an absurdly neat village around a rolling green and a pleasing stream. In the 1930s, when it was frequently featured as the ultimate pretty village, photographers ensured that any vehicles were parked almost entirely out of sight.

Now Lewis joined the fight against turning the water meadows into a by now essential – if highly contentious – car park for visiting day-trippers. The parish council in its wisdom suggested the tarmac be stained green. The proposal was scuppered and later Lewis helped to buy some land, including the water meadows, and maintain them for wildlife and poplars (for profit). He was far more engaged in his village than he was prepared to admit.

There is no record of what Lewis' old friend, the American humourist Sid (S. J.) Perelman, visiting from Manhattan with his wife in 1960, made of picture-postcard Finchingfield or of Norman Lewis so incongruously planted there. We only know they were disconcerted by the extreme cold in the house and by having every complaint dismissed out of hand by their ever-contrary host. Very late in life Lewis described his home of forty-five years, as an 'intellectual tundra', and yet productive of an 'introspective, almost monastic calm.' A kind of Shangri-La – which was, as it turns out, closer to Essex than we might have imagined.

5   HEAVEN WITH THE GATES OFF

Fresh Starts in Essex

There are Shangri-Las everywhere. A global hotel chain has taken the name, as have takeaways throughout the United Kingdom and hair salons in Canada. Proffering a generic paradise, the name even ornaments a cattery and a caravan park in Essex, which is at least marginally more appropriate, since Shangri-La's creator, the novelist James Hilton, wrote his hugely successful novel *Lost Horizon* nearby.

It's likely that Hilton's travels in Pakistan's Hunza Valley, and his studies of a 19th-century Tibetan travelogue provided a dash of inspiration for his tale, although he wrote it while living down a modest cul-de-sac in Woodford Green. At best, he might have caught views out over a westerly, sylvan slice of Epping Forest, but for the rest he fell back on his imagination. His second success *Goodbye Mr Chips* was rooted closer to home, based around his father's years as headmaster of Church End School, in nearby Walthamstow. The two books sold in phenomenal quantities and lent themselves easily to Hollywood film adaptations. Hilton was soon able to move a world away from Woodford to his own version of Shangri-La, working as a screenwriter in California.

Essex itself has often been a Shangri-La, an imaginary place in which everything would turn out better. The recent unlikely tale of optimistic ultra-orthodox Haredi Jews leaving their traditional, but now overpriced and overcrowded areas of Stamford Hill and Tottenham for Canvey Island suggests that the search for paradise is ongoing. In this case, the old sinews binding Jewish East London and Essex come into their own. Haredi Jews in Canvey find themselves surrounded by many people who are a few generations, at most, away from the old East End. There's nothing untoward, for them, about the pattern of life, religious observance or dietary preferences of their new neighbours, who are, by definition, self-contained as a community but also very positive about their move. In his essay 'Essex, an Island off London', the journalist and author Tim Burrows quotes one of the incomers saying that the islanders 'know about the bagels and the fish. They know more about the Jewish community than our old neighbours did.'[1]

Media coverage of the community move has tended to make much of Canvey Island's existing homogeneity. In a world of detached Sans Soucis and Shangri-Las, where the flag of St. George flies high, only the house names stray far from home. The island is 70% white, one of the five most pro-Brexit constituencies in the country, yet there are some obvious parallels between the established population and the incomers. If Canvey Islanders are traditional types, who stick to their own and keep a certain distance from outsiders, then exactly the same applies to the orthodox Jewish colonists from Stamford Hill. There's no reason why two groups should not be insular on the same island.

The transit route from overcrowded East End to rural space and peace in Essex is nothing new. In the 1890s, many working-class Londoners had a yen for rural life (probably having left the countryside hardly a generation or two earlier) or were eager to improve their living conditions however they could. A left-over bit of railway land in Leyton, at Lea Bridge Gardens, was known as Bungalow Town and its almost seventy shacks gained charm with their DIY verandas and cottage gardens. Begun in the 1880s, it was all gone by the 1930s. Perhaps the residents moved on, out to the banks of the River Lea or the seaside, to fulfil their dreams?

Shades of the Orient, in Leyton: self-built cottages at the end of the 19th century

Trains began to run regularly out of Fenchurch Street, Limehouse or East Ham stations to farm sales in south-east Essex – the tickets often offered *gratis* by wheeler-dealers who had spotted a golden opportunity. Strips of poor-quality land, the remnants of larger holdings abandoned by bankrupt farmers, could be secured for a deposit and regular modest payments – a Never-Never system for a nebulous rural dream.

After a free lunch, and perhaps a drink or two, potential bidders were herded into a tent, soon to find themselves committed to the purchase of two or three long thin plots, the land heavy clay, the facilities negligible. The promises proved flimsy, too; often 'mains water' was revealed as no more than a standpipe on the main road a mile or more away, while 'roads' consisted of unmade earth tracks which dissolved into a swill of deep mud after rain. The legal arrangements for purchase were frequently non-existent or non-viable, since the agents and opportunistic developers who had clambered onto this lucrative bandwagon were often inexpert or, on occasion, dishonest. But to be in Laindon or Pitsea, Woodham Ferrers, Jaywick or Canvey Island with land of their own was, for families from the squalid Victorian 'rookeries' or 'stews' of Limehouse, Whitechapel, Poplar or Bethnal Green, sheer bliss. In an early echo of the Canvey Island story, one farm sale at Benfleet in the 1890s was aimed squarely at Jewish families, so recently hounded out of eastern Europe, with handbills printed in Yiddish and the suggestion (apparently unfulfilled) that Thundersley House could serve as their synagogue.

Canvey's development, meanwhile, owed a little to the entrepreneurial spirit of Frederick Hester, who bought up 500 plots of cheap farm land at the beginning of the 20th century. Hester's intention was to rebrand the island as a sort of continental enclave of sophistication and healthy living, where smog-choked Londoners could come for a holiday, rest and cure. He commissioned a history of the island to be written, making much of its connection with the Dutch engineer Cornelius Vermuyden (who had spent a couple of years assisting with land reclamation works on Canvey and across eastern England in the 17th century), and fusing a scattering of history with his own roadmap for a glorious future, to include Winter Gardens on Canvey Island, a monorail (always a sure signal of a futuristic imagination tipping over into fever) and street canals, á la Venice or Amsterdam (signifying a retrospective heritage tendency well ahead of Walt Disney, let alone post-miracle China). Like many a chancer's illusions, Hester's came to naught, or in this case, the bankruptcy courts. Elsewhere in the county, the pre-war trickle soon became a flood, the whole business of taming the wilderness in many cases proving a kind of self-administered therapy for survivors reeling back from the front. East Enders arrived off the train or bus, weighed down with planks and building materials – in one case, salvaged from the

demolished wreck of a once-elegant Georgian house in Battersea within whose library William Wilberforce and his Quaker
colleagues had planned their anti-slavery campaign. The Settlement, Canvey Island, was built in 1905 by the unstoppable
Mrs. Sarah Stevens and incorporated doors, windows and even
carved panelling from the very room in which those good men
had brought about emancipation. No doubt some settlers saw
their journey to Essex in the same light as they piled into the
motorcycle sidecars which many of them used to bring their
families and their supplies out east.

Every story spoke of dreams and determination. Lydia Bon-
net was interviewed for the 1983 London Weekend Television
programme 'The Making of Modern London' and is quoted
in Gavin Weightman and Steve Humphries' book of that title.
She remembered that in 1924 her father had been tipped off by
his foreman at work, after seeing an advertisement for £5 plots
in Dunton in the *Hackney and Kingsland Gazette*. Her parents
went out to have a look the very next weekend and Mr. Sawyer,
the foreman, bought some 'but Dad couldn't afford it. Anyway,
the next weekend Dad took Mum to Dunton and she fell in love
with the place. Secretly she got a part-time job in a jam factory
and saved up the money.'

With equal discretion, Lydia's resourceful mother bought some
plots, next to Sawyer's, and when the family went there next, she
said to her husband, "'You would like some of those, wouldn't you
Bill?" "Yes". So Mum said, "Don't just stand there, get cracking, you
want some posts and barbed wire, it's yours, I've just bought them.'"

They started with a tent, occasionally sleeping on a friendly
neighbour's floor when it was too cold, and then they set about
building their bungalow. Lydia's mother put on her husband's
old trousers, sat on the roof ridge and cemented in the tiles as
he handed them up.

Most of the little houses were fragile, for the new weekend-
ers had reached the limits of their ambitions. Gradually, rough
ground with a tent or lean-to in the middle became cultivated
and perhaps the site of a modest dwelling, while, more widely,

communal arrangements evolved. Sometimes developers inter-
vened. In the late 1920s at Jaywick, the opportunistic F.C. Sted-
man offered those buyers who could afford it a standard chalet
or bungalow design, but the roads on the Brooklands Estate
named after motor cars (the west end) and flowers (the east
end), wittily linked by Gorse Way, remained ironically unmet-
alled, unadopted and as a result often unsuitable for four-
wheeled vehicles.

Following the second war, tens of thousands of plotlanders
from the interwar years were forced by circumstances to recon-
sider their rudimentary summer houses as permanent homes
and to scratch a partial living from their orchards and smallholdings. But there were no amenities, since these residents had
not paid any rates. Toilet facilities were best described as 'bucket
and chuck it' and little had changed since the interwar years.
But now the land, and its doughty occupants, had become ripe
for the picking.[2] The government had big plans for the counties around London, and most particularly for Essex after much
of the East End and docks had been pulverised during the war.
The Town and Country Planning Act (1947) gave it the teeth
required. But a visionary was needed to steer the legislation
through parliament, and the man in question, a modest, quietly spoken solicitor, was the Labour politician, Lewis Silkin.
His own background mirrored that of many east Londoners: he
was born in Poplar to immigrant parents, Lithuanian Jews. Following election to the London County Council (LCC) in 1925
and to parliament in 1936, he became the highly effective, and
committed, minister for town and country planning in Clement
Atlee's government.

It was, and is, rare to hear works of literature evoked on the
floor of the House of Commons, but on May 8, 1946, the second
reading of the New Towns Bill, Lewis Silkin described Thomas
More's 16th-century utopian blueprint of fifty-four new towns,
twenty-three miles apart, each divided into four neighbour-
hoods, all with a local centre. While admitting that some might
consider an early Renaissance ideal society to be a far cry from

postwar new towns, he suggested that it was high time for such ambitions: 'it is not unreasonable to expect that "Utopia" of 1515 should be translated into practical reality in 1946.'

The problem for those planning the new world was London. It had been pushing too hard, spilling too far. Silkin reminded the House of the 'ill effects of the growth of London and other large towns', as yet little controlled by the (no more than virtual) Metropolitan Green Belt. Professor Patrick Abercrombie, the very model of the town and country planner, with his monocle and bow tie, had overseen the magisterial *Greater London Plan 1944* – essentially the text to Silkin's proposals. (The planner in Halas and Batchelor's brilliant film animation for the Central Office of Information, 'Charley goes to New Town', looks very much like him.) The two men were in close agreement; Abercombie was sure that 'a new series of Becontrees would be fatal'. Becontree was the largest public housing scheme in the world, built in loosely cottage estate style by the LCC and on the ground well before its key employer arrived. Ford's Dagenham car and engine factory agreed to set up there in 1929, to open in 1931; by 1935 its population was approaching 100,000 and Becontree was becoming, by default, a Ford company town, though desperately short of the amenities that might be expected of such an enterprise, either in the public or private sector.

Motivated by, amongst many things, the fear that the Depression-hit working class might turn to Bolshevism, the LCC, led at the time by the principally right-wing Municipal Reform party, provided well-built cottages with gardens at Becontree, all of it 'council' housing. It was bold in scale but undeniably tame in its cottage-style brick architecture, repetitive avenues of semi-detached houses with gardens front and back, meandering streets and cul-de-sacs, a massively inflated version of the munitions estates built at speed late in the First War. Becontree had been conceived in the immediate aftermath of that war: the centenary of its founding is in 2021. Yet, as the social scientist Terence Young pointed out in his 1934 study of the estate, had Becontree been in the USA it would have attracted glowing 'articles and newsreels… containing references to the speed at which a new town of 120,000 people had been built. The work of the firm of contractors would have been shown as an excellent example of the American business ideal of Service to the Community.' On the other hand, had this Becontree been in Vienna, 'the Labour and left Liberal press would have boosted it as an example of what municipal socialism could accomplish… But Becontree was planned and built in England, where the most revolutionary social changes can take place, and people in general do not realise that they have occurred.'[3]

The childhood home of actor Dudley Moore and the former Archbishop of Canterbury George Carey, Becontree was flawed, though not quite the monolithic planning disaster that Abercrombie and Silkin saw. Plans for a church, shops, 25 schools and a civic centre were delayed or cancelled, those very elements that would have helped it cohere. Until the borough of Dagenham was formed in 1938, the sprawling mega-estate fell under the control of three separate district councils. Only bureaucracy could distinguish between them. Yet many residents were happy to live there, compared to the previous conditions in east London. One correspondent told Young that her mother described it as 'heaven with the gates off'. A survey in 1947 found that 85% of tenants liked their houses (which were actually built in 91 different styles) and 63% liked their neighbourhood.

Nevertheless, the lack of amenities, the uniformity of the housing stock and the lack of any attractive natural or landscaped features (despite the proximity of that once desirable leisure feature, the Dagenham lakes) continued to cause complaint. Bye-laws required weekly washing of windows and cultivation of front gardens (especially clipping the privet hedges) and placed strict limits on the number of public houses. By the time the final Ford Fiestas came off the line in 2002, those front gardens had long since become hard standing for cars, the Right to Buy revolution had unpicked the homogeneity of the houses and more widely, the future was not looking too bright. Over the years skilled work gave way to low skilled jobs in warehousing or logistics and there is little on the horizon to reverse that pattern.

For Silkin as for Abercrombie, Essex was where the wrongs of Becontree were to be put right. 'This is our last chance… if the existing evils are not to be aggravated.' The New Towns were a national task. He dreamed that the new houses, jobs, amenities and a simulacrum of the close, familial society out of which so many had been torn, could combine 'the friendly spirit of the former slum' with enormously improved health and 'a broadened spirit embracing all classes of society.' And the towns must be handsome, offering 'a grand chance for the revival or creation of a new architecture.' And not just a new architecture: Silkin also looked forward to the emergence of 'a new type of citizen, a healthy, self-respecting, dignified person with a sense of beauty, culture and civic pride.'

In 1898, Ebenezer Howard, who worked as a court stenographer and Hansard reporter, and had lived in progressive Chicago for some years, published a book titled *Tomorrow: a Peaceful Path to Real Reform*. In 1902 it was republished with the clearer title, *Garden Cities of Tomorrow*. His solution was to separate the city from the country, a rational plan offering zones for the different aspects of life, home, work and leisure. The First Garden City, at Letchworth, his greatest achievement, was an attempt to solve the problems of relentless urban expansion; at its core was a vision of the investment of the rising value of the land into the fabric and civic amenities of the town itself. Underpinning that was one of the many –isms of the age, Georgism, an economic philosophy with which Howard had become enamoured during his Chicago years, which held that earnings from labour should not be taxed, while the value derived from land and buildings should be distributed communally.

Romford Garden Suburb was the nearest Essex ever came to a Garden City. Sir Herbert Raphael, a Liberal MP, a councillor on the new LCC and then on Essex County Council bought Gidea Hall and its 480 acre estate in 1897, and launched the venture, packaged as an architectural exhibition, with his two partners, also Liberal MPs, John Tudor Walters and Charles McCurdy. They had sloughed off Howard's essential principle of distributing development value – possibly unnoticed by those who, despite their widely Fabian persuasion, vouched for it so enthusiastically.

Their own promotional material made much of old Romford, a provincial market town still enveloped in 'pure country air' and where the nightingales sang as they had when Edward the Confessor (allegedly) prayed at Gidea Hall (demolished in 1930). In prose that would not go amiss in a 21st-century developers' brochure, readers were asked to imagine it built: 'where last year there were meadows, to-day there are pleasant groups of houses and cottages, every house or cottage noteworthy as the realization of an architect's ideal.' Many of the houses, comfortably set together along meandering avenues looked, reassuringly if superficially, quite like the larger houses in an Essex village, with their half-timbered gables and fancy brick chimneys.

Romford Garden Suburb was eager to set itself apart. Nearby Upminster Garden Suburb (an almost random example from the explosive suburbanisation of the Essex fringes) aimed to house 'a desirable class... the blossoming lower-middle classes – the clerks, shop workers, teachers, salesmen and others' who would travel to and fro the capital by train from there. But the promoters at Romford aimed to transform standards of space and domestic design, considering that housing for the 15,000 families who were estimated to be moving to outer London annually could no longer be left to the 'uncertain, unscientific, uneconomical, unsocial and inartistic activities of the Speculative Builder.'

By the time of Herbert Raphael's publication, both a manifesto for better housing design and a promotional document, *The Book of the Exhibition of Houses and Cottages* (1911) one hundred and forty 'model' small houses and cottages had been built to the designs of a hundred architects at what would become known as Gidea Park. The liberal great and good were asked to specify, first, what they considered the worst aspects of the average house and second, the greatest improvement. George Bernard Shaw and Thomas Hardy, Arnold Bennett and H. G. Wells, playwright Arthur Pinero and suffragist Millicent Garrett Fawcett were amongst those who responded. They agreed on draughts and distant bathrooms as negatives, while close-fitting casement windows, tiled surfaces and kitchens as neat and compact as those 'on a rich man's yacht' were positives. An emphasis on practical domestic design for the modern woman, now coping without live-in servants, was the most progressive strand.

The masterplan was by Raymond Unwin, working with his architectural partner Barry Parker, giving Romford Garden Suburb a shared pedigree with Letchworth and Hampstead Garden Suburb. If none of the luminous names on the rollcall of supporters had decided to test out arcadia in Romford, it still had one important consequence. In 1918 John Tudor Walters gave his name (as chairman) to the report which established basic housing standards in Britain, applied to all council housing from then on. But in pre-war Romford, for all the ambitions, the result was little more than a superior suburban estate and even the promised shops, located conveniently close to the new station, were never built.

In 1934 Romford Garden Suburb was firmly and definitively renamed Gidea Park (to match the underground station that had been clumsily, if cutely, named Gidea Park and Squirrels Heath) and thirty-five houses added, a contemporary model cottage exhibition to demonstrate 'all the wonders of modern home planning, building, furnishing, decoration.' Yet the architectural pilgrims who head to Gidea Park on annual Open House weekends will find only one or two 'white modern' houses to admire, though a more aware generation is beginning to remove the ersatz decoration, the Spanish tiles and fake beams that had obscured any trace of modernity. Outstanding among them is the house designed by Tecton, now listed: 64 Heath Drive. It was given a prize. But flat roofs, sun terraces, white plaster render, Crittall metal windows and free flowing internal plans were not for middle England or the conservative buyers of the interwar years. Now thoroughly disguised behind pebbledash and PVC windows and doors, stranded in the subtopia of outer suburban London, they share their views onto the A12, possibly the least appealing trunk road in Essex.

There was no hesitancy when the Bata Shoe Company, readying itself to sell and make shoes all over the world, settled on the site of a 600-acre potato farm, close to the Thames at East Tilbury in 1931. European architectural modernism arrived ready-made in Essex together with a largely Czech workforce from the original home of Bata. Czech architects designed the factory village to look as like its parent, Zlín, as possible. The flat-roofed two storied houses, white rendered as if to emphasise the link to European modernism, were very modest-sized although they came in two categories: either 'basic' or 'managerial'. The latter benefitted from balconies and quite generous gardens, and the largely Czech early occupants quickly planted fruit trees – a reminder of home. Even at one third of its intended size, the company provided sports facilities, a Community House with shops on the ground floor and a cinema next door, (later to be, respectively, hotel and village hall), as well as a school, farm and technical college. It was enough to make the residents of Becontree green with envy.

Centre-stage, both visually and functionally, were the three five-storey factory blocks. But hardly had construction begun on the Thames than the visionary founder Tomas Bata was killed in a plane crash in 1932. His son Thomas took over, and in 1938, faced by the Nazi threat, moved the company headquarters from Czechoslovakia to Canada, where Batawa, eastern Ontario, was established in 1939 – along the usual lines of Bata company towns from Batadorp near Eindhoven to Calcutta's Batanagar (where Vikram Seth, another child of Bata, set his novel *A Suitable Boy*).

Sir John Tusa, later to become CEO of London's Barbican Centre and Controller of the BBC World Service, was born in Zlín in 1936, but the family soon moved to England where his father ran the company at East Tilbury from 1939 until 1969. When, in the course of preparing an article for the magazine of the Twentieth Century Society, he and his brother, with their families, visited the village in June 2014, they were struck by several things, including the road names – Queen Mary Avenue, King George VI Avenue and Princess Margaret Road – tactfully chosen to underline the patriotism of the new Czech arrivals in Essex[4].

During the war the British Bata Shoe Company was extremely profitable, due to valuable government contracts for military footwear (previously, in the 1930s, Bata factories had supplied Mussolini and his army with jackboots). In 1962 someone had earmarked the nearby Coalhouse Fort as a casino but, less ambitiously, it became a handy store for surplus Bata stock. The Bata factories did not close until 2006. One has been recently renovated and is used for self-storage, that most inert of all modern industries. Another is likely to become a residential conversion, while the third awaits its fate.

Clocking off: Bata's workforce at East Tilbury in the 1960s

Bata-ville: we are not afraid of the future (2005) is both a documentary film and a performance piece. Dressed smartly as 1960s air stewardesses, two Royal College of Art students, Karen Guthrie and Nina Pope, chaperone a group of elderly Bata shoe company employees from East Tilbury and Maryport, Cumbria, on a coach trip to Zlín. The adventure did everyone nothing but good. Yet one January morning in 2017 a car was, unaccountably, driven into East Tilbury Library, where the Bata archives were housed, and then set alight. No one knows who did it, or why. That unsettling catastrophe apart, the village and its environs, a Conservation Area since 1993 and a regular destination for devotees and students of architectural modernism, appear to be on the upturn. New white housing, as flat-roofed as anything that emerged in 1930s Czechoslovakia, cordons the north of the site from the swathes of conventional houses beyond. Persimmon Homes' surprising venture, clearly a nod to conservation sensitivities, and named the Boulevards at Bata Fields, offers a respectful if superficial nod to the history of this location. The statue of Tomas Bata remains, watchful, on site.

Tomas Bata at East Tilbury

Written off in a few unenthusiastic words by the exacting Nikolaus Pevsner in his first edition of the Essex *Buildings of England* volume, Bata's factory village at East Tilbury was a firm favourite for maverick architectural writer and former RAF pilot (of Meteor jets) Ian Nairn.[5] He included it in his 1964 London Transport guide to modern architecture (even though the place was not directly served by LT). He described the 'extraordinary company town… that has somehow never got the notice it deserves' and revealed that the neat linear lay-out had once helped a pilot 'fumbling his way over the smog in the Thames Estuary'. That pilot was of course Nairn himself, who frequently undertook hair-raising journalistic forays for his employers, the Architectural Press, in hired planes with a stalwart photographer alongside. On the ground on this occasion, he considered the factory blocks still looked well while the 30-year-old housing demonstrated 'a period charm of its own.' In fact, it was hard to believe that you were in Essex, rather than somewhere in Central Europe. 'It is like a New Town with all the sense of close community that the New Towns lack.' Then he went on to Harlow to test his prejudices.

Gibberd's head, sculpted by Gerda Rubinstein, amid the foliage at Marsh Lane

The master planner of Harlow, first of the two Essex New Towns, had been waiting in the wings for his call to arms. There was enormous goodwill towards the ambitious New Town programme, a central plank in the Welfare State, but it needed persuasive and even charismatic figures to drive it on. Frederick Gibberd, born in 1908, judged unfit for war service due to childhood rheumatic fever, was the man for the job. He had spent the war years teaching and was actively involved in the design of prefabricated housing and important prototypes for the nascent new towns such as the Lansbury estate in Poplar, known for a while as the *Living Architecture Exhibition* since it was part of the 1951 Festival of Britain. Gibberd immediately began to combine energetic publicity for Harlow New Town (writing most of the critical accounts in the professional press himself) with design of certain key elements. Gibberd was everyone's image of the architect with his jaunty handlebar moustache and abundant grey hair – there was a hint of Frank Lloyd Wright's flamboyance in his demeanour. He confessed to being 'a complete autocrat', not unlike his chosen hero on 'Desert Island Discs', Giuseppe Verdi.

Harlow may have been Gibberd's creation throughout, but he was merely the designer, the ring master of its architecture and planning, rather than the funder, employer and paternalistic begetter of a model community, such as Frank Crittall had been at Silver End. Impervious to rebuff and determinedly hands-on, Gibberd designed the Lawns, the first residential tower block in the country, as well as several low-rise schemes. He also brought in some of the ablest architects in the country, many hardly back from the war and several of them women, to help with a plan that, to quote the sour description of 'Desert Island Discs' presenter Roy Plomley, 'stuck' 80,000 people in open countryside. The majority of the population came from east London but John Grindrod's *Concretopia* reveals that significant numbers came from elsewhere in Essex, while many of the earliest residents were the families of men who were building the New Town itself. Rural poverty and hardship in the postwar years has been largely overshadowed by the plight of Londoners, but the new and expanded towns offered better lives to country people as well.

Gibberd himself lived on the outskirts of the town and stayed at Marsh Lane for the rest of his life. Now run as a charitable trust, the garden is strongly architectural in its layout of rooms and passages, culminating in the immense classical columns and urns from his firm's work for Coutts Bank on the Strand, an operatic effect at the end of the garden, and a screen for the busy railway line that runs close to the boundary.

The New Town itself was rather more mundane but the carefully retained green wedges of countryside, planned by the pioneering landscape architect, Sylvia Crowe, were defining features although the (vocal) critics felt that they detracted from its urbanity. More to their taste would be the handsome stepped water gardens around the Town Hall, added later on but demolished in the early 2000s to make way for an unlovely car park, despite strenuous opposition. Gibberd set up the Harlow Art Trust in 1953, and the brown signs for Harlow read 'Sculpture Town': a walking trail allows visitors to take in some 66 public works as they traverse the town, while a gallery of works on paper presented by the Gibberds is housed in the replacement town hall where Henry Moore's splendid 'Family Group' is now lodged, looking wistfully over the car park.

People were led to expect a better life in Harlow, a generation on from the grateful LCC tenants at Becontree, who had been freed from the squalor of Victorian urban poverty. The amenities were impressive, but it proved harder to build up a fully balanced demographic. *The Daily Mirror* quickly labelled it 'pram city' and the high proportion of local authority tenanted housing allied to relatively unvaried house types, did not help. A BBC 'Panorama' programme from 1959 sent a typically cut-glass interviewer with a microphone onto the Harlow streets, where his most apt question (addressed, of course, to a group of women) was, 'How do you get babysitters when there are no old people here?' He had a point of sorts, and it echoed the tropes about council housing aired in the sociologists Michael Young and Peter Wilmott's 'Family and Kinship in East London', the highly contentious book published two years earlier.

For Young and Wilmott, comparing life in the unsanitary conditions of Bethnal Green with those on the modern estate which they disguised as 'Greenleigh' (actually Debden, conveniently located on the Central Line) the trade-off had not been worthwhile. The networks of support and assistance that had defined the traditional East End communities had been uprooted, and the clean Essex air and modern kitchens were scant compensation.

For their part, the Harlow women being interviewed seemed to be singing the same note, albeit with tongue in cheek. 'We don't go out,' they said, when the BBCs man raised the point about babysitters and when he asked them what they did instead, the reply came back loud and unanimous. 'We watch you on the telly.'

If these residents accepted their new lifestyle with stoicism and humour, others were less positive. The social historian David Kynaston, author of *Family Britain 1951-57* quotes an employee of a firm which was moving out of central London. In 1951 Sunvic Controls offered their Covent Garden based workers a glimpse of the promised land: a visit to Harlow New Town and the smart, purpose-built factory that was to replace their current warren of urban workshops. One was dismissive, viewing it as the 'sort of thing the planning boys dream up, but which doesn't work out. Social classes all mixed up… nobody likes that, you know, people like to keep to their own class in practice.' Yet two-thirds of Sunvic's workforce opted to go. Despite the continuous prodding of television journalists and sociologists, the new town population tended to stay doggedly traditional, crowding their open plan living spaces with familiar possessions. Echoes of this came from communist Romania, where the authorities had bulldozed rural gypsy villages and forced the residents into poorly constructed concrete blocks, only to find them still keeping horses on their balconies, while sheep and goats often reside on Cairo rooftops. Buildings can rise, landscapes can change in a matter of months, but people adapt more slowly.

By the time Ian Nairn arrived to look at Harlow, it was almost ten years old. He found the New Town satisfying from a purely formal point of view. Views from the 'pleasant' market square were 'stopped by taller buildings in the distance, and a pleasant relationship to traffic, with the pattern arranged so that a very small number of cars trickle along one side.' But behind, around the service roads, 'everything is still a mess, and not a lovable human mess either.' However, he acknowledged it to be work very much in progress. When the market stalls were up, all was well (Nairn loved a market, none more than Romford's) for there 'human nature can overcome the lack of feeling. And there are several architectural felicities,' amongst which was the 'Painted Lady' (Nairn doesn't say so, but all the pubs in Harlow New Town were incongruously named after butterflies). Several 'crisp' blocks around the centre and the Town Hall (still being built then) added to the scene, and lifted his mood: 'It gets better as it goes on, and no final judgement is possible.' He then returned to the new railway station, Harlow Town, and (irrationally) lambasted its designers for trying too hard to emulate Frank Lloyd Wright.

Many of Harlow's difficulties were, and remain, those of any town with disproportionate numbers of disaffected youth. Hugh Kerr, Labour MEP for Essex West and Hertfordshire East from 1994–99, had moved down to Harlow with his family in 1960, 'a working class 16-year-old from a small Scottish village.' He found it a place 'full of interesting people... socialists and peace activists who made 1960s Harlow an exciting place to grow up.' He particularly remembered Leo Kersley, a teacher who produced community ballet, complementing Harlow's 'rich musical life, which by then included the Alberni String Quartet, Harlow Chorus and Symphony Orchestra, and music schools in every comprehensive.'[6] Kerr was a Board member of Geoffrey Jellicoe's fledgling charity, the Landscape Foundation, which I ran in the mid-1990s. At his suggestion we held several summer events in Marsh Lane, the Gibberd garden, and I remember his pride in Harlow and its achievements at a time when I was still largely ignorant of the town.

Heading to the Ritz... Visions of Ongar New Town in Abercrombie's Greater London Plan

Ongar was going to be the second New Town in Essex. The rising architect-planner (and landscape architect) Peter Shepheard showed it in elegant, colour washed perspectives and aerial views, a constellation of six, ten-thousand-person neighbourhood units surrounding a pedestrianised civic centre. Somewhere in all this, the remnants of old High Ongar stayed, 'preserved as a small residential unit on its own; it has a picturesque character, and screened off by trees from the industry' while the ancient log church of Greensted is 'preserved in a park'. The location has the advantage of being 'far enough from the metropolis to be completely surrounded by a countryside of its own, and to sustain its own separate life.' But that was the problem. Ongar was blighted (or saved) by poor public transport. The small station, currently headquarters for an energetic steam train preservation group, was inadequate, being merely the terminus of the London and North-Eastern Eailway, Epping and Ongar branch line. Proper transport meant electrification and a new line to Chelmsford, some eight miles away, all at huge cost. As the plans for Harlow progressed, Ongar New Town faded away, and is now long forgotten.

Looking around for an alternative, planners fell upon an area further south around Laindon and Dunton. South-east Essex was awash with plotlands, pocket handkerchiefs of land surrounding a hut, shack or bungalow. At a time of housing need, such settlements were easy targets for compulsory purchase. In 1950, Bernard Braine, the Conservative MP for Billericay, strongly anti-municipal (and specifically, anti-Silkin), argued on behalf of the doughty 'freeholders'. He pointed out that 'their homes are the result of the labour of their own hands. These people came from the East End of London and from metropolitan Essex in the 'twenties, and they built their own homes during the week-ends. In all cases their property represents a lifetime of abstinence and thrift'. Many were already pensioners and for Braine, politically emblematic since they were 'proud to own their own plot of English soil.'

As Colin Ward and Dennis Hardy observed in their memorable book on the subject *Arcadia For All: The Legacy of a*

DUNTON
PLOTLAND
TRAIL

THE HAVEN

BASILDON DEVELOPMENT CORPORATION

Plotlands Trail brochure from the mid-1980s

Makeshift Landscape, plenty of plotlanders were rooted, but others were ready for something better. The father of Roy Hollowbread, a genial, bright blue-eyed volunteer at The Haven, Langdon's excellent plotland museum, was the local farm bailiff, who'd married a girl from Poplar who came out east for family holidays. Roy worked as a carpenter, then had a market stall. As a boy he sold flowers off his father's land but, he remembers, the sheep on the farm had to be kept off the plotlands, not all of which had boundaries. Late in their lives, Roy told me, his parents had been delighted to swap their prewar self-built dwelling for a neat house with modern conveniences in Basildon New Town, and took pleasure in watching the cars and buses pass their windows, even though his father was the third generation in his family to work the land. Roy, and his colleague Fred, a skilled technician who left Tottenham for a job in Basildon in 1963, take enormous pride in the stories they tell, and the interest that they conjure up in The Haven's weekend visitors, who often include fellow former plotlanders and their descendants.

The estimated 20,000 people randomly self-housed across the area were, undeniably, a ready-made population for the New Town project. (When Essex County Council built their own new town, South Woodham Ferrers, twenty years later, they also purchased plotlands, but now for essentially private development.) After a short, angry public enquiry, the site for

Basildon was compulsorily purchased and so began the laborious business of sorting out a bureaucratic nightmare – all those 'shabby' homemade dwellings without any services or proper amenities. Led by master planner Basil Spence, the design team drew up a handsome town centre in which vehicles were kept well out of sight, below and behind. To everyone's surprise, the focus was on a soaring (now listed) residential tower block, Brooke House, to link East Square and the plazas (a favourite 1950s word), low-rise offices and shops in the same idiom. That homogeneity is now threatened, just as it becomes more highly valued for its coherence, despite decades of poor maintenance.

At the time, another distinguished landscape architect-planner, Geoffrey Jellicoe, was approached by Basildon Development Corporation to graft some of his cheerful ideas onto the apparently lacklustre early stages of the town. Perhaps they hoped that Jellicoe would energise proceedings, and make a grey city green, much as Gibberd had begun to do at Harlow.[7] He sketched some entertaining doodles, but nothing came of them, let alone any of the futuristic ideas he was mulling for Motopia, a theoretical development of some 30,000 souls near Staines, which was to include traffic passing above the buildings on skyways, specially insulated to muffle the deafening noise. It was one of several experimental schemes floated, for advertising and profile raising purposes only, by Pilkington, the St. Helens glass manufacturers.

The reality at Basildon was unimaginably complex. In a tape, lodged at the Essex Record Office, the then General Manager of Basildon Development Corporation, Charles Boniface, describes the complications of acquiring over 8,000 plots, most no more than two acres each. Dodgy transactions (or ignorance) had laid a legal minefield. On one occasion two widows appeared in his office, brandishing identical title deeds to the same property. The badly wounded wartime Commando and pre-war City solicitor admitted to being continually bemused and exhausted by his task, and yet he had warmed to the challenge of building a new town – not to relieve London's congestion, as he said, but to create somewhere that was 'self

-contained and self-sufficient'. In his opinion the New Towns were 'the most worthwhile social experiment of postwar years'.

Boniface might not have welcomed the epithet for Basildon, dubbed 'Moscow-on-Thames' by the press on account of its early reputation as a hotbed of Union-fomented unrest in the local manufacturing industries. How ironic, then, that the archetype of the Essex voter of the Thatcher years, that bellwether who had sharp-turned from Labour to Conservative (or further right), and who quickly took up the Right to Buy option on the family council house, would be be labelled by psephologists and pundits as 'Basildon Man'. That the label 'Moscow-on-Thames' now denotes the influx of wealthy and entirely capitalist Russians buying up property in the capital with funds frequently originating in former state-owned enterprises is beyond ironic. Meanwhile, when tv documentary makers seek a backing track to sum up the greed and ambition of the Eighties, they frequently turn to 1981 hit 'Just Can't Get Enough' by the band Depeche Mode… the boys from Basildon.

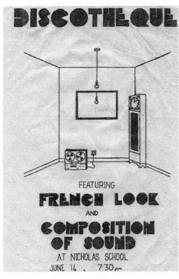

The brother of band member Vince Clark hand-drew the posters for this early gig. For a bonus point - which group became Depeche Mode?

As time passes, and the anniversaries come and go, there's a different focus placed on the Essex New Towns. Christopher Smith's thoughtful and sometimes poignant film, *New Town Utopia* (2018), makes the case for an embattled independent ethos that energised and underpinned Basildon, and produced a culture in its own image. Less mainstream than Harlow, music, punk art, street poetry and community theatre weave together strands in a scene of creative discontent and anomie, tellingly seen and heard against the recital of Lewis Silkin's elegiac hopes for the New Towns. At one moment we see, from a distance, a crocodile of Depeche Mode pilgrims as they thread through town, trying to make sense of the opaque environment and memories of 1970s adolescent rebellion. The film, like the town, is built on and around the embers of post-war idealism, but well before that, Essex had staked some small claims to being utopia.

6   A PECULIAR PEOPLE

Dreaming in Essex

Visitors to the Chelmsford Museum may be surprised to see a painting entitled 'Ear Inspection in a Russian Hospital' on exhibition. Its painter, Emily Shanks (in Moscow known as Emiliya Yakovlevna Shanks) had been the translator for an official British medical mission around 1890, hence the choice of topic for the first woman graduate of the Moscow School of Painting, Sculpture and Architecture. Her sister Louise was married to Aylmer Maude, biographer and editor of Tolstoy. The couple worked together to translate his work, another sister, Mary, illustrated some titles, and in the late years of Queen Victoria's reign the whole family would form part of a surprising connection between Tolstoyan Anarchists, Russia and rural Essex.

Essex had long been open to ideas and experiment, making it fertile ground for alternative ways of living and favouring the independent-minded. Those trying to escape the norms and conventions of society were drawn to eastern England, to its non-feudal villages where congregations of miscellaneous non-conformist chapels often outnumbered those of their handsome parish churches.[1] There was a long and honourable history of welcoming or at least not repelling outsiders, and of allowing experimental settlements to flourish, even if they rarely endured – for other reasons. Located in relatively remote and often impoverished places, they tended to be within easy reach of a way out – a station and the railway line to London, or else by sea from Harwich back to continental Europe and beyond – should the adventure turn sour or the climate unfriendly.

The so-called Great Migration of the Puritans to New England and the Caribbean was essentially one-way, but even then there were returnees who came back still more hard-line with regard to the 'rites and ceremonies of the church' than before. As early as 1632, a Thomas Sharp and his family were recorded coming back to Sandon, in full view of the village since their house was 'nearest to the church of any in the town'. They were met with widespread dismay, Sharp being well-known as a 'sower of discord and contention in the parish'. History doesn't record what drove them home again nor how they coped with the patent dislike of all around them.

Extreme puritanism manifested itself first as protest – hence the word protestant – against any aspect of Church of England sacrament or practice considered 'popish', such as making the sign of the cross at baptism, the exchange of rings at marriage or the wearing of vestments. Thus, court records reveal, a Chelmsford shoemaker tore all the pages referring to baptism from his prayer book, and two vicars refused to wear surplices or sign the cross over the infant at baptism.[2] Emigration was an alternative to a confrontation with the law – a radical, often despairing step.

The Salem Witch Trials, which took place in Essex County, Massachusetts some sixty years after Thomas Sharp made his unsuccessful transatlantic journey, remind us that some of those protesting communities failed to find peace even in the New World. Wherever they look, anthropologists generally concur that flurries of witchcraft and sorcery panic are generally a consequence of community strife, an opportunity for score-settling between factions and individuals. This was certainly the case in 1690s Salem village, described in contemporary accounts as being 'quarrelsome', with constant disputes focusing on the rights and responsibilities dividing the village and nearby Salem Town, as well as contentious land boundaries and undefined roles within the church. A succession of ministers had tried and failed to bring peace and goodwill to the parish, these tensions ramped up by regular attacks from unfriendly natives. At such a time, people found their spiritual solutions in extremism and dark doings.

You can take the dissenters out of Essex, but...
A late 19th-century lithograph of the Salem saga

The Braintree Company were Essex dissenters influenced by the charismatic Puritan preacher Thomas Hooker, who had been appointed 'lecturer' (as those who replaced the incumbent ministers were called) at Chelmsford in 1620s, before being forced to flee to the Netherlands. After carving out a reputation as a fiery and dramatic giver of sermons at St George's Church in Esher, Hooker made no attempts to tone down his content in a more conspicuous role at Chelmsford, and when he openly condemned King Charles I's marriage to the Catholic Henrietta Maria, in front of an amassed congregation of aspiring gentlemen and circuit judges, calls to silence the turbulent preacher began circulating.

Now Hooker was shifted into relative rural obscurity in the village of Little Baddow, six miles east of Chelmsford, where he started a school and showed no sign of distancing himself from extreme Puritan circles. Threatened with prison, the preacher opted to leave the country, but not before he'd had the last word in a final, excoriating pulpit address: 'For England hath seen her best days and the reward of sin is coming on apace. God begins to stir among His Noahs, which prophesied and foretold that destruction was near.'

By no means alone in identifying themselves as figures from the Old Testament, striking out with divine approval for a new Promised Land, the Essex men set sail on the *Lyon* in June 1632, heading for Boston.[3] (Hooker arrived after them in September.) Many of the one hundred and twenty-three on the passenger list, including fifty children, were related to one another, either by blood or marriage, and came from Essex villages such as Messing, Great Leighs and Braintree. They established Mount Wollaston, but soon renamed it Braintree, and founded a school nearby at Newtowne. In 1638, this school acquired what was probably the first printing press in the Americas and a year later, a new name, in honour of a local clergyman and teacher who had bequeathed a considerable sum to the college, along with his library of 400 books. We know it as Harvard, based in Cambridge, Massachusetts.

Meanwhile in 1631 a landowning Puritan, Sir Thomas Barrington of Hatfield Broad Oak, persuaded four Braintree men to join a mission to settle the mountainous island of Old Providence in the Caribbean (now Providencia, a territory of Colombia). John Beecher, John Lockin, Nathaniel Tophand and Richard Howcorner signed up, standing by to take the next ship 'bound thither'. Soon the Providence Company was reporting great success; they were already making the bricks for the most important buildings there, the church and the governor's house, and the place was proving heavenly, 'an island for pleasantness, wholesomeness and fruitfulness like the Garden of Eden.' But after ten years in this Arcadian setting, underwritten by slave labour, the Spanish fleet arrived and, despite a desperate fight by the settlers, all was lost. There is no further word of the men from Braintree. The promoters, including Nathaniel Rich and Barrington, shouldered their losses and continued in parliament, where Rich sat for Harwich and Barrington for Essex and then Colchester until his death in 1644.

Trace of those early Essex settlers remain on this remote Colombian outlier, though, with place names like Bottom House, Lupton and Morris Hill sounding defiantly un-Hispanic, and the islanders speaking a creole that mixes a predominantly English vocabulary with elements of Spanish and west African grammar. Another constant is the poverty that drove colonists to the island and today sends its young men away. When Sir Thomas began to recruit, Braintree's textile industry was in a slump; the combination of that and a disastrous harvest in 1629 had led to two outbreaks of rioting.

In 2015, meanwhile, the BBC World Service reported that some 800 men had left Providencia since 2010, many of them languishing in jails in the United States, others simply missing. With few resources, high unemployment and in-depth knowledge of the sea and coastline, some Providencia islanders carve out a dangerous and often short-lived niche as middlemen in the cocaine trade. According to the United States' consul in Colombia, there are very few enquiries about missing Providencia men, relative to the number said to be vanishing each year; are their families too ashamed, or too afraid of the truth?

Elsewhere in the New World however, Essex acorns grew into solid oaks, and within a relatively short time, bridges were being built back to the old country. In 1663, John Winthrop Jr. (born in Great Stambridge and founder of Ipswich, Essex County) was elected a Fellow of the Royal Society, the first resident of the American colonies to be so honoured. Proving a direct link to the driven, hard-nosed Puritans would become a badge of honour among US Presidents, particularly Republicans, delighted to claim descent from deep-rooted Essex families. When George H.W. Bush and George W. Bush rose in the political firmament they were quick to call up family antecedents from Messing, near Colchester. Reynolds Bush was the son of a yeoman farmer who may have left English shores even earlier than Henry Adams (great grandfather of the second President John Adams, 1797 – 1801) who was a passenger on the *Lyon*.

William Penn spent much of his childhood at his father's country house at Wanstead, Essex, before being sent on a Grand Tour to prevent him becoming 'religious in too original a way'. His father's strategy proved unsuccessful. In 1682 he sailed for Pennsylvania, to set up his 'Holy Experiment', a colony offering a safe haven to the recently founded Quakers, settling on an immense tract given by Charles II in recompense for his late father's loan. Penn's influence regarding native peoples, slaves and religious freedoms was admirably benign. He came back to England in 1684 and only returned to the colonies briefly in 1699, at which point he granted the Charter of Privileges to Pennsylvania, setting up an enlightened system of suffrage.

Perhaps the greatest transatlantic influence of all was exercised by John Locke, London-based secretary to the proprietors of Carolina, who, as we have seen, moved to High Laver to live with his patrons, the Mashams, in order to regain his health. From there, in quiet seclusion, came Locke's writings, which would substantially underpin the American Declaration of Independence in 1776.

Essex Puritanism meanwhile, became the foundation stone of both America's economy and theology. Protestantism and profit were made for each other: the notion of good hard, God-pleasing work generating profits to plough back into a growing business made for a clean, virtuous circle. Meanwhile, with its myths (George Washington and the cherry tree, the Thanksgiving Supper), its hallowed sites, solemn ceremonies and founding texts, (the Declaration of Independence, for example, is learned by rote in schools), the USA has almost created a 'civil religion', grounded in the self-identification of those first colonists with the Old Testament's children of Israel.

As a predominantly yeoman farming county, Essex didn't run to Georgian model villages or even Victorian estate cottages, but it does play a leading role in the search for utopia, or at least idealized versions of community, laid out headily in ambitious small circulation news sheets and publications, in self-built cottages sustained by an acre or two of ground, and a groundswell of memories which remain as proof of interesting settlers or passers-by.

Whiteway, the Tolstoyan Anarchist settlement that grew up on an inhospitable plateau of the Cotswolds at Miserden might never have evolved from a clutch of shacks into a village if it had not first been tested elsewhere – at Purleigh in Essex.[4]

The most radical, if short-lived, of late 19th-century community experiments began in Croydon. The Croydon Brotherhood Church was inspired by a man considered by many as a prophet for the times, Leo Tolstoy. To quote Nellie Shaw, a member and the first to tell the story of the short-lived rash of Tolstoyan anarchist ventures in Britain, it was 'inspired by a common aim, but with no religious or theological imputation.' The central principle was to hold the land in common, with the (loosely speaking) Christian society that grew up striving to operate without any authoritarian structures and at arm's length from state interference.

The Tolstoyans were very unlike that anachronistic outlier of Calvinist non-conformity, the Peculiar People, whose sect was established in rural south-east Essex just as Queen Victoria came to the throne. Picturesque as they might have seemed at a distance a century later, when John Betjeman tracked down their chapels and black-bonneted women on the Dengie Peninsula, they also embraced the unbending attitudes of an earlier century. The historical novelist Bernard Cornwell was one of five adopted children of Peculiar People at Thundersley, and his joyless, disapproving upbringing at their hands remains a source of painful memory.

Occasionally the sect took the name of its founder, James Banyard, a once-dissolute shoe-maker who experienced a Damascene conversion and set up his own chapel in Rochford in 1838, but it is the English translation of Deuteronomy 14:2 that gave rise to the group's more commonly-used name: 'the Lord hath chosen this to be a peculiar people unto Himself, above all the nations'.[5] Some members were jailed in 1910, after failing to seek medical treatment for their children, and their preference for prayer and faith healing over medicine made them a focus of fear and resentment during the diphtheria and cholera epidemics of the 19th and early 20th centuries, as did their refusal to fight in World War One. Rather less controversially, Bernard Cornwell recalled his father inserting Biblical tracts into his workers' weekly pay packets. Even more media-savvy, and better-financed, the Jehovah's Witnesses are including digital printing, video production and distribution facilities for *The Watchtower* and other publications in their enormous new complex on a former scrapyard at Temple Farm, near Chelmsford – opened in 2018, its huge gate piers emblazoned with 'JW.com'. If such millenarian movements still believe the end is nigh, then they clearly think it's worth keeping busy in the meantime.

Lacking the global reach and financial heft of Jehovah's Witnesses, the many intense small sects that have seeded around Essex were prone to frequent schisms. In 1897 the Peculiar People split, to spawn the Original Peculiar People, a rift mirrored by the quarrels that dogged the Tolstoyan Anarchists from the beginning or even those, more recently, around Brentwood's Trinity Church, known as Peniel Pentecostal Church when it was led by Michael Reid, a former police officer and insurance salesman, who had been ordained a bishop in Benin, Nigeria. The pastor attracted multiple accusations, including financial malpractice, harassment, homophobia, exerting undue influence within the local Conservative party and, of course, offering miracle cures. Reid is now confined to the internet, blogging as 'What God Can Do Ministries.' Trinity Church survives without him.

As in so many sects and circles, the Tolstoyan Anarchists split along lines of loyalty to conflicting strong personalities. John Kenworthy, the Liverpool businessman who became 'honorary pastor' of the Croydon venture, visited the influential Chertkoff, Tolstoy's aristocratic young friend and advocate in Moscow. Fired up by the encounter, Kenworthy returned to Croydon and set up the Brotherhood Publishing Company chiefly in order to spread Tolstoy's writings in English. But now it had become glaringly obvious, given the founding principles and objects of the movement, that they should concentrate on founding a land colony, built to their own requirements and administered in their particular fashion. By that means they could put identifiably Tolstoyan ideals before the public, both by example and on the page. First, though, they had to select a suitable site.

In 1896, the first three communards found a small site in Essex, about ten miles from Chelmsford in the direction of Maldon. The young colonists obtained a couple of cottages in Cockclarks, Purleigh, and lived there in a 'Spartan simplicity' that befitted their means and their ideals. They cleared three acres for cultivation over the first winter, and by the end of the year had built a house from bricks they made on site. The soil of the area was particularly suitable although treading the cold clay with their bare feet was one of many uncongenial tasks that the group faced. Around that first house grew a small farmstead consisting of a cowshed, stable, coal and work-sheds, greenhouses and fowl houses – the structures of a typical smallholding. An inheritance enabled them to buy another thirteen acres. For those who might have been weighing up a move to Purleigh, progress was recorded each month in the pages of *The New Order*, edited and published by Kenworthy. They learned that a goat had arrived in early 1897 and that the new glasshouses had become full of tomatoes and grapes over the summer, to prove their value a hundredfold when all the outdoor crops failed that autumn.

After eighteen months, the colony had expanded to fourteen members, swelled by a regular stream of helpers and also a trickle of Russian exiles, in many ways unlikely, even unsuitable, companions for a group of working-class communards whose manners were in keeping with their principles. A visitor described the scene: 'There is no reason for keeping up appearances. They do not count. So people here dress as they please, and behave as they please, and nobody objects.' In so doing they appeared to rise above the trivial and reject the norms of conventional life.

In 1897 Tolstoy's acolyte and editor Vladimir Chertkoff was sent into exile by the Russian government and, already an anglo-phile, chose to settle in England, more specifically in Purleigh, so convenient from Harwich. He set up Free Word Press, a Rus-sian-language publishing venture, in a comfortable millhouse nearby. Other exiles from Russia followed and were quickly lev-eled down to the norms of English self-sufficiency. Prince Hilkoff, who had worked as a labourer in the USA in his youth, visited on his way home to become the Russian Imperial Minister of Ways and Communications, and for a time both the Prince and Princess could be seen digging and chopping wood at Purleigh.

By the end of 1897 publicity for the colony had attracted a loose, satellite community consisting of around 35 sympathis-ers in the immediate vicinity. The presence of both Kenworthy, who had by then moved to live in the area, and Chertkoff, did not bode well for the communal venture, since neither man was remotely biddable, and each was by now at odds, even in com-petition, with the other.

To start with, the newcomers were seen by their neighbours as a curious phenomenon, industriously seeking their anarchist utopia out in the bleak Essex countryside. The Tolstoyans were keen, from the very beginning, to show local villagers how they proposed to live, to demonstrate that they were exemplifying their beliefs and their practical abilities. An open evening held in September 1897 reportedly attracted around a hundred local people, who came to enjoy music and listen to or take part in political discussion. But it was one thing to attend a meeting, quite another to cast off existing responsibilities and sail into the utopian unknown.

The following year Peter Kropotkin, the father of anarchism in Britain, visited the colony and gave a lecture, raising aware-ness of (and funds for) the resettlement in Canada of the Douk-hobors, a persecuted Christian 'spirit warrior' community who had been exiled in the Caucasus by Tsar Nicholas I. By 1898 the splits that had already shown between the original communards and the wider Anglo-Russian circle around them had fatally widened, particularly in their incompatible attitudes towards communal living. One of the former, William Hone, a practical man, derided time-wasting meditation 'coupled with vague visionary ideas that somehow things will come out right' and strongly disagreed with the Tolstoyan mantra, that of 'never actively objecting to the action of others.' Differences of opinion also opened on the acceptance of new members, again largely split along lines of class and income.

Chertkoff, in particular, alienated everyone. He was comfortably housed along with 'his retinue' as no-nonsense Nellie Shaw wrote, her lip discernibly curled. Before long he moved away to Bournemouth. More acceptable were the arrangements made by Tolstoy's translator, Aylmer Maude, his wife Louisa, (born Shanks) and four sons, who settled into nearby Wickhams Farm in 1897. The Maudes were sympathetic and generous, sharing their relative affluence, employing several young women colonists, donating a couple of dairy cows (and butter) and setting up an open-air kitchen. Both their families had been involved in Anglo-Russian business in Moscow, where Louisa had been born and where she met her husband. Under Tolstoy's influence Maude retired early from his directorship of a carpet business, and now the couple were his designated translators into English. Sudbury ('Sud') Protheroe, who would be the lynchpin of the successor colony in the Cotswolds, also joined the Maude household at this point, and became a baker.

According to Nellie Shaw, there were two essentials for a colonist: to be an energetic hard worker and to subscribe to 'the orthodox Tolstoyan views regarding sex' – essentially, abstinence. One of the Maudes' friends, pseudonymously known as Miss Clara Lee, set up in a cottage nearby, providing a welcome for those who wanted to be colonists but in a less circumscribed fashion.

With the ideal of self-sufficiency fading, the social and economic balance soured. Looking back, Nellie Shaw remarked that despite its simple start the colony was 'soon receiving help, and being almost petted by moneyed people ["honorary colonists"]'. With that, Purleigh withered away and the enterprise turned west. The £1,100 sent to help the Doukhobors reach Canada had also knocked a hole in their finances; that project, so warmly supported by Tolstoy himself, had left no spare funds to buy more land at Purleigh and must have seemed exceedingly remote from the concerns of the Essex pioneers.

Next, the hardiest colonists found a bare site on an escarpment above Cirencester and built another settlement. Loyal Aylmer Maude continued his support from a distance, heading the Board of Trustees. By burning the title deeds, in law they became jointly and irrevocably entitled to the land on which they were to build. Sud Protheroe's baking became a lifeline and a handful of Purleigh veterans came, standing, as Nellie Shaw wrote, for 'what is good and right among us. They are strong on "no force" and have discarded the use of money, as have also some of the others.' Whiteway Colony, Miserden, albeit much modified, remains to this day gathered round its frontier-style colony hall – the land inalienably held in common.

Today nothing remains of the brief Purleigh venture. But Aylmer Maude settled at Great Baddow, just outside Chelmsford, and with Louise continued as the leading promoter of Tolstoy in English, editor of the twenty-one-volume centenary edition. He held to his principles by standing on the national executive of the Fabians for some years and being a staunch supporter of the local cooperative movement. The Maudes' house, built around 1910, had Russian features, particularly a detached 'dacha' cottage in which one of their sons, Lionel, lived into the 1950s. He was remembered driving his goat off to find it a mate, the animal sitting in the sidecar of his motorbike.

Inside, Ladywell House had brightly painted, wood panelled walls with, presumably, furnishings brought from Moscow (Louise's family firm was the *Magasin Anglais*, despite its Gallic name an English-style department store). The meadows around the house became known locally as 'the Russian fields' while the Tolstoyan influence was immediately obvious in Louise's personal style. As 98-year-old Anya Troup, a Russian girl brought up in England by the Maudes, recalled in the 1990s, Louise dressed in marked contrast to her Essex neighbours, 'rather like the Russians, very tied up in a frock and boots.'[6]

If Tolstoyan Anarchy was a brief flicker in early 1900s Essex, the struggle for votes for women was a long, hard slog towards a clear conclusion. So close to London, Essex was quickly on the front line of the campaign. In November 1908, at a meeting held in Chelmsford Corn Exchange in advance of the mid-Essex parliamentary bye-election, suffragettes Sylvia Pankhurst and Helen Ogston were loudly heckled and pushed about. The following evening, their companion Flora Drummond sensibly decided to deliver her own speech from the safety of an upper window at the Bell Hotel.

Amy Hicks, born near Frinton and a graduate of Girton, was a committed member of the non-violent Women's Freedom League of which she soon became secretary. She held three meetings in Colchester in autumn 1908. Faced with the predictable barrage of banter and derision (mostly from small boys), she pointed out that she and her fellows were 'neither freaks nor frumps.'[7] Her mother Lilian had been involved in women's suffrage since the 1880s and her father had campaigned for votes for agricultural labourers.

The actress, diarist and activist Kate Parry Frye was employed by yet another suffrage organisation, the New Constitutional Society for Women's Suffrage. Essex was fertile ground, well stocked with able sympathisers and many women in the workforce at factories such as Marconi (Chelmsford) and Courtaulds (Braintree and Halstead). Frye arrived in Maldon, just ahead of the forthcoming 2 April 1911 census, a major focus for orderly civil disobedience ('No Vote, no Census').[8] She had a heavy cold and felt very alone, she confided to her diary. The next afternoon, she

Suffragettes, not afraid to state their views at the Chelmsford by-election, 1908.

went out calling. 'I disliked most of the people intensely... they are all Liberal here and say they are Suffrage but you cannot move them to do anything to further the cause and when they are men they are all Anti Suffrage while all the time they tell you they are in favour – a poor lot.'

April turned wintry, with snow dusting the pretty tiled roofs, and she lost her voice. She pressed on, distributing posters and leaflets, working from her hotel room. The meeting, despite her misgivings, was packed to the rafters. The next day she and stalwart local colleagues moved on to Witham, for another ('excellent') meeting. Solidarity was a warming sensation.

In mid-July, she was back. This time she started, much more cheerfully, from Little Baddow. 'I had no idea Essex could be so pretty – real rural England.' From there she returned to Witham, travelling to Felsted by train and happening on a vicarage tea party organized by the British Women's Temperance Association, 'a bit of luck for me'. She remained in Essex for the rest of that month, staying in Halstead and being driven around by the redoubtable Miss Katharine Courtauld who took her to visit her father, now well over eighty, in a splendid house that reminded Kate of 'Wooburn'. She was 'quite like a man, a most extraordinary person, but very nice and a beautiful face'. On two successive days

Kate Frye concentrated her energies on leafleting the women and girls coming out at lunchtime from Courtaulds' Halstead mill, 'the weaving place'. A meeting at nearby Gosfield, chaired by her friend Miss Courtauld, attracted an impressive audience of about a hundred. With Courtauld influence, all tended to go well. Suffrage was a campaign by, and for all classes.

A studio photograph of Daisy, aka Frances Evelyn Greville, née Maynard in her wedding dress in 1881.

But she encountered the hard core of the movement when she stayed with Mrs Chappelow and her daughter Grace at Hatfield Peverel. They seemed 'very Militant.' Grace had been indicted for an attempted raid on the House of Commons, and in 1912 would spend four months doing hard labour in Holloway Prison after smashing windows at the Mansion House. To Frye they seemed 'good people but so peculiar and so unwashed. Very emancipated – no servant and lots of animals and all kinds of weird theories.' In the late 1920s the pair were still living in Essex, by then at Ramsden Heath, keeping goats and selling the milk from the back of a tricycle.

While Kate Frye struggled around the halls of mid-Essex drumming up support for universal suffrage, and Sylvia Pankhurst retreated to the obscurity of Woodford Green with her Italian anarchist lover and child, another influential woman was comfortably at home indoors at Easton Lodge, near Dunmow, writing (with help) an appreciation of William Morris.

By then Daisy, Countess of Warwick had nearly spent two immense fortunes: her own, inherited from forbears at Little Easton, and that of her titular husband, the Earl. At fifty, stately but no longer the great beauty of her youth, she continued to milk her notoriety as a favourite mistress of the Prince of Wales (whose dalliance with her possibly inspired the ditty 'Daisy, Daisy, give me your answer, do…;') but was admirably, if naively, spontaneous in her support for radical causes and people. She was a charitably inclined, stupendously rich woman of her time; her modern equivalent might be more discreet, but Daisy was no egalitarian and she exploited her status for all it was worth, though usually in the service of others.[9]

Her neighbour, R.D. Blumenfeld, the American-born editor of the *Daily Express*, caught her contradictions, seeing her as 'a most assiduous Socialist who is, at the same time, also a meticulous conservative.' At the turn of the century she spent prodigious sums commissioning Harold Peto to landscape her garden in the full-blown Edwardian style. He included a number of Japanese features, fresh back from a visit. There was a teahouse on stilts out on the lake, reached via a wisteria-clad pergola and guarded by Japanese warrior statues. The glories of the garden only survive in the superb monochrome photographs seen in *Country Life* in the 1920s: a folly memorialized.[10]

Like its owner, the garden combined profligacy with charitable impulse, with the latter gaining the upper hand. The work was carried out by the so-called 'inebriates' from the Salvation Army Colony at

Hard work at Hadleigh

Hadleigh Farm, set up in 1891 near the ruined castle painted earlier by John Constable, seemingly pitted against furious seas. (The farm venture continues, in modern guise, incorporating a Rare Breeds Centre, to this day). The camp was run for men in desperate straits as part of a wider scheme, devised by William Booth, whereby rescued souls were rehabilitated firstly in city missions, then in the countryside before being sent abroad.

Daisy, in the face of furious local opposition both towards the evangelical low church army and the employment of perceived 'wastrels' was determined to give the men work and support. Thanks to Lady Warwick, that year the Salvation Army could offer respite to an additional fifty men over the hard winter months. Wooden sheds and a tin hut for the supervisor rose on the lawns outside the windows of the Victorian mansion, and the garden work began, closely observed by a steady stream of curious journalists. As they observed with a shiver of *schadenfreude*, many, even most, of the unfortunate drunks were middle-class professional men like themselves.

Daisy Warwick remained a staunch advocate of the Salvation Army's mission, publishing an article on her own experience with them in the hope that others might follow, and maintaining an interest as in the 1920s, Hadleigh Farm gave itself over entirely to training boys between 14 and 19 for farm work in the colonies.

Rare breeds at Hadleigh farm today

Otherwise the Countess continued to pursue what she considered her apolitical path, while being solidly committed to 'labour representatives who knew the needs of the people.' She spoke at the Co-operative Union conference in Braintree in 1903, making a stirring speech about the 'enormous power' they shared thanks to the pioneers of the movement. In November 1904, apparently persuaded by the elderly socialist activist H.M. Hyndman, she joined his Social Democratic Federation. She found no difficulty in supporting their programme, which included the nationalization of land – she owned some 13,000 acres – as well as the abolition of the House of Lords and the disestablishment of the Church of England, both institutions with which she had familial ties.

Hyndman's snaring of the notorious former royal mistress was something of a coup and helped fill halls for his party on dark wet winter evenings, for, as he observed, 'the woman does not know what fear is.' Paradoxical and inconsistent as her socialism was, Lady Warwick now became the planet around which a constellation of (mostly) left-leaning individuals revolved, all of whom lived locally, permanently or in transit, in the villages of Great and Little Easton and the market towns of Thaxted and Dunmow.

Her most impressive and focused act to date had been to set up a pioneering agricultural and technical school in 1897, a co-educational boarding establishment based at her farm at Bigods near Dunmow. She put £10,000 (perhaps £1 million in today's values) into the venture, having been inspired by a speech given by the eminent scientist, Professor Raphael Mendola, in which he argued for technical and scientific education to promote recovery in depressed agricultural areas. The formerly rich arable acres of north and central Essex were, by then, becoming as afflicted as the miserable south east of the county – and would remain so into the 1930s. Yet, despite the high hopes attached to it, the school was consistently at odds with bureaucratic norms, from the highest levels down. In 1904 the Board of Education withdrew its £113 grant, citing the neglect of traditional arts subjects in favour of science and agriculture. That was a signal for Essex County Council to pounce. Six members of the higher education committee were appointed to inspect the school in 1906, of which just one attended. Dr R. Wormell complained that he met with discourtesy, observed slackness and lack of supervision and then, in something of an oxymoron, declared 'that when the Countess's maternal care was withdrawn from the school, and her energies were devoted to other philanthropic schemes, the efficiency of the school would flag.' His 'report', far from shifting the financial burden from the shoulders of the enlightened private donor towards the security of a County Council grant, was an opportunity to close the school, too irregular to sit within the current rigid classification of education.

Yet, one year on, the Board of Education had a change of heart, deciding that it could categorize the school as a technological institute. But by then student numbers had plummeted, the Countess's debts were mounting and Bigods had reached the end of the road. A beacon in the field of higher education for boys and girls, the only secondary school in the area at a time when Essex offered fewer than a dozen secondary school places per thousand children, at a time when illiteracy was still a dark stain on the area, it was snuffed out in 1907.

Unusually, given his retiring nature and background role in their family life, Lord Warwick (an active Trustee) wrote to the Chairman of Essex County Council to gently berate him for the lack of support. 'An institution which was doing so much real good should have been much more generously supported.' In the 1920s, his successor had the nerve to write to Lady Warwick: 'If only we had your school now. You were twenty years too soon.'

Lady Warwick's role as lord of the manor of Easton included her patronage of four local parishes, and she grasped the opportunity to offer livings to socialist-minded churchmen (although Great Easton went to one of her Maynard relatives). At Tilty, a lime-plastered church formed from the monastic chapel of a long-dissolved Cistercian abbey, she nominated Edward Maxted, whose previous ministries had been in poor London parishes in Lambeth and Battersea, and whose beliefs were rooted in the Christian Social Union movement (a re-established wing of Christian Socialism). In 1913 Maxted stood as a socialist candidate for Essex County Council and received a respectable 378 votes (against the Conservative's 443 and the Liberal's 435). A couple of years later he gave a sermon, admitting that however heartfelt prayers might be for a cause and, however just that cause, there was no reason for it to prevail. He was, perhaps, defeated by his parishioners, steeped over many generations in rural conservatism.

At Thaxted itself, the Countess offered the living of the stupendous parish church, St John the Baptist, to Conrad Noel, whose Anglo-Catholic tendencies, in particular his fondness for medieval ritual (including incense) and his hatred for privilege, had sidelined him as a curate for fourteen years. Paradoxically, in Coggeshall, he and his wife lived in Paycocke's, home of a successful medieval clothier (now in the hands of the National Trust) while he attempted to preach socialism to the textile workers of Braintree, Bocking and Halstead. Nevertheless, in Thaxted, his first parish, where he remained for thirty-one years (having tolled the bell nine times on his induction, the number of years he intended to stay), he caused Lady Warwick some disappointment. He enjoyed village responsibilities and the glorious building, the fostering of music and traditional rural activities, including morris dancing. His patron's exhortations, to busy himself campaigning for socialism while leaving parish work to a curate and lay secretary, went largely unheeded. But the Easter Rising in 1916 and the Russian Revolution the following year energised him greatly and he advertised for a missionary priest to support his core activities, seeking an 'active revolutionary, good singing voice.'

Due to this, Thaxted was placed under an interdict, a relic of Catholic canon law that restrained excess, but Noel was more than a match for the authorities and continued to hoist the Red Flag – alongside those of St George and Sinn Fein – in the church and argue his corner against all comers. In 1921 questions were asked in the House about taking action against this latest Essex rebel's preaching of sedition. (No action was taken). On Empire Day he habitually tolled the church bell to mourn those, as he put it, sacrificed to imperialism.

Meanwhile Lady Warwick was nurturing an ambition to write, in order to set the world to rights. She enlisted the help of a motley crowd of helpers. One of the most faithful and steadfast was Samuel Levy Bensusan, whose father had been an orthodox rabbi turned feather merchant, and who was himself a lawyer turned journalist. One of his sisters, Esther, was married to the painter Lucien Pissarro and lived in Epping for some years.[11] Pissarro's paintings of their forest-fringe surroundings offered a fresh eye onto the English landscape with more than a dash of the French *plein air* approach of his famous impressionist father, Camille. Another sister, later Dr Ruth Bensusan-Butt, was a pioneer of family medicine and social care in Colchester, a Fabian and a suffragist. A blue plaque was recently put up in her honour at the city's Minories Gallery, which occupy the house where she and her husband lived for over forty years. She was also the first woman invited to attend the famous Colchester Oyster Feast in her own right, in 1921.

Her brother Samuel rented a house locally in 1899 and in 1906 bought Brick House Farm, Duton Hill, which included 50 acres of land. Bensusan began to write about farming and rural Essex life, including dialect and traditions, and became the agricultural correspondent of the *New Statesman*. Some of his columns were published as *Latterday Rural England* (1927) and they record the independence of the Essex farmer ('most are their own landlords') and their worries as men began to leave the land, largely due to the frequently atrocious conditions in which they were forced to live and work.

Bensusan had encouraged his patron to write about William Morris, and of their various co-writing ventures this seems closest to the nominal author's interests since, in her words, Morris was 'a perfect expression of the type of personality to which the Utopian impulse of the reformer is forever seeking.' In 1910 Lady Warwick offered H. G. Wells the tenancy of Easton Glebe, at Little Easton. She had him in her sights as another collaborator.

She had not reckoned with such an awkward customer as Wells. One autumn day in 1915, Arnold Bennett drove over from his own house on the coast to visit his friend. They walked in the park which, since it was the rutting season, proved to be disconcertingly full of life. 'All the bucks were roaring like lions, and we were somewhat intimidated'. But despite Wells' landlady allowing him and his family to use her park as if it was his own (which involved him leaving gates open and causing animals to escape) he told told Bennett he thought her park should be 'taxed out'. Meanwhile at H.G.'s 'showcase for weekends', Easton Glebe (which he rented until 1928) the writer entertained streams of the famous, including Charlie Chaplin and the American novelist Sinclair Lewis. Bennett, coerced into playing hockey or Wells' invention, 'his own pat-ball', considered the former rectory ('partly steam-heated') very light and 'fairly comfortable.'

For all the champagne socialism of the incomers, in 1912 the country was faced by stern reality and gripped by a rolling wave of strikes. The proximity of Essex to the docks, and her socialist impulses, led Lady Warwick to offer her park as a campsite for up to a thousand strikers' children, while organizing boarding-out in neighbouring villages for many more. But by the summer the strikers had been beaten and went back to work. Next winter, the middle-aged Latvian-Russian-English composer Gustav Holst decided to explore north Essex.[12] Perhaps he had heard of Lady Warwick's reputation as a patron. He walked from Colchester to Thaxted, a journey that took him five days. On arrival he encountered that irregular priest, Conrad Noel, advocate of plainsong, folk dancing and socialism, and it proved a happy and fruitful encounter. Bensusan's cottage at Monk Street was available to rent, and in these surroundings, with the spectacular church spire in full view and the 'thatched cottages that looked as if they'd grown there' as his daughter Imogen remembered, Gustav Holst began to compose the Planets Suite. The Holst family settled in the town, and helped set up an ambitious Whitsun Music Festival, held in the church, the germ of the modern Thaxted Festival, an annual summer event stretching over three weeks.

Meanwhile, at the turn of the century, there was a growing sense of the loss of tradition, in music as elsewhere. Cecil Sharp's English Folk Dance & Song Society placed the emphasis on fieldwork and one of his most energetic and active supporters was young Ralph Vaughan Williams. As early as 1902 he described folk music, in a lecture to a Brentwood girls' school, as 'real music' rather than 'the off scourings of the classics.' Among his audience was the daughter of the rector of Ingrave, just outside Ingatestone, where the remarkable 1730s church had been built and possibly designed by the 8th Lord Petre. Inspired, the schoolgirl invited Vaughan Williams to one of her father's parish teas, where he met a seventy-five-year old shepherd, Charles Potipher. Later, the composer visited the old man in his cottage and heard him sing 'Bushes and Briars', an experience which proved cathartic. In 1904, Vaughan Williams took a ten-day cycling tour in mid Essex, via Ingrave, Willingale, Little Burstead, East Horndon and Billericay. As he went, he jotted down words and music on paper, recording up to a hundred local songs for posterity, their tunes and poetic phrases often passed down through several generations of a family but now on the brink of disappearing along with the oral tradition and dialect of each area.[13] Although he ranged widely around England, Vaughan Williams was back in Willingale in 1906 to hear 'Sweet Primroses.' In the new English Hymnal published that year, many of these tunes, so comfortably familiar, were threaded into modern arrangements, and are still sung wherever traditional church music continues.

The composer William Byrd's years in Essex, three hundred years before, had been spent just seven miles away from Ingrave. Byrd lived at Stondon Massey for the last thirty years of his life, under the patronage of an earlier member of the Petre family, one mark of the considerable debt he owed to his Catholic patron being the pavan and galliard entitled 'Sir William Petre'.[14] A William Byrd Anniversary Concert is given

A fragment of Byrd's motet Ne Irascaris Domine, in a 16th-century music book

annually by the Stondon Singers, who frequently include work by Vaughan Williams in their other programmes.

At Easton Lodge in those years, Lady Warwick's indebtedness was causing growing worries, she was nearing bankruptcy and required new sources of earned income. In October 1913 the patient Bensusan agreed to be her literary mentor, to edit her and her husband's memoirs and to ghost-write a weekly series of articles under her name in the *Daily Sketch*. While a swirl of drama and scandal enveloped Daisy, Bensusan was unfailingly loyal, despite her continual complaints and changing commands that saw him confiding in his diary, 'a little tired of strenuous effort!!!' In February 1918, part of Easton Lodge was burned down, possibly by the Countess' pet monkey overturning an oil lamp. According to Bensusan, she was considering how to rebuild the wing by the following day.

At the nearby Manor House, Little Easton, Daisy's 'arranged' tithe barn had, from 1913 onwards, made a passable theatre. The Dunmow and District Progressive Club was a typically creative invention of Daisy's, here supported by her husband, and was dedicated to all manner of folk revival, pageants and plays in the vernacular. The stellar raft of honorary members included Sir James Barrie, Arnold Bennett, Dame Ellen Terry, George Bernard Shaw and Cecil Sharp. In the interwar years the manor would become the home, and the hobby, of Basil Dean, the actor and producer who set up ENSA in the second war. But the first performance on the new stage in 1913 was by the Dunmow Players for which the ever-amenable Bensusan had been asked to write a play entirely in Essex dialect, *The Furriner,* staged in the summer of 1914 and in which, the programme note claimed, 'almost all the characters... are required to speak the Essex dialect. This dialect is gradually being impaired in many places, and it is believed that the present attempt towards its preservation will be appreciated by Essex people.'

Preceding Bensusan's efforts, the solicitor and anthropologist Dr Richard Stephen Charnock had brought out his *Glossary of the Essex Dialect* in 1880, focusing on the north of the county. Charnock noted a tendency to lengthen vowels, so that 'made' and 'make' would be pronounced 'maade' and 'maake', along with frequent transpositions, with 'from' turning into 'frum', and a 'ballad' becoming a 'ballet'. He also spotted what he thought were old Germanic plurals, such as 'housen' for houses and 'shoon' for shoes, and detected distinct qualities to the tone of Essex speech. 'The people do not speak in the often subdued tones of Londoners,' Charnock wrote. 'Indeed, they more frequently scream their words and remind one of the Venetian gondolier or the French poissonière.'

While 'The Furriner' (which is the Essex word for a foreigner, as in, throughout East Anglia, anyone not from those parts) was being written and performed, the Rev. Edward Gepp, vicar of High Easter, was busily collecting words from the surrounding area. He also engaged in barbed scholarly exchanges with Chelmsford-based polymath, Miller Christy, who had been writing his own magnum opus of county dialect since 1875.

In this atmosphere of heightened concern for rural traditions and language, Lady Warwick and Bensusan had hopes that the staging of 'The Furriner' might be the starting point for an indigenous school of playwrights and actors, an effective way of preserving and celebrating the fragile remnants of local phrases and intonation. Bensusan continued to pursue the project, recording dialects and frequently adding the vernacular, in words and diction, to his enormous output of plays and novels. In the 1920s he read dialect works on the newly-created BBC.

Another witness to the enduring power of local dialect and terminology was Geoffrey Barber, who arrived in Dunmow as the new GP in 1930. His memoir *Country Doctor* was written to conjure up, without sentiment, the pre-war Essex he had encountered forty years before. His responsibilities stretched to High Easter and so he recognized some of the Rev. Gepp's terms on their home ground, especially those applied to health, such as 'bangled' for knocked out, 'mosey', meaning not too good and 'bindley' for weakly. Later Dr Barber saw how broadcasting and teachers (often with cockney accents) had taken their toll, but even in the 1970s as he prepared to retire, one ancient patient still utterly defied his comprehension.

Recently BBC Essex spoke to four people living on the (still isolated) Dengie Peninsula. Their accents, they agreed, bore no resemblance to 'Estuary Essex' imported from London. They still employed dialect words like 'shink' (I should think) or 'cleant' (past tense of clean) but used the more accepted version of the Essex accent, with dropped 'T's and 'H's, at work or in the pub.

During wartime Lady Warwick had continued true to her humane, impulsive form. She visited German POWs outside Dunmow, chatting to them in German, even while her sons were serving at the front. After the war she was offered the Labour candidacy for Walthamstow East but withdrew, instead standing for Warwick and Leamington, despite the uncomfortable fact that her husband's baronial seat, Warwick Castle, dominated the sky-line, if not the allegiances of the constituency. Unsurprisingly, she came third, behind the victorious young Conservative, Anthony Eden. The invalid Earl, her patient, often confused husband, died with impeccable timing a few weeks after the 1923 poll.

In these years of mounting financial worry, Lady Warwick had become desperate to offload Easton Lodge. Pathé News-reel footage shows a group gathered round the Italian Garden, a large rectangular pool with a stone balustrade, filmed on a winter day in late 1923.[15] Beatrice and Sidney Webb are easily recognisable and Arthur Henderson, soon to be Home Secretary, is there with his wife. Beatrice, to whose causes Daisy had been so generous in the past, remained loyal, disputing H. G. Wells' dismissal of her as 'a spoilt child... moved by a desire for notoriety', rather considering that she was 'a benign and hard-working old woman who has gained the respect of her neighbours by a sterling public spirit.'

Daisy's putative donation of Easton Lodge to the new Labour party as an alternative 'Chequers', a country house convenient to London for weekend gatherings and official invitations, was not accepted. When Labour took office for the first time in January 1924 Beatrice and her widowed sister, Kate Courtney had concluded that the 'almost degenerate luxury' of the house – as well as its impracticality – ruled it out. But between 1924 and 1926, the Independent Labour Party had no compunction in using the luxurious mansion for its summer schools. Attendees of the stimulating month-long sessions included young lions of the ILP like Clement Atlee and Jenny Lee. Over three years of protracted negotiation, it was the TUC that came closest to

Daisy, with Margaret Bondfield, first woman Chair of the TUC's General Council and Mary Quayle, Women Workers' Member of the General Council, optimistically discussing the handover of Easton Lodge in 1926

accepting Easton Lodge as a bequest, until arrangements came unstuck at the last moment.

Dr. Barber, who found himself Daisy's local GP as she aged, recorded her kindness to someone 'at least half a century' younger than herself. Their first, rather startling meeting was outside the old Town Hall, where he found an old woman struggling with her new car. She couldn't find either the lights or the starter. When he went to visit the Countess, having identified the inept driver, he found hordes of animals, many of them ill (including the 'revolting Pekinese dogs' that the Fabian, Margaret Cole, remembered with distaste) ranging over the remnant of the house in which she still lived. But Dr. Barber was also invited to memorable events such as a party supposedly for Daisy's granddaughter's 'Coming Out' held between 3 pm and 1.30 am in August 1936, where the gardens were garlanded with coloured lights loaned by Basil Dean from the Ealing Film Studios, a band of the Grenadier Guards played outside, while the 'Olde Tyme Singers' carolled indoors. Her granddaughter had been allowed to invite just one girl to 'her' ball; all the other guests were Daisy's, the local great and good ranging from the Mayor of Southend to innumerable County Council officials and church dignitaries. Two summers later Daisy Warwick was dead and her remaining monkeys were shot.

Like Lady Warwick, Arthur Heygate Mackmurdo had grown more aware of his responsibilities over years of high-rolling extravagance (though in his case the fortune was his wife's). Mackmurdo was a progressive architect and a tireless rural reformer, who had busied himself bettering the scant facilities in the Essex village he knew best, Great Totham. He designed village halls, social housing and other facilities there and elsewhere, as well as straying into self-indulgence by designing a handful of idiosyncratic houses, none odder than his own. Great Ruffins was marked by a lofty campanile, and was, as the architectural historian James Bettley aptly put it, the sort of residence that would 'look at home on Lake Garda.'[16] To build it Mackmurdo had made considerable inroads on his wife's large purse (she was a D'Oyly Carte) and in fact they never lived in the house, settling on something far more modest nearby.

Follies aside, Mackmurdo's concern for the countryside was genuine. He believed that, if mishandled, rapid progress would be a death knell to rural society. In 1929, well into his seventies, he founded the Rural Community Council of Essex, whose purpose was to reanimate rural life, by then under enormous pressure. RCC initiatives were varied. During the Great Depression they joined forces with the Society of Friends to set up an allotment scheme, distributing the equipment needed to cultivate a plot successfully. By 1934, there were fifty centres. On Osea Island, they supported an initiative to help the unemployed return to work. Their aims were high and wide, secular and apolitical, essentially practical.

Of all the colonies and turn-of the-century idealistic enterprises on the Essex coast, only William Booth's 1891 Salvation Army outpost at Hadleigh still functions, running a farm, rare breeds centre and tearoom. The valuable enterprise offers training and opportunities to those with special needs. In his television film *The Joy of Essex* (2013) Jonathan Meades – along with his viewers and reviewers – found it easy to poke fun at the wilder shores of communitarian zeal, but Hadleigh Farm has disproved the nay-sayers while at Bradwell, the Othona Christian settlement, dedicated to Anglo-German friendship, has endured since its foundation at the end of the last war.

Of Tolstoyan Purleigh and its supporting Anglo-Russian coterie, there remains no trace beyond the thin thread offered by Emily Shanks' painting in Chelmsford museum. In Thaxted, Conrad Noel's efforts to introduce red-blooded socialism may have failed, though the music and morris dancing continue. Easton Lodge lost its park to a WW2 airfield; much of it is now a large quarry and soon will come an enormous residential development.

After major demolition in 1950, the house remained as a fragment, Lady Warwick's 'Great Room' standing as a modest reworking of the west wing. In 1971 it was bought by a retired businessman who waged a long and arduous campaign to restore the gardens. Now a large part, including grounds down to the lake, is in the care of a Trust. Volunteer numbers testify to the survival of the strong practical communality that Daisy would have been thrilled by. The walled garden and the distant lakeside area are being put to rights; cheerful amateur croquet is played on the lawn again; a new Tree House has been built and the Italian garden, where the guests in 1936 tried to dance on the wet flagstones, is being repaired and replanted.

But Daisy's living memorial is the Countess of Warwick's Country Show. Held over two days every August Bank Holiday in Little Easton, it is a remarkable mirror of rural life in northwest Essex. Although it was only instigated in its current form in recent decades (inspired by the Countess's Bank Holiday Flower Show and Fun Fair in her own park and garden) it is an enormously extended village fête, serving as it does, five local parishes and its profits going to the maintenance of all their exceptional churches. The attractions, weather allowing, include something for everyone – things to wonder at (classic and vintage cars), things to compete for (tug of war and ploughing matches), prizes for excellence (fine animals from sheep to rabbits, home-made wine and flower arrangements) and a full range of food and drink, in which passing fashions play their part as pulled pork and craft beers and gins now jostle with the staple homemade jams and chutneys.

By combining strands of the traditional country show, agricultural and horticultural as well as parochial, with publicity for the varied charitable organisations that thrive in this now prosperous corner of the county, including the continually expanding group that looks after and opens Daisy's own garden at Easton Lodge, it offers something for everybody. On such a grand day out, it's hard to remember that the local countryside, and its population were once so desperately impoverished or that Essex, all of it, was on the frontline of the 20th century's two bloodiest wars.

DARLEY'S DAYS OUT

Walks and Wanders Around Essex

NORTH WALK

Start: Red Lion, South St., Mistley
End: Harwich Redoubt
Length: 14.3 miles

The Stour, the Orwell and the World: a River Trail

In its top right-hand corner, Essex faces off Suffolk across
water, to contrasting effect. Near Dedham, the modest River
Stour runs through water meadows Constable might still
recognise, while further on, the ghostly gantries of Felixstowe
whisper the story of global trade, for better or for worse.

Take a train to Mistley (change at mainline Manningtree to
avoid a long plod through dull recent housing estates) and
head east. **Mistley** itself is well worth a glance, having kept
evidence of its Georgian confidence, an intriguing mixture of
the elegant with serious eighteenth-century ship building.
Staying close to both river and sea, the route partially follows
the final leg of the Essex Way, which begins in Epping. At
intervals, **swathes of green or blonde reeds** (depending on

the season) blur the lines between marsh and firm ground, visually at least, though the aged trees offer reassurance. Some, especially the oaks, almost seem to be grazing in the river. Nearing Wrabness, you can walk along sandy 'beaches' and be caught up in the frenzied excitement of **sand martins**, dizzying to watch, as they swoop in and out of their front doors on these modest banks. Humans have their own seasonal dwellings on the bank around Wrabness, too, less beach huts than expanded allotment huts or garden sheds, a nod back to the ad hoc ingenuity of the county's interwar plotlanders. Then the prow of the idiosyncratic **House for Essex** sails into view, set well above both path and river, part Russian church, part little gingerbread house.

Soon you are approaching both Harwiches – **Harwich International** indissolubly linked to the Hook of Holland, **Harwich Town** pinioned between the rivers Stour and Orwell, a medieval planned town with a quay at its head. There's something distinctly Dutch about some of the older buildings, their wavy pantiles and soft tomato brick might have served as ballast across the North Sea. There was ambition here too, in the towering mid-Victorian **Great Eastern Hotel** (now flats) and the ground-breaking **Electric Palace Cinema** (1911), while **a row of wood-clad houses** donated to the town by Norway remembers the terrible East Coast floods of 1953. The burly **Redoubt** (1807-9) reminds us that this coast was once, justifiably, nervous of its continental neighbours, but today's Harwich hooks Essex up to a world far wider than its own hinterland.

NORTH WANDER

Hidden Gifts and Brightly Hued Houses: Saffron Walden

In the 1960s Saffron Walden was described as 'probably the best looking small town anywhere in Essex or East Anglia', and that accolade, from the *Shell Guide: Essex*, still holds. It helps that all routes converge on the market square, with an

open market held on Tuesdays and Saturdays and plenty of **small independent shops** keeping things humming for the rest of the week. On a stage set by the exuberant **Town Hall** (which plays host to concerts and comedy nights) there's a sense of purpose and lively confidence here that many towns would envy.

Architecturally, **castle ruins** and an **enormous church** apart, most streets are an entertaining mix of scale and ambition. Oliver Cromwell allegedly quartered at the former **Sun Inn** during the Civil War; if so, we must hope the riot of decorative plasterwork there, and on several other town buildings, cheered the dour Puritan. Elsewhere dozens of modest cottages, individual in detail and material, colour and pattern, jostle along the pavement. This is still a town where people live and work.

With so much to look at, unsurprisingly **7a High Street** was, from the 1980s, the home of Jack Cardiff, considered by Marilyn Monroe (and many others) to be the 'best cameraman in the world' and a pioneer of Technicolor, from his 1936 travelogue on Vesuvius onwards – which was filmed so close to the active crater that the tripod feet were melted by the lava.

From his handsome Georgian front door Jack could, like any visitor today, cross the main road and dive down a little garden path to the lead-clad **Fry Art Gallery**. This holds an unrivalled collection of 'North Essex artists' – formerly 'Great Bardfield artists', after the village where most of them lived – the best known being **Eric Ravilious** and **Edward Bawden**. But as with many provincial towns, Saffron Walden's treasures tend to be little known, existing for the benefit of residents. The glass-fronted bookcases of the recently renamed **Gibson Library** (formerly the Literary and Scientific Institute) are a reminder of how thoughtful people (often Quakers, like the Gibsons) shared their advantages with others less privileged. Now it sits alongside the modern public library, another generous amenity for the town. Even better hidden, though outdoors and accessible to all, is **Bridge End Garden**, also a Gibson gift, containing a **hedge maze** which, along with a mysterious turf labyrinth coiled in a far corner of the Town Common, has encouraged Saffron Walden to claim itself as a capital of mazes. It has had similar claims for wool, for brewing (those Gibsons again) and, most obviously to us, saffron, the commodity that gave the town its name. From the fourteenth until the seventeenth century, glorious 'smiling' fields of pale mauve *crocus sativus* grew there – described by the historian and topographer William Camden in 1586 – their interior parts used in medicine, in the kitchen and above all as a dye. The red threads, or *stigma* of the plants were dried and used in industrial-scale production by the Essex textile industry – itself long disappeared. Not hiding, just modest and unpretentious, is the town's newest amenity: a **concert hall** attached to the secondary school, universally praised for its acoustic and presented, anonymously, by someone local.

EAST WALK

Start and Finish: St. Mary's Church, Mundon
Distance: 28.5 miles

From Wasabi Snacks To Atom-Smashers: A Pilgrim Path On The Dengie Peninsula

For walks on the Dengie peninsula, there is but one perfect destination, the magnetic **St. Peter-on-the-Wall**. Most of the way – and it's a very long way, so do consult the online map if you're seeking a shorter sample – you'll follow the path by the sea wall: to your right, mauve and brown drifts of **sea lavender** and tough, salt-tolerant plants; left, **a brilliant emerald inland sea**, vast fields regularly planted with two very modern seams of agricultural gold: alfalfa (horse fodder) and sugar peas (destined to be dusted in wasabi).

St. Mary's, the tiny timber church at Mundon (cared for by the heroic Friends of Friendless Churches) provides a first taste of magic, although it's a relative newcomer from the 15th century. '**St. Peter's Way**' – as maps call it – is also of recent vintage, a council branding exercise from the 1970s, but follows ancient paths tacking eastwards past Mundon Creek like a pastoral *via sacra*. I suggest all but the hardiest long-distance walkers drive to Tillingham, where the track leads through **St. Nicholas' churchyard** and towards the sea wall; once there, a tiny dot starts to magnify as you walk towards it. If St. Peter's is open, you will find yourself in a single cell building, its unplastered walls a palimpsest of materials, initially from the detritus of the earlier Roman fort and later – some time after it fell into disuse under the Tudors – anything to hand when a farmer repurposed it for a barn. Nearby **Bradwell beach** has a cockle spit consisting of thirty acres of nothing but shells, the famous local oysters adding to the mix. Like much that's good in the Essex countryside, it's managed by the Essex Wildlife Trust. Bradwell A, the decommissioned nuclear power station sits just out of sight but, if eventually built, the huge mushroom forms of **Bradwell B**, much closer to St. Peter's, would loom over, and destroy, this very special, remote and delicate site.

The return walk passes **Bradwell-on-Sea**, whose **village hall** (1932) looks like something from 1900s Vienna, while **Bradwell Lodge**, a handsome Georgian rectory with a glazed belvedere, was once home to Maldon MP Tom Driberg, a fitting candidate for that description originally invented for Lord Byron, 'mad, bad and dangerous to know'. Despite that, Driberg was a tenacious advocate for Essex and a fierce opponent of the 1950s power station. Food for thought on the walk back.

EAST WANDER

Woven from Wealth: Coggeshall (with a trip to Layer Marney)
Coggeshall is one of several Essex towns that grew prodigiously rich from textiles in the late medieval period – Hollington Brothers operated a factory there until recently, and their on-site retail outlet kept going until early 2018. The town is stuffed as full as a bale of wool with **elaborate timber-framed houses**, whose exposed, carved oak beams shout out great wealth and age, although sometimes they are fibbing. The façade of **Paycocke's**, seemingly the most spectacular of all, is a heavy-handed restoration from the early 20th century. That only proves a wider point about the town, though: Coggeshall's built evidence, of almost every date, style and material, points to prosperity and employment continuing over many centuries. The wealth wasn't concentrated solely in the hands of the few, either, as we are reminded by the central cluster of **nonconformist chapels**, built by public subscription.

Yet the town around the central crossroads – marked by Queen Victoria's **Golden Jubilee clocktower** (1887) – is only part of the story. For the first chapter, you must walk a bit further, over the infant **River Blackwater**, up the hill (taking in the 13th-century **Grange Barn** on your right) and then along an unadopted lane which reveals itself to be the exact mid-point of the Essex Way – and leads to **Coggeshall Abbey**, central to life here until Henry VIII's Dissolution. All that now remains of the Cistercian monastery are a handsome, slightly incoherent farmhouse and outbuildings combining fragments of the old monastic buildings and, on the other side of the track, a **distinctly incongruous Victorian factory chimney**, perhaps the last gasp for the older watermill alongside it.

No such prolonged adaptation for **Layer Marney Tower**, eight miles south of Coggeshall by road, and somewhere no visitor to these parts should miss. Sir Henry Marney's meteoric rise through the courts of Henry VII and VIII emboldened him to build a grandiose mansion, of which only the soaring brick and terracotta gatehouse was completed before his interment in the adjacent rebuilt church. The planned mansion was stillborn, since Henry's son died two years later. In the intervening centuries, the Tower has faced challenges, not least the 1884 earthquake, but surmounted all, standing proud like a fabulous hatstand, looking out over distant water. The water in question is **Abberton Reservoir**, the heart of an immense late 1930s damming enterprise based around Layer Brook. With it came a scattered, bespoke collection of **Art Deco water treatment and pumping stations**: an unexpected, eastern counterpart to the 'Golden Mile' of 1930s industrial buildings on the edge of West London. A modern water supply here was, itself, pure gold.

SOUTH WANDER

Tilbury and the Forts that Never Fought

Tilbury is crammed with forts and fortification, west to east, a reminder of how tempting the Essex bank of the Thames has always looked to invaders. The jewel is **Tilbury Fort**, Daniel Defoe's 'key of the river', built in response to the people who'd given the country such a fright by appearing at Chatham in 1667: the Dutch. In 1670 plans were hatched by Sir Bernard de Gomme (himself Dutch) to replace Tilbury's dilapidated Tudor blockhouse with

After De Gomme's map 1670

a mighty, star-shaped, brick and stone fortification featuring double moats and four huge bastions. These outward-projecting 'legs' were a Dutch innovation, too, although the intended quintet had to be reduced due to the tidal challenges posed by the Thames. By the end of the century, the fort bristled with countless powder magazines and some 272 guns; none was ever fired (a success, then, in defence terms).

Don't be deterred by the surrounding industrial landscape of **wind turbines**, **Amazon warehouses** and **container parks**: Tilbury Fort is an incongruous and astonishing mix of utility and ornament. Take its eye-catching **Water Gate**, built of fine white Portland stone, decorated with sculpted bundles of gun barrels and armour, and ennobled by a plaque to Charles II. Stranger still, it's all a deceit: this elaborate entry fronts a modest brick house, pleasingly Dutch with its mansard roof and sash windows.

To the west is the towering **1930s Cruise Terminal**, multi-storied cruise ships queuing nearby, while a purposeful little gantry leans over thick tidal mud to deliver passengers onto the car ferry, a short hop to Gravesend. We have reached, so the white weather-boarded pub tells us, the **World's End**. Heading east, the next fort lies three miles along the Thames coast path (and much further by road). **Coalhouse Fort** is menacing, built of deep grey granite and as compact and (seemingly) impregnable as Tilbury Fort is extended and complex. It was built, and rebuilt, later than its neighbour – in the first half of the 19th century – but with a far older enemy in mind: France. Typical of government infrastructure projects in any century, it was finished too late to be useful, although it found new purpose in WW2 when it housed a 'degaussing' system to render ships invisible to deadly German magnetic mines in the Thames. These days, it crowns a **peaceful park**, with long watery views to the distant derricks and toy-brick containers stacked colourfully at the **DP World port facility**. The only invasion, these days, is of cheap goods from afar.

SOUTH WALK

Start: Benfleet Railway Station
Finish: Ye Olde Smack, High St., Leigh-on-Sea
Distance: (inc. Hadleigh Castle) 8.6 miles

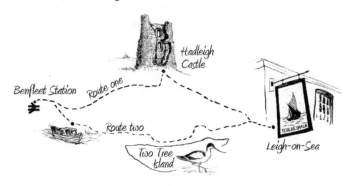

Boats, birds and buckets of bi-valves: Benfleet to Leigh

This walk works best with a measure of flexibility, and the train is the answer, since it allows for last-minute changes to the route and variable length of time. The lines to South Essex depart from Fenchurch Street, one of my favourite London terminals, if bafflingly hard to find.

The well-marked path from Benfleet station takes you past an intriguingly ad hoc collection of river craft, ranging from **mould-covered hulks** to much-loved little **pleasure cruisers**, usually with girls' names. You have a choice: keep on the straight towards Leigh-on-Sea or make a big loop up to the (surprisingly) high ground, visiting the substantial ruins of **Hadleigh Castle**. The **Salvation Army farm colony** just behind it, founded in 1891, is a reminder of troubled lives in the past and a continued mission in the present. A serious agricultural business, the farm has **rare breeds** and a **tearoom** for visitors just when you need it after the climb. John Constable sketched the castle in 1814, then returned to it 15 years later in a furious explosion of oils. If his Hadleigh works say something about humans' impermanence, so does the castle – it was the show-home of Hubert de Burgh, King John's Chief Minister, who later lost his lands and titles after falling out with his former ward, Henry III.

The walk directly to Leigh takes you along **the seawall**, constructed from compacted landfill, solidly sealed with clay. This walk is, depending on the season, **bird watchers' heaven**, offering an immense screen, a kind of ornithologists' Imax. The Essex Wildlife Trust maintains **Two Tree Island**, close by, as a winter refuge for waders and wildfowl and, in particular, as a breeding ground for **avocets**. Depending on the time of year, myriad different flocks come and go, such as curlews heading for northern moors, while an immense core brigade remains as resident foot soldiers, working along the rim of each retreating tide. They feast on the shellfish that sustain so much activity in **Leigh-on-Sea**, a busy mix of bucket and spade, fishing village charm and hard work (all assisted by a rail link, one stop on from Benfleet). Wherever you look here, fish is demonstrably centre stage – either being eaten, preferably as an outdoor pub lunch with a view of the water (Ye Olde Smack boasts an estuary-facing terrace, but there are many other eateries similarly well-appointed), or being dealt with in a series of olive-green sheds, military-looking and serious, as the trade still is, in these parts.

WEST WANDER

Not So New: Henry Moores and Hellenic Follies in Harlow

Harlow New Town is seventy years old now, but it's stuck with the adjective. As Norman Scarfe wrote in 1968, 'creating a New Town is a most exciting activity in any age', and he reckoned it would need another two decades for Frederic Gibberd's 1947 masterplan to mature. It's hard to grasp Gibberd's enormous achievement and easy to be swayed by bad publicity, but I hope you will follow me down this modern(ish) rabbit hole. Gibberd was adamant about preserving the 'genius loci' and his scheme envisaged a contoured tranche of Essex countryside, with mature trees and grassland acting as a unifying thread to the town, enhanced by his landscape consultant, Sylvia Crowe.

The central **Water Gardens** (now listed) were a key feature, an echo of Venice's Piazza San Marco with three terraces of canals, fountains and ponds forming a bold contrast to the rural landscape beyond the town. Extra car parking in the early 2000s did much to undermine their effect; today, the surviving marketplace, its clock and the nearby church of **St. Paul's** give a better sense of the original town centre. The church is lit by slivers of coloured and clear glass, a touch of le Corbusier's Ronchamp chapel in eastern France, while **John Piper's huge mosaic of the Risen Christ** dominates the east wall, gem-like, with shimmering golds and greens. Secular, but equally surprising is **the Lawn,** Britain's first residential tower-block, built in 1950. The public housing preference of the time was for two-storey homes, and Gibberd's plan, for mixed housing styles and a sizeable proportion of flats, met considerable opposition. The block's unusual butterfly shape allows for every flat (four to each of the nine storeys) to have a south-facing balcony.

Many distinguished architects contributed to the town's design, but prolonged poor maintenance has done the build-ings no favours. Interest is growing, though, and with it pride in the place and its achievements, especially in the arts. Har-low bills itself the world's first 'sculpture town' with self-guided trails that are an excellent way to grasp the essentials. One starts in the remnants of the **Water Gardens**, another, the **Hep-worth Walk**, sets off from the Town Park. If you arrive by train at Harlow Town, you can take the River Stort trail from there, heading for old **Parndon Mill** to find one sculpture per lock as well as a graceful sculptural footbridge over the weir. (An ele-gant map and guide are available, in print as well as online.) **Marsh Lane**, Gibberd's cleverly architectural garden, features even more sculpture, the most eye-catching being **a pair of full-height Corinthian columns** and four urns, which Gibberd salvaged from the exterior of Coutt's bank on the Strand whilst his firm undertook a redesign. Transporting them to Harlow was, the architect noted in his diary, a costly business, all the more so after the delivery lorry 'demolished three trees and dumped a pile of huge fragments in a ditch outside [Gibberd's] gates.' Perhaps it was, as he called it, 'an expensive folly', but it's also a dream-like fragment of ancient Greece in an Essex garden. And all the stranger on the edge of a New Town.

WEST WALK

Start: Epping Station
Finish: High St., Chipping Ongar
Distance 7.5 miles

Epping Station

St Andrew's Church,
Greensted

Chipping Ongar

Contrasting views and a decent spread of transport options make this a favourite way to explore **Epping Forest**. It alternates gently between wooded areas and farmland, sweeping views across Essex and the teeming, chattering business of the forest. Treats for eyes and ears alike.

The footpath soon leaves housing and traffic behind, although even at this early stage, some ramblers can fear they've gone astray. Epping's 'forest' is not Hansel and Gretel material; originally the word meant any area where the king's deer roamed. We're swiftly into the trees, though, and one of the most striking parts of the managed forest: **a stand of pollarded hornbeams**, the clear ground below their venerable trunks a stage for their beauty. Silky-barked hornbeam is an ancient native species, one of the hardest woods, showing no signs of age beyond its girth and the marks of prior lopping or cutting. This stand reminds us of a time when the forest was far from peaceful: in the late 19th century, Epping's landless folk lost their last access to common land, and with it, centuries of traditional grazing, coppicing and lopping rights.

En route, tiny **Greensted** is also linked to Victorian social upheaval. After public outcry at their harsh sentences, some of the Tolpuddle Martyrs were given farm tenancies here. **St. Andrew's** church deserves viewing, too. The tiny log-walled church, at first glance more Norwegian than English, dates from the 11th century, though excavations tell of far earlier origins, going back to Saxon Christianity.

If you've planned ahead, your arrival at **Chipping Ongar** could be crowned with a trip on the **Epping-Ongar heritage railway** (steam or diesel). Alas, you cannot chug all the way back to Epping until they've built a platform, but if you alight at North Weald, you can bus it back to the tube station, or hop on the railway's equally **vintage Green Line bus** for a veritable nostalgia overload.

7 DO SOMETHING FIERCE

Essex at War

In 2003, a Saxon king turned up just outside Southend. Preparatory works for a road widening scheme of the A127 and A1159 at Prittlewell uncovered the burial chamber of a very grand individual who died in the late sixth or early seventh century. Initially described by the tabloids as Southend's 'King Of Bling', the then-nameless remains were swiftly demoted to the more modest 'Prittlewell Prince' after the discovery of an even more lavish burial in a field near Litchfield. According to the latest archaeological thinking, though, the princely label is appropriate, as the grave is believed to belong to Seaxa, brother of the Saxon king Saebert, who ruled between 604 and 616.

This man was interred in some style, with more than 60 high-status objects including bronze cauldrons, gold foil crosses, glass jars, drinking horns, bone dice and gaming pieces and a sword and shield. Due to the acidic soils of the area, there was no body of any sort to be found, only some fragments of tooth enamel, but the archaeologists excavating the site still described an eerie thrill as they found copper alloy bowls, hanging on the chamber walls where they'd been placed, 1,400 years before[1].

Artist's impression of the original grave, with bowls hanging on the walls

However little of Seaxa there might be in the grave, its other contents mark him out as a sophisticated European: an Italian type of folding stool, Merovingian gold coins and a Byzantine bowl announcing his far-reaching connections and clout. Comparing the Prittlewell site and goods to other Saxon burials at Sutton Hoo and Taplow, archaeologists also detected clues suggesting links to Rome, and Christianity: there were few signs of personal adornment apart from the crosses (thought to have been laid over the man's eyes or affixed to clothing long since perished), little of the martial hardware that typically accompanied Saxon warriors to the afterlife; instead of the battlefield, grave goods like the stool, along with golden spoons, a candelabrum and a scythe pointed towards Southern European civilizations. This was not a Christian burial, but it bore signs of being the burial of someone who had become Christian, and who seemed to be shifting away from the customs of his ancestors and looking towards new horizons[2].

His ancestors, of course, would have come here from the continent themselves, part of an almost geological process, whereby incomers have been slipping ashore on Essex's fractured coastline of inlets, shifting tidal mud flats and intermittently treacherous salt marshes, to become absorbed into the population yet staying on the edge, gazing outwards. People came this way in boats large and tiny, fleeing persecution or terrible events in Europe, to escape justice or exploit new opportunities. Over the centuries, the coastline offered them makeshift refuges, shepherds' huts and wicks (dairies) which stood empty much of the time, preserved by homespun coastal defences and useful to miscreants, vagrants and smugglers.

Those who came and went from over the water, legitimate or not, often married Essex girls and settled down in the area. Later they often became publicans – former smugglers knew their brandy. After involvement in punishing continental expeditions in the medieval and Tudor periods, the returning conscripts and mercenaries, soldiers or sailors, tended to be offloaded in Essex, too. They were long gone before their vessels docked in London, soon absorbed into the mist and the empty acres. This potentially troublesome, but vital and opportunistic element fed into the demography of Essex, sometimes emerging as lawlessness, sometimes as the kind of cussedness that is, as I write, propelling a number of Canvey Island independent councillors to form a break-away local interest party, inspired, they say, by the Catalans.

Nowhere around the intricate coast of islands, inlets and estuaries can compete with the strange isolation of the Dengie Peninsula or the disconcertingly atmospheric Mersea Island. In the 1870s the Reverend Sabine Baring-Gould, Exeter-born writer of that most stirring of all Victorian marching hymns 'Onward Christian Soldiers', became the furiously disaffected rector of

Mersea today, still wild, but with regular mail…

East Mersea. Baring-Gould, a collector of folk songs, an archaeologist, speaker of Basque and the father of some 15 children, had been sent into the wilderness by his ecclesiastical superiors, apparently due to his 'old-fashioned high church views' (as John Betjeman put it). During the decade he spent in Mersea, before retreating to the west country – where he inherited not only the family estates but the right to appoint himself as the local Vicar – Baring-Gould lamented the lack of what he termed the steadying hand of the landed gentry (or resident titled incumbents like himself) 'to civilise and restrain' behaviour on these wild eastern fringes. He channeled his desperation, but also a fascination with the folklore of the place and its people, into his historical novel *Mehalah: a story of the Salt Marshes*. It was published in 1880 but purported to be set a century earlier. The book, by far his most successful (of a huge output, including *The Book of Werewolves* and *Curious Myths of the Middle Ages*), was compared to *Wuthering Heights* in its bleak and tragic romanticism, played out against the timeless, unforgiving landscape.

Mersea Island helped give a raw emotional charge to the melodramatic narrative of a girl undone by a rough but fascinating loner. A solitary house may once have existed on Ray Island, as the author describes (he was also an antiquarian), while there is evidence to suggest that the characters, particularly the dastardly Elijah Rebow and the eponymous heroine Mahala (the actual spelling of a local ferryman's daughter's name) were based on figures well known by reputation on Mersea, even if the actual events described were entirely fictitious.[3] Baring-Gould described the locals as 'dull, reserved, shy and suspicious – I never managed to understand them, nor they to understand me.' For all that, he seemed mightily to enjoy going for tea with Mahala's father and stepmother and recounted with great glee how the latter returned to the boat drunk on one occasion, only to have a bucket of water thrown over her head by her husband. Like many an author, it seems, Baring-Gould was poised awkwardly between observing and belonging.

One modern edition of *Mehalah* was introduced by the novelist John Fowles who, though firmly associated with the

West Country in his own life and work, had been brought up in Leigh-on-Sea after his mother fled London for coastal Essex for fear of the deadly Spanish flu epidemic in 1919. He admitted to a 'bleak sort of affection' for the Dengie landscape but in his preface to *Mehalah* he observed that the true source of evil in the story was the surroundings, and not the people.

Others, like Fowles' mother, saw the empty wastes of Essex as their salvation, and 20th-century escapees from one plague or another were merely part of a longer, older chain. In 1665, after a working visit to a Naval Board colleague at Dagnam (close to modern Harold Hill), Samuel Pepys confessed in his diary that he had reassured everyone that he lived 'wholly in Woolwich' given 'how all these great people here are afeared of London, being doubtful of anything that comes from thence or that hath lately been there.'

As he travelled around, Pepys was continually quizzed about the progress of the plague, 'a sad question to be so often asked.' Understandably, people in the countryside were terrified of the plague. A friend of his told an unnerving story that conveyed the chill reality. Two coaches were passing one another in a narrow lane, and the other being heavily curtained off, a young man cheekily thrust his head through the window, hoping to expose a dalliance. He was horrified to discover that the darkened interior contained a neighbouring family's maid, 'very ill, in a sick dress and stunk mightily', being conveyed to the 'pest-house'.

But nowhere was immune. Colchester, like Braintree, became an epicentre of plague. It raged for fifteen months, killing nearly five thousand, a higher proportion of deaths than in London itself. Commerce (particularly the trade in local, sought-after oysters which Pepys, a man of so many appetites, greatly enjoyed) was badly affected. Estuaries and ports had to be strictly policed. Londoners were escaping by water in droves, so anyone who could not prove definitively that they were plague-free was prevented from landing; there were fights and scuffles as each vessel moored. But some people showed great bravery.

At Wivenhoe, one Thomas Clarke refused to help an official prevent infected passengers landing while a captain, Thomas Collin, 'took his boat and therein fetched divers of the passengers on shore from out of the packet-boat[4].' Humanity had overcome prudence and both men found themselves standing trial at Colchester Quarter Sessions. We do not know their fate.

The battle against the elements was as unrelenting as that against contagion from the city. As early as the 13th century, it was common knowledge that sea levels were rising (or perceived to be doing so, since the land was also shrinking as a result of better drainage). Local people were required to contribute, according to their means, to the upkeep of sea walls. In the medieval period Essex defended itself from the North Sea in a relatively *ad hoc* fashion, but at the turn of the 16th century, local landowner Sir Henry Appleton and a Dutch cloth merchant named Joas Croppenburgh set out to solve the problem.

The partners entered into an agreement for reclamation works at Canvey Island. The task, carried out under the supervision of the young engineer Cornelius Vermuyden and a team of men from the Netherlands, appears to have been complete by 1622. Two so-called 'Dutch' cottages survive, thatched and octagonal, with a chimney stack in the middle, all at sea among the bungalows of Canvey Island. In the 1930s, the same decade that a casino, helter-skelter and amusement park were established to reinforce the holiday spirit, and boost some family fortunes, several more cottages were added, in the 'Dutch' style so confusing the picture somewhat. But the memory and the bloodline of Dutch engineers still lived on. Women on Foulness, living on an island then, as now, largely inaccessible and shrouded in secrecy due to its use for weapons testing, were recorded as customarily wearing Dutch dress and, even more steadfastly, speaking Dutch, until World War I. Canvey Islanders continued occasionally to don Dutch dress, at least at carnival time, into the 1950s.

One of the remaining 'Dutch' cottages on Canvey

Meanwhile, the incessant forces of erosion, driven by changes in weather and lately exacerbated by intensive agriculture, pointed to more varied strategies. A hefty wall was built in the 1930s to protect Canvey Island from the North Sea. Otherwise entirely functional, it was cheerfully embellished with a circular café cum shelter dating from 1932-33. One of the most surprising modernist buildings in Britain, the recently renovated Labworth café, cheerfully aloft on the sea defences, was designed by the young Ove Arup.

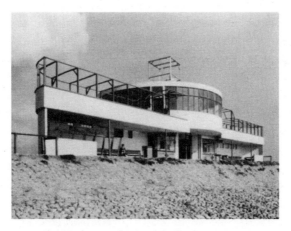

The original exterior of Ove Arup's dazzling design at Canvey

Given such preparations, it was a terrible irony that the North Sea floods of 1953, a tidal surge of unprecedented ferocity, hit

Seaside resort turned nightmare: Canvey in 1953

Canvey Island the hardest. As we have seen, it left almost sixty people dead and devastated the largely self-built town of shacks and rough bungalows. One eye witness was five-year-old John Wilkinson (aka Wilko Johnson, the demon guitarist with Dr Feelgood). 'All I remember was my mum gathering us together, and I looked out of the back window at the fields, but there were no fields, it was the sea, there were waves, waves coming in.' Despite the best efforts of the RAF with blow heaters the Wilkinsons' 'cardboard' house was a write-off.[5]

After the disaster, sea defences were reinforced and low-lying areas of the coast further fortified. Operation King Canute, the plan instigated well before the floods and which had its local operational headquarters in the Red Cow pub on Canvey Island, had to fulfil its purpose. It was the threat from the landward side, the bottling up of rivers and submerged fields by the sea wall, which had driven joint planning between the RAF and the waterways authorities. Meanwhile, the work continued over decades, always to keep the sea at bay[6]. Christine Townley was a young civil engineer whose Northumbrian firm sent her south in 1978 for site experience, an important step towards becoming a chartered engineer. The job involved building two new barriers – one, Easthaven, from the mainland to Canvey; and a further two kilometres of flood wall which would mean an unfortunate loss of views. To begin with this initiative had seemed an opportunity for creative thinking. There was talk of lifting the Lobster Smack pub on stilts, while Binnie and Partners (Townley's employers) had extensive talks with Pilkington of St Helens (the Motopia people) about the use of toughened glass in the floodwall but 'the glass was going to have to be very thick and would have cost a fortune... so sadly that great idea never happened.' In her opinion, her colleagues and the client played disappointingly safe: 'no stilts... no glass.' It could have been much more fun.

Compared to the devouring incursions of the North Sea, the intermittent threat posed by human aggressors from over the water might seem more easily thwarted. In the third century, the Romans, now fully at home in Essex, constructed their own defences against the dreaded sea rovers, or pirates. The site of their Othona fort at Bradwell-juxta-Mare, the English Bradwell-on-Sea, gives its name to a Christian community living close by, set up in 1946 by RAF chaplain Norman Motley, to promote Anglo-German friendship and understanding. Motley was drawn to the spot by the sole ancient landmark on the entire Dengie peninsula at this point, the tiny church of St Peter on the Wall, built by St. Cedd in 654 CE and sited, as the name suggests, on the foundations of the west wall of the fort.

Cedd, a monk from Lindisfarne in Northumberland, became bishop of the East Saxons, establishing minsters at Bradwell-on-Sea and Tilbury and giving Essex a sprinkling of institutions bearing his name, from primary and preparatory schools to Masonic Lodges. In fictional Chadfleet, the Essex village setting for P.D. James' first detective novel, *Cover Her Face* (1962), the St Cedd's church fête, held as usual in the grounds of medieval Martingale House, becomes the overture to the crime – enter DCI Adam Dalgleish.

Most of the surviving materials in the fabric of St Peter's are clearly Roman, neat little tile bricks like filo pastry, and lumps of suet-like septaria, the hardened river mud that stood in for stone around here. Only the nave remains, and on approach it looks more like a barn – which is what it was until the early 1900s when the Office of Works (antecedent of Historic England) stepped in to piece it carefully back together. The fort's loss was to be the church's gain. It was re-consecrated in 1920 and has immense presence, despite its diminutive scale and raw state.[7]

The Chapel of St. Peter on the Wall, Bradwell-on-Sea

Near these evocative remnants, a convivial group of bird watchers is often to be found, gathered to observe the vicissitudes of migratory birds off this coast as well as the local comings and goings of part-time residents such as the opportunist peregrines who lived for a while on Bradwell nuclear power station just round the headland, the honey buzzard that only a true ornithologist (my walking companion on one occasion) would recognise and, an easy one for me, unlettered in birds, a kingfisher flashing home along the water's edge. Walking on the raised seawall path on Dengie, one brilliant autumn day, heading for the little chapel shrunken to a pinhead in the far distance, we passed a stunted apple tree, bearing a single ostentatiously red and shiny apple and, just below it, an adder. As if to build on the biblical analogies, massive flocks of dunlin wheeled incessantly above, collectively turning their silvered wings as angels might, beating and unfurling high overhead.

Did they also provide aerial distraction for the participants in that disastrous event, the shakily recorded, and even less certainly located, Battle of Maldon? The Vikings, who had already had a try at seizing Colchester and Mersea, now sailed up the Blackwater towards Maldon to be met by the stalwarts of the Essex militia, the *fyrd*, mobilised to defend their land and led by Byrhtnoth, the elder of the shire. The engagement was short, brutal and futile. It lives on in the name and fragments of an Old English poem 'The Battle of Maldon'. Without an exact locale for the battle, in recent years the National Trust and Maldon Council have settled on it being at Northey Island. As the plaque near the causeway onto the tidal island, (one of six in Essex) puts

it, 'on and around this spot an army of Danish raiders and the Essex army commanded by Earl Byrhtnoth fought on 10th August 991 AD. Byrhtnoth's heroic defeat and death became the subject of a great Anglo-Saxon poem.'

Opinion divides as to whether the poem is a contemporary account or one written in the rearview mirror. When its author introduces certain characters, such as the cowardly Godric – who flees the battle on Byrhtnoth's horse – he does so as if the outcome is already well known to his audience. Why tell us, upon arrival as it were, that this Godric is the coward Godric? But there are two Godrics in the narrative, one yellow-bellied, one a hero, so perhaps the author is merely trying to make things clear. And if this is a work addressed to an audience well familiar with all the details, why is King Aethelred not graced with his usual 'Unready', or

Statue of Byrhtnoth at Maldon – resisting beyond death

more accurately 'ill-advised' (a play on his name, which meant 'wisely counselled')?[8]

The poem describes how the advancing Vikings are held off at a bridge, but request permission to cross in order to wage battle; a request Byrhtnoth grants due to his 'ofermode', a term variously translated as pride, over-confidence or excess zeal. It certainly seems that the suicidal heroism and loyalty Tacitus had noted in the Saxons a millennium earlier was still going strong, recalled in verse if not elsewhere, and in that sense 'The Battle of Maldon' illustrates the main political division of the era. Men like King Aethelred and his dubious advisers followed a *realpolitik* strategy of paying off the invaders to avoid bloodshed – the so-called Danegeld. Men of Byrhtnoth's stamp – and possibly the poet's – believed in resisting until death. The Danes kept demanding more money and Aethelred kept paying, the result of which was that Aethelred kept his throne for 37 years, a regal record not surpassed until Henry II in the 13th century. So, who was wiser?

In 2006 the episode at Maldon was commemorated, for a modern audience who may have been blithely unaware of the weight of history here, when an immense statue of the vanquished leader was erected. This was the work of locally born sculptor John Doubleday, whose other Essex-linked subjects include cricketer Graham Gooch in Chelmsford and crime writer Dorothy Sayers in Witham.

Of Sir (Ralph) Norman Angell (Lane), writer, editor and internationalist whose heirs presented Northey Island to the National Trust in 1976, there is neither sign nor word, far less a statue to the Nobel Peace Prize winner of 1933. During a career which combined the roles of cowboy, wine-grower, Paris editor of the *Daily Mail* and Labour MP for Bradford, Norman Angell, as he preferred to be known, bought the island in the early 1920s and designed himself a house there[9]. His best-known book (of many), *The Great Illusion* (1910), was a hugely influential argument for European integration and the benefits of economic cooperation. An ardent pacifist, his reasons for purchasing Northey Island, with its connotations of that famous battle, remain a mystery. He rarely visited it after the 1920s although he lived on until 1967, much of the time in the USA.

No uncertainty dogs Colchester's claim as a battle site. The vicissitudes of this, the first recorded town in Britain (as the brown signs tell all who enter), have been extreme, but never more so than during the terrible Civil War siege. In early June 1648 thousands of royalist troops, under the leadership of George Goring, poured across the Thames from Greenwich. When they arrived at Colchester after more than a week on the road, they found the gates shut – to be reopened after 'a brief skirmish'. The plan was to stop briefly, take on supplies and add more men to their number, particularly needy weavers. But their adversaries, parliamentarian forces led by Thomas Fairfax, arrived just two days after them. They did not, could not, leave. And the siege began. By mid-July the starving town was cut off from all outside supplies, including water, and the cloth trade was on its knees. The siege lasted until the end of August, at terrible cost. After the surrender the relatively small Dutch population, known as the 'congregation', was forced to pay half of the immense fine, possibly because although Protestant they had been keener to retain something of their textile trade than to help resist the siege. Meanwhile the Royalist leaders, Sir Charles Lucas and Sir George Lisle, were summarily executed.

Almost a century later, Defoe described a town still in mourning, since all the buildings outside the fortifications had been razed, leaving 'battered walls, breaches in the turrets, and ruined churches.' Some stabilised ruins, such as St Botolph's Priory, remain as evidence to this day.

While eastern England had readied itself for successive incursions from across the sea, nothing could be more terrifying than the prospect of Napoleonic invasion – from the air. Napoleon's forces had begun to use hot air balloons,

named after their makers, the brothers Montgolfier, for observation. Happily, though seemingly unknown to the British,
the French balloon corps had been disbanded in 1799, but from
1805 onwards – and ironically, after Napoleon's naval defeat at
Trafalgar – a chain of defensive structures, known as Martello
Towers, was built along the south coast, extended to the east coast
in 1808 and designed to be early warning stations against invasion from the sea or even from the air. Of a total of twenty-nine
in eastern England, eleven were in Essex. Six of them survive.

The man who master-planned the location of the Martello
Towers was an unlikely candidate for such a sensitive stra-
tegic role. General Charles-François du Périer Dumouriez
had been the commandant of Cherbourg, from where he
had devised a plan to invade Britain, before returning to revolutionary Paris and joining the Jacobin Club. His military
career was unconventional from beginning to end. In 1804
he arrived in England, settling near Henley-on-Thames, to
become a trusted adviser to the British War Office, in which
role he drew up the structural chain-link fence that was to
be wrapped around the most exposed parts of southern and
eastern England.

Martello Towers, impressive drum-like forms, are
three-storey brick structures protected by tough render,
and the Admiralty had become persuaded of their usefulness while assisting Corsican separatists against the French
in 1794. Coastal villages and towns on the island had been
building similar, circular structures since the 15th century
in order to watch out for marauding north African corsairs,
and the one at Mortella Point in the north of Corsica was
unsuccessfully bombarded by two British warships, before
finally falling to a land-based assault after two days of sustained fighting. Impressed, the British copied the design, and
the name of the place where the battle had raged – but they
made a spelling mistake.

Imported onto the south and east coasts of England, the towers are reminders of the prolonged state of alarm during the

Napoleonic Wars. Children growing up in the area before the last war were still being told to be good, or 'Boney' would come and get them. In Essex, old threats die hard.

Jaywick's Martello Tower during World War One, camouflaged and occupied by the men of the Essex Rifles, with bicycles

From Harwich, where the elaborate Redoubt is the key structure in the chain, the towers extended south to Jaywick and Clacton and round to St Osyth. A number have been lost and one of the three at St Osyth, at Beacon Hill, was demolished as recently as 1967. In peacetime their location made them well-sited coastguard bases; once the country was at war again, they became pillboxes for the Royal Observer Corps, optimistically camouflaged. More recently, they found an even darker use, as monitoring points against nuclear fall-out in the Cold War. The turncoat General had done his job better than even he might have imagined. Nowadays some have been converted for peacetime purposes: the Martello Tower in Jaywick is a flourishing community centre, while Clacton's, which boasts a drawbridge and moat, was a restaurant for a while.

In between wars in the mid-19th century, there were domestic battles to fight, involving matters such as the franchise, the right of women to hold property, and the private enclosure of public land leading to the loss of common rights. A fierce fight was erupting in Epping Forest, and D.W. Coller's monthly part-work, *People's History of Essex* (1858 onwards), set the tone.

A journalist on the *Chelmsford Chronicle,* Coller argued in 1861 that the people of Loughton were cosseted by their proximity to the forest. They exhibit a 'want of energy, and an unwillingness to move from their native place.' While this attachment to a single spot might seem admirable in general, Coller considered that their immobility demonstrated a lamentable lack of social ambition – perhaps a case of pot and kettle, given his own *curriculum vitae,* 40 years on the same newspaper. He writes: 'the pretext of procuring firewood by means of the loppings of the trees, which the inhabitants claim a right to cut during the winter months, encourage habits of idleness and dislike of settled labour... Enclosures, however, seem to be commencing in the neighbourhood, which will probably check these irregular and, to a certain extent, demoralising tendencies.' Coller believed that the commoners, cut off from their source of livelihood and domestic comforts, would pull themselves together and become upwardly mobile, ambitious and restless. It all suggests a close reading of Samuel Smiles, the Victorian high priest of self-improvement and the inventor of the term 'Self Help'.

In this climate of self-serving moralism, it is perhaps no surprise to discover that the man who enclosed more of Epping Forest than anyone else was a local cleric. The rector or, as Mark Girouard neatly puts it in his book on the Victorian country house, the 'squarson' of Loughton, the Rev. J.W. Maitland, had fenced off the not inconsiderable area of 1,300 acres, leaving just nine for the village recreation ground. He believed in living well, commissioning W.E. Nesfield to design him a pleasant, but rather grandiose Queen Anne Revival country house in Loughton, well beyond the ambitions of the usual rector. Loughton Hall and its land were bought by the LCC in 1944, to become an 'out-country' cottage estate of over 4,300 dwellings[10]. Did the residents know that they were living on a famous battleground?

Although Epping Forest was still Crown land, from 1860 the lords of the manor were free to buy forest rights, and so enclosure had gathered momentum – whether it was still woodland or not. Hainault Forest had been enclosed in 1851 and now followed the last remnants of Waltham Forest, once an immense royal hunting zone. The threat of wholesale privatisation – to use the modern term – alerted a group of public-spirited individuals, who took up the cudgels. George Shaw-Lefevre, Lord Eversley, a Liberal MP and lifelong public servant, along with Robert Hunter, the lawyer to the Post Office, jointly founded the Commons Preservation Society (CPS) in 1865, the first national amenity society in the country (almost in the world) to respond to the mounting threat to common land and other public rights of access.

In Epping, they used a single case to illustrate the point. A typical labouring family, the Willingales, depended upon lopping rights for their livelihood and *pace* Coller, had no plans to move elsewhere, let alone climb the social ladder. In a carefully coordinated move, Thomas Willingale broke through the Rev. Maitland's fence at precisely midnight on 11 November to secure the commoners' right to lop branches any day between then and 23 April.

When proceedings were taken against him, the CPS stepped in. It was a long case, and costly, and they called up the financial backing and support of the Corporation of the City of London, which already held commoners' rights over 200 acres in Wanstead and had much deeper pockets for protracted legal argument. When judgement was finally given in the summer of 1874, the commoners were victorious. The Master of Rolls remarked unambiguously that 'the Lords of the Manors have taken other persons' property without their consent and have appropriated it to their own use.' All enclosures since 1851 were now overturned and the CPS continued to fight for full public access to the Forest. A handful of high-handed, well-placed individuals were thereby prevented from wrecking the remaining open space on this eastern flank of London.[11]

Making the Queen welcome at Epping, May 6, 1882

On May 6, 1882, the royal opening of Epping Forest at High Beech sealed the transfer of royal privilege to public rights. The Crown ceded to the populace, and Queen Victoria declared it to be 'the people's forest'. Edward North Buxton was a verderer (that is, an official of the forest in charge of common land), as was his brother Thomas. He had first drawn the attention of the CPS to the plight of commoners in Epping Forest and played a major part in placing it in the control of the Corporation of London. Once he had achieved that, he turned his conservationist energies to securing the future of Hatfield Forest, while the CPS, named the Open Spaces Society since 1899, continues to defend public rights of way and access to common land to this day.

From 1882 onwards, incursions into the Forest, much of which was in fact open pasture by then, would be more likely to serve the public interest. During World War I, the outer edges of Epping Forest were cut into elaborate earth and turf trenches, dug by large numbers of volunteers with the Artists' Rifles, and duly recorded by official government photographers. Yet it was questionable how prepared Essex was for the very serious threats posed by the war. At first the county played to its strengths. The 8th (Cyclist) Battalion, the Essex Regiment, was assembled easily, one of 14 such battalions (all from southern

Troops of the 1st Battalion County of London Volunteers digging trenches at Epping Forest in 1917

and flat regions of England), yet their usefulness in trench warfare conditions was quickly seen to be, at best, limited.

Arnold Bennett, since 1912 living near the east coast at Thorpe-le-Soken when not buzzing up to London by train (the village has a working station to this day) to keep himself in work and abreast of events, recorded the ineffectual preparations with chilly eye and lacerating pen.[12] 'Generals came down from town,' he noted on August 9th, 1915, when he was just back from a month's writing assignment on the Western Front. A member of the Essex Emergency Committee since the early days of the war, he was shocked that the military 'have not yet got their transport into order; they admit that it will not be in order for 2 months.' Confusion reigned on emergency arrangements: a secret word, without which 'no order to evacuate was to be considered genuine', turned out to be unknown to the relevant officer. Even the number of horses available for the ammunition column was a mystery, while their feeding depended on local goodwill. But Bennett was told, 'You must never say "I don't know" in the Army.'

Continual vigilance was essential, despite the farce. Two men were seen up to no good in the local ammunition store near the station, where some 300,000 rounds were kept. 'Clacton was called up by telephone, and kept up most of the night… The missing men were supposed to correspond with [descriptions of] two interned Germans escaped from Dorset.' One, it was said, walked soundlessly on rubber soles and carried a rope.

Soon after, in late February 1916, local garrisons were doubled on the expectation of 'small German raids.' Two batteries stood in readiness for two days and reinforcements from Colchester, (the major garrison town of East Anglia) proved to consist of 'convalescent wounded gunners from the front, appointed only to light duty and to extreme emergency duty.' Soon afterwards, the ammunition column was ordered to move on. Transport was by mule-wagon; on the top of one was perched the OC's servant holding his dog and a large photograph. 'The departure had the air of a circus departure badly managed,' wrote Bennett.

To its evident surprise, Frinton-on-Sea, like Clacton-on-Sea, was on the front line and the Bennetts attended several fundraising concerts, usually for the Red Cross, in which the music was of variable standard and the locations offered outstanding discomfort. The ladies wore unnecessary evening dress, while the parson had a tendency towards 'speechifying.' Soon, at Mrs. Bennett's instigation, they diverted events for local troops to their house, Comarques, offering them a stage, a piano and games. A Chrysanthemum Show for the Red Cross, selling only their own plants, struck Bennett, by then earning prodigious sums from his writing, as 'a strange, though ingenious way of getting money.' The takings were £23 net. Meanwhile his splendid Dutch yacht, the Velsa, formerly moored at Brightlingsea, was brought inland in order to avoid it being commandeered by the enemy.

The overhead threat was more urgent. The slightly fanciful notion of a fleet of hot air balloons heading into English airspace from France had turned, a century on, into a very real prospect of Zeppelin attack. By mid-September, central London had been hit and, reported Bennett, 'it was said in the village that a Zeppelin hung over the village church for an hour on Monday night, but I did not believe this.' When he went to collect his wife from the station, the porter told him that they had been telegraphed to keep the platform in darkness. 'This mysteriousness of unseen things known to be coming – such as Zeppelins and trains – was rather impressive.'

A month later, Zeppelins hit the military camp in Epping Forest, drawn by the lights left blazing in the Officers' Mess. They dropped four or five bombs, weighing a hundredweight each. None exploded and the men nonchalantly dug them up with picks and shovels. But Zeppelins introduced Essex to war on its own soil. The intended targets included munitions factories such as Hoffmann Bearings in Chelmsford. Airfields were targets too, the Royal Flying Corps (from 1918, the RAF) at Hornchurch, Wormingford, or North Weald Bassett. The entire area was, by default, highly vulnerable as the dirigibles went to and from their targets along the Thames or into central London.

On the night of 23 September 1916 two were brought down over rural Essex[13]. Twelve gigantic airship bombers had set out from Germany. L32, heading for London but deflected

Zeppelin L33 at the crash-site

by the anti-aircraft barrage, dropped its bombs near Purfleet and then, illuminated by searchlights in the night sky, was successfully targeted by a routine RFC patrol, to come down, a ball of fire, on farmland at Great Burstead near Billericay. There were no survivors from the crew of twenty-two; all were buried at Great Burstead but later exhumed and moved to Staffordshire.

The second of the pair, Zeppelin, L33, had been bombing the East End of London but crashed at New Hall Farm, Little Wigborough, a few yards from a house. The occupants, the Lewis family, escaped harm, while the crew of the immense inflatable simply walked away, having set it alight to prevent it falling into British hands. They later admitted that this wasn't easy, as matches and lighters were understandably forbidden on airships. Police Constable Charles Smith – thereafter known as Zepp Smith – boldly intercepted them as they set out towards Colchester to hand themselves over. A conversation between equals ensued, as one German officer asked him, in English, what his countrymen thought about the war, before shaking his hand.

The only armed Germans to land on English soil during the First World War, Käpitan Alois Böcker and his crew were well looked after, accommodated, thoughtfully, by the Vicar of West Mersea in the parish hall while his wife Nancy organized meals for the men and treatment for crewman Artur Piepkorn, who had a fractured rib. It seems strange to think that these men were returning from a mission which had killed six civilians, destroyed a pub and set an oil depot on fire. Equally odd were the actions of Alois Böcker who, moments before the Zeppelin went up in flames, had reportedly taken the trouble to knock on several nearby doors to warn people of the impending explosion. Rather like the famous Christmas football match in the trenches, the honourable elements of war are somehow just as, if not more unsettling than the slaughter.

Meanwhile in a farmhouse at nearby Great Wigborough, a Mrs. Clark gave birth to a baby girl. Given the significance of the night, her GP, Dr Spinks, suggested an appropriate name might be Zeppelina and her parents agreed. Zeppelina Williams (her married name) lived until 2004 and her memorial is to be seen in Little Wigborough church.

By 3am on the morning of 24th September, carloads of curious Londoners had started to arrive at the crash sites, and by 8am, soldiers were trying to prevent souvenir hunters from pilfering mementoes. Canny lemonade sellers set up stall throughout the next day and New Hall's owner, Charles Hutley began charging admission of 2d, donating the proceeds to war charities. Rather less honorably, two local men described as 'Jack Lewis, postcard vendor' and 'Edward Shandling, innkeeper' found themselves in court on 7th October 1916 for offences under the Defence of the Realm Act, namely being in possession of and attempting to sell fragments of the crashed Zeppelin.

Despite the conscientious efforts of her crew to destroy evidence, and people like Lewis and Shandling endeavouring to dispose of it by other means, the wreckage of L33 would provide inspiration and study material for several misguided British forays into airship construction, culminating with the R101, which came down in northern France en route to India in August 1930.

A little further north, Harwich, a naval base and the closest harbour to Germany, was continually on high alert. That worry rose to a crescendo, as recorded by Arnold Bennett, when a meeting of the Emergency Committee in April was alerted to 'the strong probability of an invasion between Harwich and Maldon in July or August.' The Great Eastern Hotel became the Garrison Military Hospital. But the invasion was a scare, useful to assure readiness but groundless. As a town and a port, Harwich remained remarkably unscathed.

Immediately after the Armistice, the River Stour at Harwich provided a parking lot for some 160 surrendered German submarines and so was known for a time as 'U-boat Avenue' – at its peak extending for two miles, each craft being 100 metres long. The crews returned to Germany on transport ships without having set foot on British soil but empty submarines and backup craft now required disposal. Some were sent to France, others displayed in various ports, but most were dismantled, providing useful scrap metal for postwar industries desperately handicapped by lack of materials. Quite recently, one appeared lying insouciantly on mudflats off Kent, on the Isle of Grain. In 2018 the event was memorialized by a life size willow U-boat, destined to degrade into the mud with time, on the beach at Dovercourt.

U-boat crew awaiting a lift home at Harwich

If eastern England was relatively calm again during the 1930s, there were continuous repercussions from a series of dire political events in mainland Europe. With the Spanish Civil War, Leah Manning, a redoubtable figure particularly in the field of education, and later to serve briefly as Labour MP for Epping after Winston Churchill, became secretary of the Spanish Medical Aid committee. She organised the evacuation of almost 4,000 Basque children in May 1937 after the bombing of Guernica, an event she had witnessed in person. The SS *Habana*, in which Manning travelled north with the refugees, docked in Southampton.[14]

After some weeks in tented accommodation on a nearby farm, the children were dispersed in many directions, to seventy so-called colonies. These were anything from rudimentary huts to redundant country houses, set up and funded by sympathisers, who ranged from Quakers, pacifist organisations, convents and the Salvation Army, to unions, political parties and groupings of the left. There were at least three in Essex. One was at Hadleigh Castle at the Salvation Army farm, another at Langham, near Colchester, where members and sympathisers of the Peace Pledge Union housed and supported sixty children. When it closed in the autumn of 1939, some of the older children, those who still could not be repatriated, were taken in by local pacifist families and others transferred to other colonies, still supported by the PPU, at the rate of ten shillings a week for every child.

Another camp, more directly under the aegis of Dame Leah, occupied a large Victorian house, Woodberry, at Theydon Bois, on the edge of Epping Forest, and was supported by the National Union of Teachers. The group of twenty-one children was given lessons by their own teachers at the house, with some extra afternoon sessions at a local convent. The boys were keen on football and their team was soon playing against neighbouring schools. Most of the colonies were temporary arrangements, constrained by the limits of local fund raising, but in 1951 it emerged that 270 of the 4000 children who had disembarked in Southampton were still living in Britain. Some never left.

In the anxious months of summer and autumn 1938, preparations for war – be it dealing with invasion, chemical attack or the housing of homeless children from the vulnerable areas around the docks and East End – gathered momentum. The crime writer Margery Allingham, though only recently settled in the remote village of Tolleshunt D'Arcy, found herself in a central, even commanding role.[15]

Episodes veered between high farce and administrative brilliance. The village policeman was detailed to distribute official documents, a fearsome package that included, among much else, a list of the terrifying effects of phosgene and mustard gas, starting with gangrene. There were first aid instructions and rules for effective decontamination of everything from clothes to buildings and vehicles. On one occasion Margery's husband, Philip (Pip) Youngman Carter, member of the A.R.P., received a peremptory message from Maldon: 'Collect seven hundred gas masks for your area and fit.' The prospect of the marshes filling with deadly gas was a demonic version of the fogs and 'haars' (heavy sea mists) with which the locals were all too familiar.

Allingham, using any spare moments to write about the doom-laden atmosphere and mounting fears, asked her English, but America-based editor at Doubleday, who was raging against Neville Chamberlain's apparent capitulation, to consider his views more carefully. He might try and picture himself putting 'six hundred old ladies, yokels and school kids into gas masks, explaining to horrified country folk that the food they eat, the crops they grow and the animals… cannot be protected in any way' and then be very glad he was living in America.

Preparing sufficient accommodation and adequate practical support for the vulnerable Londoners, whenever they might come, with little idea of the numbers involved, was a huge headache. The village butcher Mr Doe had been appointed billeting officer, and Margery volunteered to be his assistant, setting up accommodation in advance for up to one hundred and twenty children. Based on her experience, Allingham wrote a national report on the topic for the WVS, emphasising that those housing the incomers must be willing volunteers, not coerced because of the size of their properties or the presumed depth of their pockets.

Mainstream newspapers were unwilling to pick the story up, touching as it did on social and class sensitivities, but local newspapers were more amenable. Allingham tactfully suggested that the problem was distrust, a fear of strangers, and that preparatory measures, such as twinning between urban and rural organisations, should be taken head on. 'Let us meet them not as Government boarders, nor as invading foreigners but as ordinary other people who may, Heaven knows, in many cases be extremely nice?'

During the unsettling months of the phony war of 1939, Allingham and the butcher pressed on with their preparations for a large influx of Londoners. Once war was declared, Civil Defence measures were rapidly put into place ahead of the expected air raids. Supplies, from oil skins to bomb maps, from wellington boots to first aid kits, were stored in D'Arcy House, which also, having one of very few telephones in the village, became the Warden's Post. Margery's husband Pip was Chief Warden.

When the evacuees arrived, the reality was a 'ramshackle caravan of double-deckers carrying hundreds of luggageless mothers and children' as well as their dependents. Eight buses brought three hundred people to the village, twice the number expected. Ministry officials followed with money. But the families, their physical state and their expectations, were far beyond the experience of rural Essex. One group consisted of nineteen family members who refused to be parted and others included pregnant mothers with numerous small children in tow. Many people were judged to be 'verminous'. As Allingham recorded after a single night, 'the original emotional pity of the hosts had turned to alarm and exasperation.' Doe, the butcher, resigned his post. The replacement volunteer was Jane Degras, a left-wing economist and a newcomer to the village. The two women formed an uneasy, but effective coalition and efficiently dealt with reality. A house was set aside as a maternity home and Allingham was instructed in emergency midwifery, although despite the births of five children there that winter she was not required to practice her new skill.

Margery asked her editor at *Time and Tide* to bear with her and be flexible, since writing to deadline was difficult 'when all your neighbours are mucking about in the dawn looking for nuns with sub-machine guns and collapsible bicycles to arrive by parachute.' The inhabitants of Tolleshunt D'Arcy could see with their own eyes, all too vividly, the menacing German bombardment of east London. The local bomb map was spotted with black flags, often the result of homing bombers. From early on Margery Allingham was heavily involved in the full range of war-time functions in the village, as she recounts in her only non-fiction book, *The Oaken Heart: The Story of an English Village At War* (1941). Yet after overseeing emergency rations, the village pig club, organising land girls and carrying out scores of urgent local tasks, she was still able to summon the courage to review Martha Gellhorn's *A Stricken Field,* with its graphic descriptions of man's bestial behaviour to man.

Not far away, a Ministry of Information photographer was sent to Springfield, outside Chelmsford, to record English village life under wartime conditions. By August 1941 people were keeping calm and carrying on as instructed. To modern eyes looking over this photographic record, there is a *Dad's Army* element in the line-up outside the church before the assorted volunteers mount, full tilt, their attack in 'sunny parkland'.

They don't like it up 'em, Mr Mainwaring

Elsewhere, as an ARP Warden reports to the Chief Warden, members of the WVS are busy cutting out hospital clothing from donated American cloth, carefully following paper patterns under the eagle eye of one Lady Ritchie, 'chief cutter'. In another scene,

Women's Institute members are shown, beyond parody, making chutney in the rectory garden. A group of London evacuees is working in the Victorian conservatory of a large house, making luxury goods for the American fashion market. Beyond all this, the village green is dotted with sign posts, removed from their actual locations, apparently to prevent enemy aircraft landing on the grass.

Village life in wartime, recorded by the Ministry of Information

The war had changed everything, not least the existence of large houses. Audley End House, the nearest to a palace that Essex could muster, experienced a particularly surreal period between 1942 and late 1944, during which it was known as Station 43, a secret training college for the Polish SOE Underground Warfare section, the last stop before their active deployment as members of the *Cichociemni*.[16] A constant stream of trainees came and went at six-monthly intervals. The first test often involved getting to Essex, and the house, by covert means. One unfortunate Pole hitched a lift in a motorcycle sidecar, only to be promptly delivered to Saffron Walden police station and placed under arrest as a German spy.

In view of its historic and architectural significance, the

Office of Works had prepared Audley End carefully for military use, a measure which let it emerge relatively unscathed after the war years. Inside the principal rooms, a protective shell of plywood was inserted to protect panelling and historic features, and the contents were removed. Nothing much palatial remained; it was as spartan as any Nissen hut. There was no heating, the men slept on mattresses on bare boards and washing facilities were rudimentary. A truck took them periodically to Cambridge to use the public baths.

The Poles were mastering an impressive array of skills including microdot photography, the use of invisible inks, lock picking, radio communications and every aspect of covert and overt attack, both physical and psychological. The staff and instructors settled down in Saffron Walden, attending the Forces Club, local pubs and regular dances at the town hall. In contrast, the trainees were obliged to stay within the grounds for their entire six-month course, passing their spare time playing football and volleyball (on the tennis court) and holding sports days. In the surrounding park, a British tank crouched menacingly in the now tangled vegetation of the Elysium Garden, and the fuselage of a Halifax bomber was set down neatly on the cobblestones near the stables.

One of the 316 *Cichociemni* who were parachuted back into Poland from 1941 onwards, Aleksandr Tarnawski, was still successfully making parachute jumps as recently as 2014. Others may be alive to this day, but many changed their names and made a point of never discussing their wartime exploits. This was pure expediency rather than stiff upper lip, as over a hundred of them were either killed during the remaining years of the war, executed by the Gestapo or were condemned to long periods in prison at the hands of the Soviets and later Soviet-backed regimes, who regarded them as British spies. This treatment was especially misguided in the case of the Polish agents, who formally ceased to belong to SOE the moment they landed back on native soil and became members of the 300,000-strong *Armia Krajowa* resistance.

No single engagement during the war touched eastern England more directly and physically than the evacuation off

Cichociemni trainees at Audley End

Dunkirk. When the call for help came, local fishermen and yachtsmen formed an instant voluntary force, many heading out from Tollesbury when the tide allowed, while on the last day of May 1940, Leigh-on-Sea cockle fishermen received official instruction from the Navy at Southend. Eric Osborne, one of a Leigh cockle fishing family who sailed with his cousin Horace on his father's 1927 ship the *Resolute,* recalled that long night many years later.[17] At eight o'clock, they were instructed to go to the pierhead, where they would be supplied with fuel, rations and an extra hand, before being given an escort across the Channel. Their Bawley-type sailing boats were broad and flat bottomed, specifically designed to be beached at high tide on sandbanks, from which fishermen could easily collect shrimps (in the winter) and cockles (from Easter to October). That made them, like the equally shallow-draught spritsail barges that plied the Thames and the Blackwater, ideal for the task ahead.

Six cockleboats formed the little fleet for Operation Dynamo, ordinariness their best protection, looking to all appearances like French fishing vessels rather than a naval operation. Only their lofty names marked them out. *Resolute, Reliance, Defender* and *Endeavour* had received their unlikely handles from famous J-class racing yachts, on which the fishermen used to crew for extra cash in the 1920s and 30s.

Crafts and crews were both more accustomed to estuarial waters, so the crossing was a major undertaking. Fortunately for them, the cockleboats had strong motors. Their role on arrival in Dunkirk that evening was enormously important, providing undercover transport between the men waiting on the mole to a series of trawlers, coasters and other larger vessels out to sea. Some men actually refused to be rescued by such unlikely looking craft. On the way back, in the dark at almost two o'clock in the morning, the *Renown* hit a mine and exploded, killing its crew of four. The tragedy is marked by a memorial in St Clement's church and an annual service held on June 1. In 2016, the *Endeavour* returned to northern France to take part in the filming of *Dunkirk*.

The crisis of Dunkirk sounded the alarm and triggered a major civil engineering effort to protect the vulnerable country, while armaments were in desperately short supply.[18] On land, Essex was protected by a series of fortifications, starting with a coastal 'outer crust', and working inland, in a series of oblique lines running north west to south east, first by the Eastern Command Line (past Colchester), then the GHQ Line (Saffron Walden to Chelmsford and on out to Canvey Island) and finally the Outer London Defence Ring (Nazeing to Chigwell Row).

The latter was an immense anti-tank system, consisting of great ditches – unless there happened to be a river at hand to serve the same purpose. Hundred upon hundred concrete pillboxes of various designs formed the hardened field defences. Many still stand, being effectively indestructible, and often listed as being of historical importance. They are startling in a quiet pastoral context, dotting areas such as the Chelmer Valley. Out to sea, in 1942-43 a series of Maunsell Forts (named after their designer Guy Maunsell) appeared in the Thames Estuary, including one in British (and Essex) territorial waters: Nore Army fort.

Maunsell Fort in wartime

The only actual struggles those extraterrestrial structures saw occurred in later years, and were between vying pirate radio stations, buccaneering enterprises in tune with the early 1960s, operating from international waters where they rocked in the heady freedom of unlicensed broadcasting. Radio Caroline broke the silence during Easter 1964, opening with the Rolling Stones. For stranded rural mid-teens such as myself, broadcasts from the good ship helped pass the hours, and when Ronan O'Rahilly, founder of the station, tried to storm a Maunsell Fort to oust his rival Paddy Bates, the whole business felt both belligerent – and fun. It was certainly living up to its piratical name.

Bates was an unlikely counter-cultural hero: a wartime Army major, whose first foray into broadcasting began in October 1965, with a station called Radio Essex, which beamed from a Maunsell Fort called Knock John. Conditions for those early pirate DJs were harsh in the extreme: the forts had been stripped of all comforts, not to mention most essentials in the postwar years. Cranky generators provided patchy power and heating, and fledgling broadcasters endured solitude and spartan conditions, often going without supplies when the seas were too rough. To add to the difficulties, Bates' own musical preferences (unlike his audience's and probably his DJs', too) were ballads and easy listening rather than hard rock.

Despite a change of name to Britain's Better Music Station, advertisers became wary after Bates was hit with fines for broadcasting within territorial waters; he struggled to pay them, let alone his DJs, and resorted to recording advertisements in his sitting room in Westcliff-on-Sea. The station went off-air abruptly on Christmas Day, 1966.

Bates then decamped to another Maunsell fort, known as Roughs Tower, which was safely in international waters, but before he could begin broadcasting, new laws came into effect declaring all pirate communications from British citizens to be an offence, wherever they were beamed from. The Navy began systematically to destroy other Maunsell forts in the area, and in the midst of this, Ronan O'Rahilly, charismatic Irish proprietor of Radio Caroline, staked his claim on Roughs Tower, a structure where he'd previously built a helipad and which he had envisaged as a supply depot for the Caroline network.

Having repelled the Caroline assault with molotov cocktails, Bates declared Roughs Tower to be a new, independent nation, the Principality of Sealand, and he set up home there with his wife 'Princess' Joan and their two children, Michael (Prince Regent) and Penelope.

Radio signals never came from Sealand, but bullets did: in 1968, Bates and his teenage son faced Chelmsford assizes after the younger 'Prince' of Sealand had fired shots at a naval vessel passing close by. The Judge, noting that the case seemed to belong more in the previous Elizabethan age than the present one, found that the incident had occurred within international waters, and dismissed the charges. Bates died in 2012, in a care home in Leigh-on-Sea, by which time, according to his obituary in the *Guardian*, the Prince Regent had added to his dominions a couple of fishing boats and Princess Penelope a dog grooming parlour. Sealand, with its national anthem and a thin stream of revenue from sales of data and, more fruitfully perhaps, peerages, endures. As the website proclaims, 'Upgrade the way you live with a title pack from the Principality of Sealand.' It may be located off the Suffolk coast, but it's a peculiarly Essex phenomenon, belonging yet not belonging, absurd yet admirable[19].

More serious confrontations were brewing inland. Opened in 1964, the University of Essex was one of the so-called 'plate glass' generation of new universities. The six svelte dark brick towers (only a third of the quantity proposed in the original plan) rear up in the distance over the Hythe. The architect, Kenneth Capon of the Architects' Copartnership, was reportedly keen to shake up the staid notion of a campus, wanting 'a certain amount of controlled vulgarity' and to avoid what he termed the English tendency towards softness and the 'shaggy'.[20] The intention behind the campus architectural approach was 'to do *something fierce*'. He had not, however, intended to design a student battleground.

Yet politics arrived on the campus with a vengeance, a conjunction between outside events and the vigour and radicalism of its internationalist social science faculties, brought together by Vice-Chancellor Albert Sloman, who in spite of his (relative) youth, overt liberalism and radical vision for the new university, eventually became a figure of hate for the student body.

There can hardly be any doubt that the Vice-Chancellor, aged just 41 when he took the job, was in step with the spirit of the age. He recruited brilliant and controversial young academics to the university staff, including the sociologist Peter Townsend and the economist Richard Lipsey, he insisted that undergraduates should sample a broad range of subjects before specializing and, partly because of his own experience in Hispanic studies, broadened the Humanities and Social Science curriculum to include the in-depth study of cultures abroad. Measures like this, and mixed-sex accommodation blocks, may be taken for granted by today's students but at the time, Sloman's vision was bold and, depending on your own age and background, either inviting or terrifying.

It seems that Sloman's commitment to – or understanding of – free speech was at least part of his undoing. Scuffles had occurred in 1967, over the honorary degree awarded to Harold Wilson and the price of food in the cafeteria, but the flashpoint, surely, came in February 1968, when a speech by Enoch Powell was interrupted by a student, dressed as Guy Fawkes, carrying a fake bomb, which was actually and fairly obviously, a grapefruit with a sparkler attached. To shouts of 'Racist!' Powell wisely fled the stage, and in the aftermath, seven students were suspended.

Three months later, a talk by a scientist from the Porton Down research facility was disrupted. A group of students had predicted that their interventions would be interrupted, and therefore had armed multiple members with copies of the same printed indictment so that, as each one was dragged away, another took the stand to castigate Porton Down and its representative for its crimes in chemical warfare. The police eventually broke up the meeting with dogs, and in the aftermath, another three students were suspended.

Had Sloman, an inexperienced administrator, dealt with this more efficiently then – who knows? – the University of Essex might not have acquired its, in some quarters, proud reputation as a hotbed of activism and unrest. At any rate, his insistence that the protestors had violated a serious taboo by preventing an invited speaker from speaking remains, for some, a moot point. How free is free speech meant to be? That question rages on, half a century later. At the time, even that most traditional of voices, *The Times*, was certain that Sloman and the university authorities had acted wrongly in suspending the students without giving them a chance to explain their actions or to appeal against the decision.

Further demonstrations, aided, as demonstrations always are, by warmer weather and lengthening evenings, led to an emergency meeting of the university Senate, an immediate rescinding of the suspensions and, for a brief period, à la Sealand and other Essex utopias, the existence of the 'Free University of Essex', wherein the normal timetable was suspended, and day-long teach-ins, discussions and seminars involving students and staff debated the issues that had arisen from the foregoing crisis. Gone by the summer holidays, the experiment was reignited in

February 1969 in the three-day Revolutionary Festival, visited by sympathizers from other universities and filmed by the suitably radical director Jean-Luc Godard – for whom the students obligingly set light to a Fiat 500 in the central fountain. (This marked a high point in his Essex film oeuvre – his next offering would be 'British Voices', of 1970, in which disgruntled employees of the Ford Dagenham works debated – or rather, just related – their workplace woes while a child recited excerpts from Marx and Engels. Its principle value is in the field of dialect, rather than dialectics, as some of the contributors can be heard speaking a pure, broad Essex rarely heard these days.)

Regardless of its reputation, seemingly to blame for low undergraduate applications for the next three decades, disappointing levels of endowment, and scant goodwill from the local community, Sloman stuck with Essex University until 1987, an unusually long term for someone in his role, expanding the number of graduates and actively encouraging students from overseas. In 2012, the year he died, the *Times Higher Education Supplement* ranked Essex as 20th out of a hundred of the world's universities established in the past 50 years.

Meanwhile the Cold War threat had already escalated towards the unimaginable consequences of nuclear engagement. In a prophetic inversion of Dunkirk, H.G. Wells' Martians in *The War of the Worlds* (1898) had stomped east from the capital to be faced by 'a dense swarm of boats' assembled in a 'huge sickle-shaped curve' around Harwich, Walton and towards Foulness. Essex could defend itself, whether in the wildest reaches of science fiction or from a real threat of cataclysm. Two bunkers had been constructed, one at Mistley (recently on the market) and the other near Brentwood at Kelvedon Hatch. Built in 1952-53, it originally housed the RAF's intricate subterranean radar system, ROTOR. Disconcertingly (to modern eyes at least) it masqueraded as an inconspicuous farm cottage with a cosy dormer window in its tiled roof. This was the entry point to the elaborate premises below, which later became one of several Regional Government Headquarters, large enough for several hundred personnel, both military and civilian, to live and work on the premises and over-see national survival after a nuclear attack. Access was by Central Line train to Ongar. Kept on standby at considerable expense, it was not decommissioned until 1992.

It is now advertised by those trusty brown tourist signs as the 'Secret Nuclear Bunker' and operates as an unusual, not to say peculiar self-service museum, organised and run by the Par-rish family, the farmers upon whose land it lies. Ingeniously the women in the typing pool are represented by a bevy of half-length mannequins on office chairs, wearing neat van Heusen shirts. The rest of the multi-level accommodation, quite chilling in its detail, is shown in its labyrinthine complexity. The visitor route is prescribed, with the bunker's various functions and activities described along the way, before you are eventually disgorged in the café and shop. Here you and your fellows make the first con-tact with a museum employee since buying the entrance ticket. The whole, impersonal experience is mildly unnerving – as if the bomb had already dropped. Now the bunker helps to earn its keep as a regular location for any television drama in which a menac-ing, subterranean setting is required.

But before writing off the bunkers as post-modern light enter-tainment, consider, admire (and fear, just a little) the Soviet map of the Essex (and Kent) banks of the Thames estuary and beyond, drawn up on the basis of the Ordnance Survey, the place-names rendered phonetically into cod-Polish. When the time came for the Communist bloc to rise triumphant over us, these maps would help the new arrivals on their way.[21] The ren-dering of the place-names has a sinister charm all its own: from Typtri (Tiptree), via Czelmsfed to Klekten-on-Sji. *The Red Atlas* represented a 40-year labour by spies covering locations across the country (and elsewhere in the world). In use until 1989, the maps are chilling. And how did Tiptree, the heartland of Essex jam-making, become ear-marked as a key target for the Soviet bloc? Maybe by that stage there was a joker in the pack.

Socialism comes to Saufend (-On-Sji)

8   CREPES, GRAPES AND
       SALT FLAKES

Making it in Essex

For John Evelyn, 17th-century diarist and an expert in grow-ing and preserving vegetables and herbs, salt was invaluable as 'a resister of Putrefaction.' Without it everything soon rotted, leaving people deprived of fresh supplies during the long winter months. So essential was the supply of salt that routes had worn their way into the landscape, known as saltways, intricate cat's cradles intersecting with the drovers' roads. From Chaucer's time, and maybe even before, travelling salt merchants had a reputa-tion as love rats, arriving on the farm, seducing women and girls, before pressing on with their endless packs of horses to the next farmstead, village or town. What they sold was rough stuff too, rock salt. Best quality sea salt, and the manners that came with it, were quite another thing.

Maldon sea salt was the gold standard and already a beacon of excellence at the Georgian table. In 1747, Mrs. Hannah Glasse author of the *Art of Cookery Made Plain and Easy* (the Mrs Bee-ton, nay the Jamie Oliver, of her day, the book running to nine editions in less than twenty years), praised it highly as the final touch in flavouring and preserving, whether for York ham or Suffolk butter. More than two hundred years later, and even after domestic refrigeration was the norm, those with discerning palates were seeking out and specifying the one and only sea salt; Elizabeth David pointed readers to it, even at three shillings for a 1lb packet in 1970 (around £4.50 at current values) in her *Spices, Salt and Aromatics in the English Kitchen*. And, said the always exigent Mrs. David, those silky flakes must never be ground, merely pinched between the fingers.

CAME ASTRAY,

On the 26th of December, 1783, to the Salt Office at Heybridge, near Maldon, Essex,

A Brace of POINTERS; the Owners describing their marks, and paying the charges, may have them again, by applying at the Salt Office aforesaid; and if not claimed within one month from the date hereof, will be sold to pay the expences.

March 25, 1784.

Notice from Maldon's Salt (and Missing Mutt) Office, 1784

Along the Essex coast, there is evidence of salt panning stretching back to the Bronze Age, the earliest of all being at South Woodham Ferrers, dating from around 1500 BC. With salt water lapping around the estuaries, people in this part of the world had to be resourceful, and the sea, so often a menace, was in this case a blessing. Originally the sea water was dried in shallow hollows, from which the brine was taken and put into terracotta vats. Once the salt was removed, piles of brick and ceramic spoil, charcoal and general waste were left behind – the so-called 'Red Hills'. These shallow mounds, the remnants of the salterns, once rimmed every estuary. A few survive, such as on Mersea Island and Peldon, while potsherds still regularly emerge on the shores of the River Blackwater. In stormy weather, these manmade 'hills' used to serve as refuge for panicked animals as the sea broke through to submerge their grazing land. So, as you crown your breakfast boiled egg with a satisfying crunchy pinch of Maldon sea salt, you continue a long story.

Room for one more? 18th century statutes attempted to control the enthusiasm

The Domesday Book recorded forty-five salt pans in Maldon alone. With the later discovery of enormous salt caves in north-west England, the commodity travelled east from Droitwich and the 'wich' towns of Cheshire to be shipped out of Harwich, while sea salt was of more immediate use to east coast fishermen, whose (now preserved) haul then headed off elsewhere. As an invaluable commodity, salt was repeatedly taxed, and a prized source of revenue until the final repeal of the salt tax in 1825. After that, it became more economic to mine rock salt and the advent of 'solution mining' – effectively flushing the caves out with water to obtain the brine – led to mass production of table salt, treated to run smooth, albeit with a metallic aftertaste, whatever the weather.

In Maldon the heyday of quality sea salt seemed to have passed with that, but some of the salt panning families kept the tradition on as a sideline to more profitable ventures, such as selling coal. Perhaps it was alongside a consignment of the black stuff that a few boxes of white Maldon crystals ended up in Harrods, whose purchasing department began to stock it in 1900, and wrote a congratulatory letter to the coal merchants Bridges, Johnson and Co., (who were also trading as The Maldon Salt Company) praising its unique flavor and efficacy in the pickling of beef.

By the 1960s, The Maldon Salt Company was in the hands of Cyril Osborne, who features, brylcreemed and gumbooted in a Pathé newsreel from 1968, cornily entitled 'Salty Business', raking the flakes in what the narrator describes as a 'factory' but seems little more than a small shed. In spite of the humble appearance of the enterprise, viewers are informed, the Osbornes can't produce enough Maldon salt to satisfy global demand. One has to wonder where all this demand was coming from. In Sixties Britain most people were content with Saxa in its functional red drums. Like olive oil, which in my country childhood was only available from chemists for the treatment of ear ache, sea salt was a commodity sold in health food shops and by discerning grocers, people such as the comfortingly rotund Mr Kisby, who presided over the family store, E. W. King on Market Hill in Sudbury.

Father and son, Cyril and Clive Osborne, raking the salt pans

At a certain point, though, Maldon sea salt joined a range of products that were transformed from the status of delicacies into staples of the British grocery cupboard. Cultural historians and food writers may have all manner of theories; it seems clear, though, that Maldon salt must have followed slightly a different path to products like olive oil and pesto, which people would have encountered thanks to cheap travel abroad, perhaps even brought home in their luggage. Was it all down to one TV chef recommending a pinch of Maldon, one supermarket being besieged by eager sea-salt buyers the next day and one newspaper picking up the story? I'd hoped to pin it on the (otherwise) ridiculous Craddocks, Fanny and Johnnie, but could find no proof.

21st century salt rakers, who hand-harvest the world famous Maldon Salt flakes

Whatever lies behind Maldon's healthy profits today, a former City bond trader – Cyril Osborne's grandson Steve – now oversees the operations in Maldon and up the coast at Goldhanger. There've been changes: natural gas is used to heat the brine instead of coal, cheaper, more environmentally friendly and easier to regulate temperatures; 37 pans now operate where there were once just three. For all that, the process is much the same as it was in the 19th century or even under the Romans. Seawater is filtered, then heated and reduced. The super-salty brine is raked for its salt crystals, which are then drained and dried. A little over 3,000 tonnes of salt leave Maldon that way every year, 60% of them destined for Spain, the USA, Scandinavia, Germany and France. Unsurprisingly one of the most persuasive advocates for its use is Jamie Oliver, that internationally respected cookery superstar hailing from a pub in Clavering. Rather less expectedly, in 2015, the actress Cameron Diaz told *Cosmopolitan* magazine that she carried Maldon salt everywhere in her handbag, and born-again lifestyle expert Gwyneth Paltrow has recommended it on her website, Goop.[1] Sea salt has even left the kitchen for the health spa, where it is rebranded (and classicised) as thalassotherapy and forms part of a baffling 'remineralising' process, included within an arcane menu of salt scrubs and exfoliating treaments available, for example, at an establishment near the Essex coast, in Thorpe-le-Soken.

In the 17th century, one of the first ventures that John Winthrop Sr set up after his arrival in North America was a salt business on the Boston shoreline. Previously this essential food preservative had had to be imported at considerable expense. In the event, it proved much harder to extract in the more extreme North American climate, and Winthrop made several false starts before making the necessary adaptations. In 1641 he sailed back to England to drum up investment in another venture, this time an ironworks.

In the early days of the colonies, much of what came east from across the Atlantic was completely new to Europeans. Peter Collinson FRS was a cloth merchant by trade but a botanist by inclination.[2] He imported seeds and cuttings largely supplied by a pioneer plant hunter, the Quaker John Bartram of Philadelphia. Collinson soon became a trusted friend and supplier to a very young man with a very large estate: Robert Petre, the eighth Baron and scion of the most important Catholic family in the county. The pair found common cause in gardening. Petre inherited Thorndon in 1732, aged 19, and eagerly subscribed to the 'boxes' sent back each autumn and winter, ready for the coming growing season.

Thorndon quickly became a famous showplace for a range of exotic trees and vegetation previously unseen in Europe: tulip trees (900 of them) were just one of 50 species introduced. The landscape was transformed to accommodate the planting: there was earth-moving to create canals, lakes and mounts (each topped with a cedar of Lebanon); semi-mature trees were transplanted to form great naturalistic sweeps and glades that looked, at first impression, as if they actually were in North America.

Then, in 1742, the planting came to an abrupt halt. Petre, aged just 30, died of smallpox. Collinson was devastated, writing to Bartram: 'Send no Seeds for him... all is att an End.'

None of those rare American cultivars survived. Modern golfers negotiating the fairways and greens between the great stands of trees at Thorndon Hall, carefully retained during the 1920s redesign, are actually in the midst of a handsome late 18th-century naturalistic planting to fit James Paine's fine neo-classical house, built for a later generation. Nothing of North America lived on there.

For those whose ambitions were intellectual rather than material or territorial, continental Europe was destination enough. The ancient universities of France or Italy offered studies in classical antiquity and natural philosophy (the term for science) and plenty of exposure to the unfamiliar. The extraordinary achievements of John Ray, the son of a blacksmith father and an herbalist mother, who was born and died in modest circumstances in Black Notley near Braintree, exemplified the possibilities. Cambridge-educated and briefly serving in holy orders, he and the naturalist Francis Willoughby (his patron, travelling companion and possibly also his student) ranged across England and Wales observing thousands of species in their natural habitats before setting off for Europe in 1663 on an intensive three-year expedition, collecting and observing specimens across the natural world but especially plants.

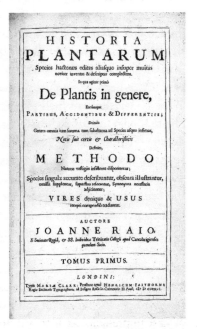

The cover of John Ray's book

On his return, Ray, like John Winthrop Jr, was put forward to become an early Fellow of the Royal Society. Proximity to London allowed him to regularly attend meetings of the learned society and spend time with his intellectual peers, an audience for his great achievements. His local friend and biographer, Dr William Derham, rector of St. Laurence, Upminster, reported back to him on the various items he had seen on display at the Royal Society on a visit in 1704, such as Isaac Newton's 'new contrivance of reflecting glasses' and was proud to report that his great work was prominent in the library at the Royal Society, 'Mr. Ray's last volume of *Plants...* is now published and is well printed.' [3]

Not as well as some would have liked, though. In his introduction to the epic *Historia Plantarum*, Ray stated his wish to 'facilitate the learning of plants without a guide or demonstrator, by so methodizing them and giving certain and obvious characteristic notes of the genera that it shall not be difficult for any man to find out infallibly any plant, especially being assisted by the figure of it.' Unfortunately, the figures, that is the intended illustrations, proved too costly to print, even with funding from the wealthy Willoughby.

Nevertheless, when the author of the multi-volume masterpiece died the following year, he was internationally renowned. Hidden away behind the Essex hedgerows, Ray had evolved a revolutionary classification system for the natural world, one that he intended should reflect the role of God, and that easily ranks alongside that of his successor, Carl Linnaeus.

Meanwhile Derham, who was the rector of the tiny Essex village of Upminster in the long years between 1689 and 1735 had time to pursue his own studies. He was often to be found on the top of the church tower armed with his sixteen-foot-long telescope. Like so many educated and somewhat stranded rural churchmen, he was an avid experimental scientist, sending his observations back for discussion and, frequently, publication through the Royal Society, of which he became a Fellow in 1703. He studied the skies, for astrological and ornithological purposes, as well as for meteorology. However, his most important contribution to science was his arrival, by 1709, at a more or less accurate measurement of the speed of sound, which he had achieved with a pair of pocket watches, his telescope and the services of obliging friends who positioned themselves a considerable way off and fired guns in his direction. Standing on the roof of the church tower at Upminster or, on occasion, in nearby North Ockendon, he watched for the flash and then timed the interval that elapsed before he heard the shot.

A modest living in Essex provided the perfect opportunity for another vicar with big ideas. After a promising start in a fast-rising architectural practice, Ernest Geldart's resignation and sudden ordination to the priesthood must have baffled some. It was merely the background, though, to a soaring passion for church architecture and interior design. This found its purest expression in the church where he served as vicar from 1881 to 1900, St Nicholas, Little Braxted, which he transformed from a plain Norman cell into an Late Victorian High Church casket, every surface elaborated within an overall scheme.

Possibly due to its location, between the capital and the North Sea, exposed and laid bare to Siberian winds and tidal extremes, the atmosphere in Essex had always been conducive to novel experiments and risk-taking. In the 1780s a trio of enquiring French visitors, two young aristocrats and their tutor, arrived in Mistley, on the south bank of the Stour inland from Harwich.[4] There they were struck by the evidence of the entrepreneurial spirit of the Rigby family, particularly Richard Rigby, Paymaster to the Forces for the duration of the American War (1768-84).

With the help of the most fashionable architect of the moment, Robert Adam, he'd built a 'spruce' town with a new quay that could accommodate a procession of craft, 'sloops, luggers, all the coaling and coasting vessels', as well as a shipyard equipped to build frigates. Among the regular cargoes on the quayside were grain and flour, and it was from here that Golding Constable, the painter's father, sent his merchandise to

London on his own pair of sea-going vessels. Heading the other way was his fleet of barges, which brought goods (including bricks) downriver on the Stour, now navigable from Sudbury through to Manningtree, close to Mistley.

Georgian Mistley has a fragmentary elegance. The romantic shards of twin towers, the remnants of Robert Adam's church, rear up over a waterside now seething with swans rather than vessels. There is very little evidence of the scale and energy of the industrial undertaking that once flourished here. Yet Rigby's enterprise extended to deep-sea fisheries and the whaling grounds of Greenland. The money he spent, in stupefying quantity, all came from the nation's purse.

Harwich, then as now firmly linked with the Hook of Holland, its twin port in Europe, had been the original entry port as Calvinist Protestants, the Huguenots, fled to take up Charles II's protection after the revocation of the Edict of Nantes in 1685. Many had been commercially successful in businesses such as wine, precious metals, banking and textiles, especially silk weaving, and while most pressed on to the capital or north to Norwich, some trades stayed to take root in Essex. There had been a French-speaking congregation in Harwich since 1683. When the three Frenchmen visited the town they were astonished to easily gain admission to the King's boatyard, where two frigates were under construction for the Navy. 'Perhaps we shall capture them,' jested young François de La Rochefoucauld; it was a joke that in 1784 could easily have been mistaken for a threat. Just ten years later, the Harwich-built *Castor* was to be boarded by a French squadron of the Brest fleet, though it was re-taken a few days later.

Essex was pre-eminently a textile area, a story starting with wool, and in many ways the first evidence of that fault-line which splits the county between north and south. The finishing trades were to the north, the marketing to the south. Clothiers bought the fleeces, and then organized the next steps, including dyeing. Halstead already had a fulling mill by the mid-13th century, a process that felted and thickened the cloth.[5] Finer worsteds and twills were brushed. Much of the labour of spinning and weaving was carried out at home. For all the strength of the Lancashire weaving industry, from the late 17th century onwards the eastern counties rapidly overtook the damp north west. The score was settled later, however, when the lack of minerals, and worse, of fast rivers, meant that the clothiers lost their advantage.

Throughout, Colchester was the centre for the manufacture of a range of woollen fabrics of different weights and consistencies, the names of which have been all but forgotten. In an indication of the scale of the trade, a 1713 Act of Parliament specifically mentioned the weekly round trips made by two Colchester packet boats from Wivenhoe to London with 'Bays, Says and Perpetuanas', and back from London 'with Wooll to be manufactured at Colchester.' Bays or baise or baize, says, similar to serge, and bocking, a finer version of baize, named after the town, supplied an immense overseas market from the 17th century onwards (perpetuana was another type of durable, worsted fabric).[6] Later on, the trade seems to have moved to the roads. The heaviest material was for blankets and floor rugs, the lighter for clothing. Flemish cloth workers (Huguenot or Walloon, so French-speaking) had made the Colchester textile industry into a world-class undertaking. The Dutch Quarter – an area of narrow lanes and timber-framed houses – survived the siege, was rescued from attrition and destruction in the 1950s by the Borough Council and carefully infilled during the

DRESS.

OCTOBER 9th, 1860.

IT is always a pleasure to us to see our workpeople, and especially our comely young women, dressed NEAT and TIDY ; nor should we, as has been already declared in a notice that has been put up at Bocking Mills, wish to interfere with the fashion of their dress, whatever it may be, so long as their dress does not interfere with their work, or with the work of those near them in our employ.

The present ugly fashion of HOOPS, or CRINOLINE, as it is called, is, however, quite unfitted for the work of our Factories. Among the Power Looms it is almost impossible, and highly dangerous ; among the Winding and Drawing Engines it greatly impedes the free passage of Overseers, Wasters, &c., and is inconvenient to all. At the Mills it is equally inconvenient, and still more mischievous, by bringing the dress against the Spindle, while also it sometimes becomes shockingly indecent when the young people are standing upon the Sliders,

FOR ALL THESE REASONS

We now request all our Hands, at all our Factories, to leave HOOPS AND CRINOLINE at home when they come to the Factories to work ; and to come dressed in a manner suitable for their work, and with as much BECOMING NEATNESS as they can.

And OVERSEERS at all the Floors are hereby charged to see that all the Hands coming to work are then properly dressed for factory work—without Hoops or Crinoline of any sort ; and Overseers will be held RESPONSIBLE to us for strict regard to this regulation.

Licking Bobbins.

WHEN a Bobbin is fastened off, it has been a common practice to touch the end with the tongue to smooth it down, and there is no harm in that.

But out of this practice has arisen another practice, both nasty and mischievous, of licking the Bobbins all over to make them weigh heavier.

And to put an end at once, and altogether, to this nasty and mischievous practice of Licking the Bobbins, we now make it

A RULE

Not to touch the Bobbins with the Tongue at all ; and Overseers are hereby authorised to enforce this rule by Forfeits.

SAMUEL COURTAULD & Co.

Prohibitions on hoops, crinoline and the licking of bobbins.

1970s and 80s; today it is an enduring monument to the Dutch contribution and Colchester's long history of both industry and integration.[7]

When the three Frenchmen reached Colchester in 1784, they found it 'one of the great towns of England'. They were astonished by the vitality of the textile industry. 'Always more work than workmen: 500 looms clattering.' Wages were high and the workforce both male and female. Four wagon loads of 250 bolts of serviceable double serge left weekly, bound for London, where the wool was dyed before export to Spain and Portugal, and from there to the religious houses of Central America. Well into the 19th century, and even during the Napoleonic wars, the principal market was the Roman Catholic church. The wool was woven in its natural state and then dyed according to requirement, despite the modern association of baize with the grassy green of billiard, snooker and gaming tables.

Silk weaving was initially a cottage industry. In the late 18th century, the Spitalfields Acts had systematized working methods and (arguably) introduced and held fairer wages, in so doing encouraging many Huguenot manufacturers to move away from the capital. Colchester, Sudbury, Halstead, Braintree and Bocking were the beneficiaries.

In the 1790s, George Courtauld – whose Huguenot family of silversmiths had arrived from the French Atlantic coastal town of Marennes in about 1688 – left east London and, with Joseph Wilson, converted a flour mill in Pebmarsh to silk-throwing for the production of yarn. It was the beginning of a transformative enterprise which, after a downturn during the Napoleonic years, became an extensive business when his eldest son Samuel converted and built a series of mills in north Essex towns – Halstead, Braintree and Bocking – many on premises previously used for processing crops. By around 1830, steam-driven machinery and a huge local labour force of some two thousand men, women and children, had turned the area into a major textile centre. The world of piecework and cottage industry had been superseded, and the faces of the towns altered, though they never approached the population levels or the abject poverty of the cotton towns in England's north west.

Courtaulds' enduring commercial success was built on death; or rather, the arcane requirements for mourning dress, affecting society from the court downwards and involving an intricate hierarchy of social status and family relationships, as well as marking the length of time since the death. Full mourning involved a three-year graduated journey, marked by wearing of matte black, both for clothing and accessories, even to the hem of a handkerchief, although permitted jewelry might help to make a woman's outfit marginally less dour as the years and months passed. With Queen Victoria's widowhood, in 1861, existing practices were further codified and tightened. As the social historian Alison Adburgham wrote in her landmark book *Shops and Shopping, 1800-1914* (1964) 'business in mourning was business worth getting'. Specialist mourning warehouses had long been in existence; there were four on London's prime shopping parade, Regent Street, while every draper in every town had a department devoted to dressing the bereaved. Courtaulds rapidly overtook the competition and were soon supplying almost all the nation's needs.

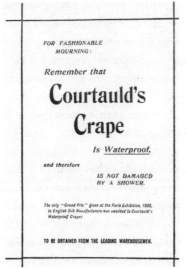

FOR FASHIONABLE
MOURNING:

Remember that

**Courtauld's
Crape**

Is *Waterproof*,

and therefore

IS NOT DAMAGED
BY A SHOWER.

The only "Grand Prix" given at the Paris Exhibition, 1900, to English Silk Manufacturers was awarded to Courtauld's Waterproof Crapes.

TO BE OBTAINED FROM THE LEADING WAREHOUSEMEN.

Courtauld's crape: fashionable and waterproof

In 1877 the leading London department store, Debenham and Freebody, published a dress code and instructions. Crape (or crepe) would swaddle a widow – and to a lesser degree her bereaved children – from head to toe, from veil to muff, for the first year after her husband's death, and then decreasingly on a sliding scale that reflected the passing of time. Eventually the crape could be set aside but, if sufficiently high quality, it could be brought out of the drawer to be used time and again, as circumstances dictated. As the store's *Fashion Book* pointed out sagely, 'inferior crape may reduce the first outlay; but it becomes shabby and loses colour so quickly that the price of replacing it should be added to the original cost.' Courtaulds had cornered the market in strong, light mourning crape of the highest quality, as well as in the argument for buying quality, and by the 1880s the firm had seen an almost 100% leap in profits over the previous fifty years. They continued to manufacture silk crape into the 1940s.

Silk was clean compared to wool or cotton, which generated contaminating and unhealthy fluff and fibres on the factory floor and around the looms. As Unitarians, the Courtaulds were outstandingly socially aware employers, who built decent housing, avoided child labour, fought for suffrage (as early as 1866 two members of the family petitioned Parliament on the subject), and in later generations became philanthropists on a large, not to say munificent scale. The women of the family were as engaged as the men.[8] Katharine Mina Courtauld sat on her parish council as well as that of her county (from 1919) and, as we have seen in Chapter Six, was an active suffragist. During the First World War, Dr Elizabeth Courtauld worked as an anaesthetist in France, at the frontline outpost of the Scottish Women's Hospital, Royaumont and like all her colleagues, received both the Legion d'Honneur and the Croix de Guerre in gratitude for the number of lives she saved.

A list of the Courtauld family's charitable donations in the pre-Welfare State era covers an astounding variety of projects scattered across the district around Braintree and Halstead. There was housing, two schools (one converted later to a Unitarian chapel), two hospitals and a nurses' home, a Roman Catholic church – regardless of the family's Huguenot origins – a literary and mechanics institute, a town and village hall (the former for

Braintree, the latter for Bocking), recreation grounds and gymnasium, drinking fountains and public gardens and, in the Second World War, a large area of (still surviving) air raid shelters in which the essential work of making parachute silk could continue in safety. It is quite a tally. By the late 19th century, Messrs. Courtauld had 3,000 employees, and in 1904 gained the patent for artificial silk, viscose, ensuring a lucrative and fast-growing future for the company – although that side of the business was concentrated at a new Coventry mill from 1905 onwards.

In 1982 the closing of Halstead mill marked the final chapter of the textile industry in Essex, though three silk weaving firms have survived within sight of Essex, in Sudbury, Suffolk.[9] They are testament to a trade that had once been as important to the region as the motor industry was to Detroit.

Everything connected: high-precision engineering, and engineers themselves, spread from the textile industry into other areas such as agricultural machinery and bicycle design (for a brief period around 1900, Walthamstow and other parts of Essex were at the cutting edge of bicycle manufacture), metal window manufacture, ball bearings and electronics. The buildings that nursed new processes frequently proved admirably tough and adaptable. The gunpowder works at Waltham Abbey were housed for centuries in what had once been a fulling mill; Courtaulds started off in a flour mill; Marconi in a disused silk mill.

The people were also adaptable – perhaps most of all those who arrived from elsewhere to successfully transform their lives[10]. The displaced Huguenots built on existing, if uprooted, networks of their own, as did the formerly prosperous Ugandan Asian community that arrived in Britain in 1972, expelled by Idi Amin with just ninety days' grace. Several of the most successful Essex businesses of recent times owe their existence to Amin's cruelty, among them the Tilda rice brand, built up in and around Rainham by the Thakrar family before they sold it in 2014 for £220 million.

Even in the early 18th century, Defoe observed in coastal south-east Essex that 'not one half of the inhabitants are natives of the place, but such as… settle here for the advantage of good farms.' This pattern was repeated in the late 19th century, when landowner-sponsored advertisements tempted farmers, often from Scotland, to convert their uneconomic arable acres into pasture. The so-called Scotch Colony were those 'men of energy, intelligence and substance' who had answered the invitation to come south, where they would benefit from 'low rents and… freedom of cultivation'. They often brought their Ayrshire cattle along, sometimes whole trainloads of them. By the mid-1890s some 125 families had settled, and many would stay.

One early arrival was a Scot by the unlikely name of Primrose McConnell. In 1883 he took on the tenancy of Ongar Park Farm near Epping and, with his father, turned it into an exemplary dairy farm. In 1905 he bought his own 500 acres at Southminster, on the Dengie peninsula, and built up a 100-strong dairy herd – exceptionally large for the time. But his fame rests on his journalism and writing on agriculture, much of it turning on the potential of farming within reach of urban markets, to prove enormously influential for his compatriots moving south to new territory. *The Agricultural Notebook* was published in 1883 and ran to eleven editions in his lifetime, remaining in print until 1996, by then in its 19th edition.

Improvements to the railways meant that Essex milk production was aimed at the capital, speeding to thirsty London. The pre-eminent name in the East Anglian dairy industry was Lord Rayleigh's Dairies. The company's signs used to feature alongside the railway line, not so far from where today the isolated Britvic Clock Tower in Chelmsford commemorates a large soft-drinks factory. To a small child of the 1950s (me) it all went to prove that milk and orange juice, both so good for you as they said, obviously hailed from Essex. The family name of the Rayleighs was Strutt (Edward Strutt was a Nobel prizewinning physicist) and their roots went far and deep in the county. The family were early Georgian mill owners from Maldon and Chelmsford, who had stepped into the breach in the 1880s, when dairy farming rescued agriculture from disaster. Their milk empire flourished across Essex and Suffolk until the 1990s.

The ostensibly conservative world of farming can be surprisingly daring when it comes to trying new things. Consider the growth of Essex vineyards in recent decades, responding gamely to the challenges of climate change. At the time of writing, a recent paper from scientists at the University of East Anglia identified 86,000 areas in Essex and neighbouring Suffolk with combinations of soil, terrain and climate that could make them ideal for the production of Champagne-style sparkling wines. Meanwhile, as the move away from meat speeds up, and gluten and allergen-free diets become increasingly mainstream, the fleet-footed, enterprising Fairs family at Great Tey – who have been farming quinoa since the 1980s and pride themselves on actively developing non-GM 'niche crops' and oils – is now expanding into chia seed, as well as running crop trials to continually broaden and improve their range.

In a similar spirit, Ashlyn's organic farm near Ongar has diversified from food production alone to becoming a family attraction, with wildlife walks and rare breeds in the fields, a soft play area and a barn-like restaurant and cafeteria supplementing the meat and vegetables sold in the shop, while a major commercial composting facility on their land, out of sight but not out of mind, processes green waste from local authorities and businesses for resale.

These innovators have plenty of predecessors. In 1841 the Essex agricultural scene was galvanized by the arrival of an Italian (with a German mother) from the City. John Joseph Mechi, born in 1802, was an alderman and banker whose rapid ascent to wealth had come from patenting a razor strop. As a child he had spent holidays in the Essex countryside, and since then had immersed himself in books about modern farming improvements. He decided to buy a modest property at Tiptree and put what he had read into practice, transforming his 130 acres into a model farm and in the process spending a prodigious sum.[11] He continuously tested out (and publicized) a maelstrom of new ideas, methods and machinery, from keeping cattle on slatted wooden floors to designing and constructing new buildings. Tiptree Hall hosted an annual agricultural show, which soon became famous. Mechi gave speeches on his theories and practice, while offering everyone a good lunch. By 1856 attendance had reached 600, and he was able to regale the assembled company with tales of dramatically improved fertility and drainage, of his use of steam power on the farm and, especially, a new system of pumped irrigation involving liquid manure. In 1859 he wrote *How to Farm Profitably*, which ran into several editions, and the following year he played a part in setting up the Agricultural Benevolent Institution to help those among his fellow farmers who had not been as successful. By 1866 he seemed to be in line to become Lord Mayor of London.

Not long after, the simultaneous failure of a bank and an

An 1860s photograph shows Mechi supervising his workers

insurance company in which he was involved forced him to resign as an alderman. He battled on, despite falling sales of razor strops (due to the fashion for military beards after the Crimean War) and the devastating agricultural depression. This Hardy-esque tale ended with Mechi's death in 1880, days after being forced to place his business affairs in liquidation. In his final months, the wider farming community had rallied round the former Chairman of the national Farmers' Club, subscribing to help Mechi through his financial difficulties. On his death, the funds were given to his widow and family.

Mechi's passionate and very public embrace of the new may have inspired quieter revolutions. Far to the north, in the Cumbrian village of Blennerhasset, the well-to-do and progressive William Lawson renamed his property Mechi Farm and used it as a testing ground for all manner of social and technical experiments from gas lighting to a farm-workers' parliament. Meanwhile, back in Essex, Arthur Charles Wilkin was the owner of a small farm next door to Mechi's, which had remained in family hands since the beginning of the 18th century. In 1862 Wilkin switched his 250 acres to fruit cultivation and planted extensive orchards. By 1885 he was producing jam on an industrial scale, the acreage much expanded. Today, Wilkin of Tiptree, royal warranty-holders, remains a family-owned company, with an employee partnership scheme and labels that still bear the much-admired original logo.

Arthur Wilkin campaigned in print and in person for small holdings and allotments, as a way to provide local families with a measure of self-sufficiency. By 1908 there were more than 250 smallholdings and allotments immediately around the Tiptree area. Now, walking down to the River Blackwater from the village of Goldhanger in early summer, you may notice a sea of shimmering plastic fruit tunnels; underneath are tens of thousands of Wilkin's Little Scarlet strawberry plants, the ingredients for a peerless jam much fought over in our house – and, if that isn't recommendation enough, James Bond's jam of choice in *From Russia with Love*.

If commercial fruit growing on this scale was new, nurserymen and seed merchants had long been well-rooted, benefitting from the lighter soils and relatively dry and sunny climate of north east Essex. Cants had set up their nursery business in the mid-18th century in Colchester, before selling the original site for building – it has ever been thus. In the late 1870s two members of the Cant family, Frank and his uncle Benjamin, began to specialize in roses, still close to Colchester, where the firm remains –

rose-growers supreme to this day. Meanwhile, the great gardener
Beth Chatto had built her reputation, nursery and garden at Elm-
stead, east of Colchester, where she demonstrated the potential
of dry, gravelly soils, and just how little rainfall a carefully chosen
range of plants needed. Sustainable gardening and the difficulties
we face with climate change come together with prescience in
Beth Chatto's internationally renowned Dry Garden.

Next to the Cants, the Buntings were relative newcomers,
starting their business in the 1820s. Young Isaac Bunting set
out from Colchester for Yokohama in 1874, where he spent a
couple of years learning the export trade from his near contemporary, nurseryman John Joshua Jarmain, whose family business was already prospering there. The time was right. Japan
was opening up to the world at an incredible pace, the Meiji
dynasty having unified the country in 1867. The Suez Canal,
greatly shortening the journey east, opened in late 1869. On his
return Isaac took his £22 savings out of the bank in Colchester
and sat for a dynastic family photograph, before going back to
Japan in 1877 to establish Creekside Nurseries. In Yokohama he
described himself in local trade directories as a 'Seed and Cloth
Merchant'; and he was indeed sole proprietor of the London and
New York Tailoring Company. It would appear he was hedging
his bets by importing readymade men's wear from Colchester.

But Bunting's heart was already in lilies, and he soon became
a master in the art of safely transporting specimens on their
lengthy journey around the world. In mid-winter the incoming cargo for Bunting and Sons at Hythe Quay would consist
of many hundreds of identical wooden crates. Inside the crates,
made of cedar wood but later, more economically, of deal, were
packed thousands of small clay lumps. On closer examination
these turned out to be lily bulbs, each clad in a porous earthen
overcoat. The packing of this treasure was a delicate art, well
suited to meticulous Japanese workers who were practised in
clay modelling.

Reputation was all. Horticulture was a small and close-
ly-connected world, and many of the leading firms operated

within mere miles of one another, in the same corner of Bunting's home county. A good bulb was a clustered bundle of clean, fleshy segments, much like a waxy, giant garlic head. The tones of the individual bulbs varied specie to specie, but the choicest specimen, *Lilium longiflorum* (the Easter lily), was a creamy colour with a brown-tinged outer scale, belying the icy blue-white of the flowers to come.

Bunting's success rested on his customers' confidence that his firm had the means to transport these beauties all the way from their natural habitat to the market, be that in London or Amsterdam, Paris or St Petersburg. Unpacking was a nervy business: what if sea water had entered the container, or other damage had occurred to the delicate bulbs? As the business grew, the Buntings built an icehouse alongside their other premises on the quayside. It ensured that their precious commodity, after the intense care given to its transport thus far, would not be lost to an unexpected last-minute change of temperature or humidity. Even so, Bunting displayed an acute awareness of the issues that could affect a trade so precarious as lily bulbs, noting to overseas customers in his 1885 catalogue that 'I... do a cash business and that only. My customers will therefore please understand that I require cash at Yokohama as soon as the goods are safely packed and on board the mail boats.'

Meanwhile in Colchester the goods would be readied for the voyage back to Alexandria, then through the Suez Canal and on to the lucrative ports of the Far East. Perhaps Isaac Bunting pursued his other stated occupation, that of tailoring, by exporting bolts of Colchester's excellent woollen stuff, so suitable for military outfitting, on that return journey.

By the turn of the century, the two Bunting sons were fully installed in the business, one in Yokohama, one in Colchester, leaving their father free, in late middle age, to explore further and wider in Japan. Isaac became an enterprising and expert plant-hunter, identifying locations for rare bulbs in several southern Japanese islands, and training the islanders to collect them from the source, wrapping them in dried sugar cane leaves

Keeping in touch with Colchester – via Siberia

for the journey back to Yokahama. So highly regarded was he, for the stream of income that changed the hand-to-mouth existence of the desperately poor Okierabu islanders, that a myth grew up around Bunting, saying that he'd been shipwrecked off the island, saved by the locals and in gratitude begun to do business with them for the indigenous lilies they'd previously regarded as weeds.

Isaac Bunting became an emperor of his trade, at least before intensive cultivation and the economic aftermath of war brought it low. At its height, the market in rare lilies had linked some of the most remote and beautiful islands in the south of Japan to unassuming but fertile north-east Essex. The name of Colchester briefly became synonymous with lilies, almost eclipsing the fame of its oysters while out in Yokohama the name of Bunting has endured through Isaac's descendants, although he and his Essex-born wife Sarah moved on, ending their days in Vancouver, to where they had moved in 1927. Nearing eighty, the old Colchester nurseryman and avid plant-hunter, shown in a contemporary photograph quite as tightly wrapped in his fox-fur-lined overcoat as one of his own clay-clad lily bulbs, apparently still had further plans.[12]

In the late 19th century, Chelmsford's star was in the ascendant.

Millwrights morphed into agricultural engineers and then found wider applications for their ever more sophisticated technology. In 1878, the Arc Works were set up by the pioneering Colonel Evelyn (R.E.B.) Crompton. It was the first electrical engineering company in Britain – the first to see that the future lay with electricity, in this case applied to industry, municipal lighting and civic buildings. As a boy Crompton had been inspired by a visit to the Machinery Hall of the Great Exhibition at the Crystal Palace in 1851.[13]

On leaving the army, Crompton returned from India, where he had closely observed the work of the Royal Engineers, and joined T.H.P. Dennis in Chelmsford, an agricultural and heating engineering company. Three years later, in 1878, he bought the company and set up Crompton & Co. Inventor and industrialist rolled into one, he built up a company that produced a huge range of electric goods, many of them innovatory, from arc lamps for the military, to the instruments and immense generators required in industries such as mining, paper and cement. Around 1880 he went into business with Joseph Swan to produce incandescent lamps. Living to ninety-four, Crompton rose to the top of his profession, twice becoming President of the Institution of Electrical Engineers and a recipient of its highest honour, the Faraday Medal. Always progressive spir-

The first radio transmitter, installed at the Marconi Works, Chelmsford, 1919

ited, he became a key figure in the Electrical Association for Women, founded in 1924 to promote the domestic use of electricity and, with it, to modernise the British home. The company he founded lives on, becoming Crompton Parkinson in 1927, and now Brook Crompton, based in Leeds.

Chelmsford's reputation for technological innovation at the turn of the century reached the ears of a young Irish-Italian physicist from Bologna. Guglielmo Marconi had a passion for wireless telegraphy and, as a result of his mother's family connection to the Jameson whisky fortunes, the means to indulge it. In 1896, at the age of 21, he secured the first British patent for wireless telegraphy, and set up in business. Marconi's Wireless Telegraph and Signal Company was founded in July 1897, typically using a disused 1850s silk mill as headquarters. Wireless transmission had caught the public imagination; it was only a couple of years before the first transatlantic transmission took place.

The expansion of Marconi's premises into the New Street Works (built on the old town cricket ground, of all sacred spaces) in 1912, and their continuous research and development into wireless technology (and soon radar, their mastery of which was preeminent) put the company into the first rank. Essex with its flat landscape and proximity to London made an

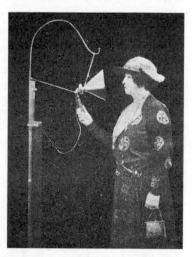

Nellie Melba over the airwaves

ideal location. Marconi was responsible for the first territorial broadcast in Britain, made on Valentine's Day 1922 from a former army hut at Writtle just outside Chelmsford, while the Australian soprano Nellie Melba had famously transmitted live from the works on New Street a couple of years earlier, singing 'Home, Sweet Home' via an improvised microphone made from a cigar box and a telephone mouthpiece. Closing with the National Anthem, her performance was heard as far afield as Iran and Newfoundland.

It was Peter Eckersley, Aldous Huxley's cousin and later fascist sympathiser, who masterminded this nascent radio station, both as engineer and broadcaster (he recited poetry and sang on air) and quickly became chief engineer of the new British Broadcasting Company Ltd. in London in December that year. A few years later Ekco (named after the combined initials of its founder, Eric Kirkham Cole, who founded the company with his future wife in 1924) began to make electric powered radios in Southend. The characteristic Bakelite drum-shaped radio cabinet designed by Wells Coates, the modernist architect, was just one of their progressive products, prominently displayed in design museums around the world. But it is Chelmsford that can confidently claim to be 'the birthplace of radio.'

Meanwhile, around the time Marconi set up in Chelmsford, a Swiss inventor, Ernst Gustav Hoffmann, patented a lathe that could produce perfect ball bearings. He left England after registering it in 1892 and went to the USA in search of his fortune. Six years later, two Chelmsford brothers, the Barretts, spotted the potential of the product within their engineering and bicycle-manufacturing business, and hauled Hoffmann back to Essex, where he set up a factory.

Even by the 1950s, when this advertisement was issued, the name 'Marconi Wireless Telegraph Company, Ltd.' sounded outdated

These two innovative businesses were first in line for important war work, in manufacturing munitions and in communications. In the 1940s the two great factories, Hoffman and Marconi, faced each other across New Street, Chelmsford, becoming prime targets for Luftwaffe missions. The Germans had obtained a set of aerial photographs of the layout, which allowed them to build a detailed scale model – Marconi's works edged in blue, Hoffmann in yellow – in the centre of Chelmsford. Armed with such accurate information, they scored a number of direct and deadly hits. After the war was over, an RAF mission discovered the actual model in a German airfield in 1945 and brought it back to the town. Now it is displayed at Chelmsford Museum, an impressive reminder of half a century of massive employment and industrial activity, not to mention two exceptional minds. Hoffmann (by then RHP) finally closed in 1989, whereupon their New Street building ('Globe House') was converted to flats and offices.

Marconi fared little better. Asset-stripped and depleted after its purchase by GEC in 1968 (later the subject of a searing television exposé) some company offshoots are still planted in local soil within BAE Systems' Applied Intelligence Laboratories at Great Baddow, and in Basildon, where the former Marconi Avionics division became BAE Systems Avionics, then Selex ES, a leader in the expanding field of thermal imaging.

Basildon's Marconi sapling became the stage for a sad tale of aborted espionage in 2002, when an engineer named Ian Parr – using the codename 'Piglet' – handed an envelope of sensitive technical information to a Russian agent called Aleksei, in return for £25,000 cash in a Southend pub. Unfortunately for Parr, 'Aleksei' was part of an MI5 sting operation, and the father-of-two was sentenced to 10 years. There was much media chuckling over Parr's codename, not to mention his army nickname 'Hazard', which proved doubly true when reports emerged that he'd tried to wire his spectacles to the electricity supply in prison by way of a suicide bid, and merely succeeded in burning his face. At the root of the story, though, was a tragic misunderstanding: Parr's rash act of treachery came about when he suspected he was going to be made redundant; in fact, he was about to be given a raise.

Long before Essex's specialist industries had become of interest, real or pretend, to foreign powers, a pioneering businessman had realized that the county offered distinct advantages. As the Peckham photographer Alfred Harman developed a system for manufacturing dry gelatin plates, he came to understand the importance of an unpolluted atmosphere. Such was not to be found in Peckham at the time, but it was – along with easy access back into the city – from a new base in the village of Ilford. The Britannia Works, opened in 1879, initially comprised a workforce of Harman himself, two men and three boys, in the cellar of his house, from which he drove a daily consignment of plates – each box of a dozen selling for two shillings – into town by horse and cart. By 1895, the site of Harman's house had become a sizeable factory, the sheds and belching chimneys shown against a reassuring foreground of allotments on the company letterhead.[14] Following a legal dispute, the firm became Ilford Ltd., and by the time ICI took it over in 1958, the colour processing business had moved to Basildon New Town, to occupy a streamlined new steel and glass panelled factory. Ilford House, the headquarters of the company, joined it on an adjoining site in 1976, just in time for the company centenary but also just as digital technology began to lay siege to analogue systems. Ilford – 'for places and faces', as the advertising slogan went – lasted just twenty years in Basildon New Town. It was better to stay with the known; in 1964, the Ford tractor plant had relocated there from Dagenham. Now New Holland, their successors, offer Essex farmers regular tours of its advanced manufacturing processes, robotics and all. Around south Essex, agriculture still calls the shots, as it did 150 years before.

Postwar, unlike the authorities in the New Towns, the LCC had no specific powers to attract industry, so the relocation of the Bank of England's highly skilled bank note printing operation from its site at St. Luke's Hospital, Old Street, to Essex was

Artist Feliks Topolski was originally commissioned for three paintings of the Debden works, but the Bank of England decided to purchase his 23 preparatory sketches as well, initially because they might be deemed a security risk

something of a coup. They were eager to take advantage of a near rural site (Green Belt, ironically) on the edge of Loughton, at Debden on the River Roding. Even more ironic was the fact that the Loughton Hall estate had been owned by the Rev. J.W. Maitland, the man who, some eighty years earlier had precipitated the court case leading to the City of London's ownership of Epping Forest. Further, Debden was Willmott and Young's 'Greenleigh' in their epochal, and contentious, social study *Family and Kinship in East London*.

Architects Easton and Robertson's handsome cathedral of a building was 800 feet long with a main hall soaring to 125 feet. It opened in 1957. New staff at the Bank visited the works during their induction, and one of them recently recalled his tour in 1963.[15] 'We walked by fields from Debden station to the works, where we were closely shepherded around the first-floor gallery of the main printing hall and able to watch through one-way darkened glass and see the printing staff minding the machinery as new bank notes were produced.' Such tight security measures proved insufficient, however, to prevent systematic theft over four years, starting in the late 1980s. About £600,000 disappeared from the incinerators, the main instigator stuffing the old notes into her underwear. It was, the court heard in 1994, her family's lavish and unexplained lifestyle that gave her away, rather than her unemployed husband's continuous trips to the bank to deposit enormous quantities of cash.

Rather more secure, the old Bank of England printing works remains in its ownership, while De La Rue maintains a contract to print banknotes from the premises until at least 2025. The handsome 1950s brick tower rises emphatically across the Roding Valley to the south. Despite the shift in the UK from paper to polymer bank notes, the factory employs a local skilled labour force utilising ever more sophisticated technology. Satisfying work so close to home is rare in 21st-century Essex, and certainly not secure. As I write, it has been announced that the company has not been awarded the contract to make the new bright blue post-EU passport.

Industry comes and goes, sometimes with dizzying speed. Tilbury, once the nemesis of the Port of London, is still an active port and the river a busy waterway. Nearby Tilbury Fort, so particularly admired by Defoe and now a key site in the portfolio of English Heritage, earned its keep by rather more than the ticket price of a few heritage-minded visitors when it acted as the setting for the Peterloo Massacre of 1819, impressively staged between and against its walls in Mike Leigh's film of that name. Appropriately enough, just along the Thames, gunpowder, and after that cordite, lay at the heart of the munitions industry at Purfleet. In its heyday, the Kynoch Arms Enterprise spawned vast factories and a workers' village, self-admiringly named Kynochtown. It was all gone almost immediately after WW1 and the village renamed after new players, the oil business in Coryton. The immense oil tanks of its refinery were the very horizon of south-east Essex when I first walked near Canvey Island, but it was all over by 2012.

Rod Holt, and a Christmas cracker destined for the window displays of the West End

Back in Purfleet, a 14-acre site now houses the Royal Opera House Production Workshop, a thriving enterprise area slotted into a farmyard, now known as High House Production Park. Scenery and costumes are made here, while the National College for the Creative and Cultural Industries at the Backstage Centre offers apprenticeships and technical skills training. Not very far away, a workshop run by Rodney Holt is the home of Mojo Creative Productions, producing the stuff of London's most fabulous shop window displays, amongst much else. Holt's father, who had trained as a French polisher, moved out of Bethnal Green to take a job at Ford's Dagenham after the war. Holt's workspace in the run up to the delivery of Fortnum and Mason's Christmas window displays looks like a child's dreamscape, a mix of chaotic heaped ladders and paint pots, props from other jobs, and for the immediate project in hand, an immense gold turkey bursting out of a cracker, a translucent tree made of glass flutes accompanied by a glittering Christmas pudding, glowing blue and spilling coins. The aesthetic is gloriously exuberant, the workmanship is the highest quality and the location, fittingly enough, turns out to be on the edge of that TOWIE heartland, Brentwood.[16]

In sharp relief, the heavy industrial scene of 21st-century estuarial south Essex is one of vast derricks and skeletal gantries set against cliffs of red and grey containers. The shoreside at the Thurrock Super Port – or DP World London Gateway, if you prefer – the deepwater port that replaced another oil refinery, Shell Haven, is overwhelming. More is planned. Since 2013 this has been the face of the Thames estuary, along the very stretch where Conrad's yawl was once anchored.

A naming ceremony for the new Hapag-Lloyd vessel at DP World London Gateway, in July 2018

Behind the port a 'logistics park' grows, and the juggernaut trucks roar on and off the miserable A13 to joust with desperado-like skip lorries. Yesterday's detritus is today's moulded landform. Beyond, the compelling, slow theatre of river business and modern industrial consumption continues. Above and away from all this, a smart, slatted-timber visitor centre with a winding ascent onto a rooftop viewing platform has been built for those wishing to survey the scene, essentially a pivotal place on the nation's economic and physical edge.

Much as a funfair comes to the seaside, only to pack up and move on, so industries die and uses change – with ever more precipitate effects. At Barking, the site of the Thames-side electricity power station, little more than a flash in the pan since it opened in 1995 only to close in 2004, has been earmarked by the City of London as the location for its main wholesale markets, Billingsgate, New Spitalfields and Smithfield. (Freeing up tranches of valuable urban land for more housing, or at least, more blocks of investment flats to be sold off-plan in Malaysia or Hong Kong.)

Barking and Dagenham's regeneration agency is called Be First. But it has not always been that way. Fords of Dagenham have gone from maximal to minimal employment, their engine plants, Lion, Tiger and the latest, Panther now employ less than 2000 people in total. But the output on the near-mile-long production line in the 'factory you thought had closed' as the Londonist website puts it, is fairly astonishing, estimated in 2017 at 750,000 engines per year. Research on emissions-cutting 'green diesel' engines occurs here too, though the main Ford research and development arm is based at Dunton Technical Centre outside Basildon.

The Ford factory at Dagenham is probably best remembered by the fight put up by a bunch of tenacious women machinists in the upholstery section, who became activists in the fight for equal pay and conditions in 1968, and whose actions led to the Equal Pay Act of 1970. Their story was filmed as *Made in Dagenham*, with a theme tune sung by a former clerk at the Dagenham works, Sandie Shaw, to lyrics by Barking's own bard, Billy Bragg, and became a West End musical. It brought the town and the works enormous pride, for equality in the workplace is an issue more enduring than the short life-span of a particular vehicle, although the fight against atmospheric pollution and global warming, subtexts of the current rebirth, runs it a close second.

9   ALL THE FUN AND MOST OF THE SUN

Playing in Essex

There have been few stranger invasions of Essex, albeit inordinately well prepared-for, welcome and long-anticipated, than the 2014 Tour de France. The terrain from Cambridge to London is gentle, a quietly swelling arable landscape where church towers and spires mark modest but picturesque villages, allowing the cyclists to enjoy a fair turn of speed with no fear of punishing hills ahead.

The route on a sunny July day ran through Saffron Walden and Finchingfield

Le Tour: considerably off-piste

(these two providing a dash of picture perfect 'other Essex' and giving a useful fillip to local tourism), then continuing to Chelmsford and onwards via a rather obscure back route. Unlikely as it might seem, this is route 1 of the Sustrans cycle map. It would take them past our own lineup for the Tour, consisting mostly of our daughter's friends – among them a couple of quite serious cyclists – and numbering over a dozen. Supplied with food and drink, streamers, folding chairs and the rest, we waited on the narrow lip of the minor lane that leads from Roxwell to Fyfield. Afterwards the Tour would head on through Epping Forest, sprint territory, before taking in Waltham Abbey and riding into the city in the late afternoon.

That morning, the entire caravan, followed by the peloton itself, sped towards us along the tiny – and heavily pockmarked – lane. Surprisingly, the previous

A motorized detachment of gendarmes drives through Wethersfield in north Essex

year's frost damage had been left untouched. At the appointed hour, helicopters churned overhead as the tidal wave of vehicles approached. It ranged from advertising and promotional lorries to cars carrying trainers, support staff and spare parts, as well as motorcycle police (including *bona fide* gendarmes). All were struggling to make any progress at all, let alone keep up the requisite pace, as they tried to squeeze through the numerous pinch points along the route.

By this stage, the partisan frisson attached to the hotly tipped local contestant, Mark Cavendish, had evaporated – Ongar's favourite son had come to grief in Harrogate and was no longer in the competition. The hand jiving teenagers liberally scattering Yorkshire Tea bags and other tidbits from the back of open trucks were becoming sluggish; they had been bopping for an hour or more. But for us and the other knots of people gathered along this stretch, the momentary flash-past by the streaking riders was a worthy climax to our excitement, and a great moment for Essex.

Brief as it was, the Tour is far from forgotten in the county. 'Follow the route of the Tour De France with a ride through Epping Forest. This emerald of luscious foliage in southwest Essex has all the ingredients of a classic short stay cycling holiday' gushed the *Visit England* website. The volume and variety of two-wheeled traffic on our small section of the route is astonishing, ranging from leisurely pairs of a certain age to feline packs of lycra-shimmering club cyclists. The numbers seem to grow exponentially year by year.

Hub of cycling, in Walthamstow

Essex, with its ideal terrain, was in at the very beginning of the cycling craze of the late 19th century. John Kemp Starley, the inventor of the revolutionary Rover Safety Bicycle, with two similar sized wheels and a chain, was a Walthamstow man. Such villages close to the countryside but also accessible for Londoners quickly became a centre of the bicycle trade. Hundreds of clubs of all stripes sprung up. Some were focused on cycling itself, their *raison d'être* being to race or tour, but others were political, with riders sharing causes or beliefs, or more often simply offering a congenial hobby, a rare but popular example of an activity men and women could do together, unsupervised by their elders.

The clubs had badges; they had favourite pubs and stopping places; some even built their own huts for shelter and rest. From the start, bicycling lent itself to eccentricity. The *Halstead Times* reported sighting a tandem: 'the lady who occupied the rear seat being attired in a large coat of fashionable cut and the most daring of "rationals", while gaiters and a pair of eyeglasses completed her costume.'

High Beech, where Queen Victoria had handed Epping Forest over 'to the use and enjoyment of my people for all time' in May 1882, soon became a favoured site for popular attrac-

Women take to the saddle

tions. One of these was a dirt track behind the Kings Oak public house. Originally laid out for bicycle races, it fell into disuse during the war years, but was then upgraded to a motorcycle speedway track, in keeping with a faster and more raucous era.

One participant on the opening day was 19-year-old Norman Lewis, the inspired travel writer and curmudgeonly observer of Essex met with elsewhere in these pages. Lewis, a devotee of speed and excitement all his life, took part in the races held on 19 February 1928. He and dozens of other riders were watched by thousands of onlookers enticed by the novelty of the event, many participants imported from Australia and the USA. The entirely unforeseen scale of the crowds caused gridlock on local roads, while the sixpenny admission tickets and programmes ran out before the first race. The organisers, Ilford Motorcycle Club, had struck gold.[1]

The oval track had the requisite cinder surface, and there was a rudimentary stand. On a dry and sunny day, most onlookers stood closely packed around the entire perimeter. No barrier had been set up to protect them from the hurtling machines, and, alarmingly for the riders, the spectators were free to wander at will onto the track. A field of novice cyclists was spiced up with 'several prominent riders', and the day's programme included races for all kinds of machine – including both solo cycles and those with sidecars – as well as for various levels of rider experience. Not altogether unconvincingly, the poster proclaimed it 'The Most Thrilling Speed Event Known.'

Perhaps with more of an eye on a good story than the truth, Norman Lewis claimed he 'could be relied upon to fall off in three races out of four.' Even Billy Galloway, the Australian speedway ace, was photographed tumbling off on one of the tightest turns. His life was saved by his crash helmet. Speedway became a grand boys' day out and continued for several decades, by then constrained behind solid barriers. On Sunday February 18th, 1968, Speedway celebrated its 40th anniversary. Soon after, the track at High Beech closed for ever.

Galloway's spectacular crash at High Beech

In earlier times, those who craved speed went horse racing, which usually took place on common land amidst a fairground atmosphere. Before the coming of railways, the horses had to walk between meetings, which were conducted in a refreshingly egalitarian spirit: no entrant was allowed to have previously won a royal plate, announced the *Chelmsford Chronicle* in 1787. From at least the mid-18th century, Chelmsford was a centre for the sport.[2] The old flat-racing course at Galleywood Common was transformed, physically and socially, once a grandstand opened in 1863, allowing for ticketed and thus slightly more exclusive events. Soon after, the course was converted to steeple chasing, over fences and ditches, imitating the realities of hunting country, including broken bones and worse.

In the 1930s greyhound racing took off, and a 'night at the dogs' became the favoured leisure activity of millions. In Essex, competition between the tracks was intense. Arthur Leggett, promoter of Romford dogtrack (established in 1929), went furthest in his efforts to grab attention – cheetah racing. The wretched animals had been brought from Kenya and subjected to prolonged quarantine. When finally set to race, in December 1937, they remained stolidly uninterested either in chasing the lure or in competing with the greyhounds (though able to effortlessly outpace them). Further outings for the disinterested felines occurred at tracks in Walthamstow and Harringay, all making for electrifying, if short-lived publicity.

One of the Leggett cheetahs, looking unimpressed by Romford

Today Essex may be an also-ran in racing, with its dog tracks reduced to only two, in Harlow and Romford, and betting more likely to be online than in person, but cricket is another matter. As early as 1732 the county had put up a joint team with Hertfordshire to play against the London Cricket Club. Today, Essex County Cricket Club, founded in 1876, is one of eighteen first-class county sides in England and Wales, proudly representative of the 'historic county' of Essex – that is the county before the GLC's dilution of the entity.

In 1825, the Chelmsford Cricket Club rules were stern. They included fines for absence (sixpence per each missed game, held on Monday and Thursday evenings at five o'clock), as well as strict guidance on dress ('straw hat, white jacket bound with purple, white or nankeen trowsers, shoes and white stockings' – on pain of another sixpence fine). Essex has thrown up more than its share of England Test captains, including Graham Gooch, Nasser Hussain and, most recently, Alistair Cook. It is, however, village cricket that knits the county together, and helps cement a strong bond between inner and outer Essex.

Individual teams may wax and wane but the Shepherd Neame Essex League lists almost forty associated clubs which suggests plenty of life and enthusiasm. The close-mown green, the lapped timber clubhouse and the echoes of applause or dismay that drift over the fields in summer months are essential ingredients of life in many Essex villages.

Team cricket is also deeply enmeshed with common rights and the village green. The Bell Common pitch, the home of the Epping Foresters Cricket Club, is little different from most but in the 1980s it found itself, to its horror, standing in the path of the projected M25. Since the land belonged to the City of London, guardians of the forest, and thus the common man, its assortment of committed cricketers, old and young, were not about to back down. The contractors were obliged to submerge their motorway beneath the old common and its cricket pitch, using engineering so sophisticated that at some points there is a distance of only 18 inches between the tunnel roof and the green above.

Bell Common Tunnel, one of only two on the entire circumference of the M25, conducts an endless flow of traffic through below and yet, when I go to watch a friendly match of second teams on a peerless June Saturday in 2018, there isn't a sound except for a polite round of clapping now and again and the suggestion of leather on willow. Only when I walk into the remaining segment of the forest, where immense ancient trees still stand, alongside the Common and then on a bit, do I hear the beginnings of a mysterious roar, evidence of something underfoot but out of sight and mind.

Up above, in the village quiet, there is a typical pavilion (a rebuilt version of the old one) with a verandah, clock and dig-ital scoring, and a convivial group of supporters in deckchairs. Just beyond the green, there rears the outline of a cottage roof. But this is not a house, not part of the surviving village, but a domestically camouflaged control centre for the various tech-nological aspects of a road tunnel, looking for all the world like the home of a slightly reclusive individual who has decided to dispense with windows onto the outside world.

The Epping Foresters won their cricket pitch back in the 1990s, but in the late 19th century the rate of encroachment on the countryside, and the losses incurred, were a continual source of fret and worry. The Essex Field Club was founded in 1880 by a doughty group of amateurs whose pleasure was to observe and record, as a spare time activity or hobby, the natural and archaeological evidence of the county, before it was lost to development. The Club depended on a network of meticulous correspondents, a regional, low-key version of the exchanges between the far-flung Fellows of the Royal Society which nev-ertheless provides, on occasion, a revealing snapshot of the conflicts of the time. Edward A. Fitch of Maldon recorded, in a letter dated September 29th, 1887, a satisfactorily encyclopae-dic day out. 'Returning from Grays by the 6.24 down train, after a day's 'deneholing' [deneholes were medieval caves and pas-sages dug in chalk], in Hangman's Wood, upon my arrival at the railway station with no time to spare, the lamps were just being lighted and I noticed two moths, a Noctua and a Geom-eter, upon the glass of one, probably just disturbed after a day's rest thereon. I picked them off and shut them up in the cover of a book I had with me.' On closer observation these proved to be relatively unusual specimens. One, a Dicycla, was 'a species I should not have expected in so different a locality as the banks of the Thames.'

But he also expressed fears that 'the large number of brilliant electric lights at Tilbury Docks will demoralize a portion of the lepidopterous fauna of the district.' Light pollution proved a worrying new menace to the Victorian naturalist.

Like Fitch, members effortlessly combined, or cross-fertilised, their interests in science with those in medieval chalk-works or entomology. Like those earlier country rectors with Fellow-ships of the Royal Society, they were living in equally intellec-tually ambitious and rewarding times. Dickens' damnation of Chelmsford as unlettered and 'the dullest and most stupid place on earth' was unwarranted: it may have something to do with his failure to find a newspaper for sale in the town on a Sunday morning. Equally, given that Dickens was at the time touring Essex whilst covering elections for the *Morning Chronicle*, he might have tarred Chelmsford with the same brush as the bel-ligerent, boorish and openly corrupt politicking of the time, in which denizens of the town were no better, but no worse, than those anywhere else. Had Dickens but known, the Chelmsford Philosophical Society was established in 1828, and its museum in the very year he penned his complaint, 1835.

Other towns followed suit with learned societies and reading rooms, including those at Colchester and Saffron Walden. As early as 1704, the estuarial port town of Maldon was bequeathed the eight thousand volume library collected by Dr Thomas Plume, a Maldon-born cleric and bibliophile. It was housed in a new building alongside the ruined medieval guild church of St. Peters and is there to this day. The newest libraries in Essex, those at Rainham and Southend, are good buildings, with one eye on their traditional bookish role and another on what might be required of them next. (At the time of writing the threat of closure is being held over many of them) Rainham's library is located within a mixed-use development, including flats and other community facilities, just off the old village centre, while at

Southend, it is handsomely lodged within the new civic complex, the Forum, together with local authority offices, bits of the university and the Focal Point Gallery.

While enquiring Victorians living in Essex towns and suburbs might have filled their time visiting libraries, attending lectures or taking part in field trips, most of the London working class would be lucky to get a taste of the countryside even once a year. Along with philanthropists and clerics, enlightened bosses offered their workers bean-feasts. The term denoted a day's holiday and was often the only break in the working year, a high point in the calendar. John Betjeman helped to conjure up a vanished, yet quite recent world, for 20th-century readers: 'Epping Forest glades

His and hers charabanc outings from the Leyton and Walthamstow areas, c. 1920s

where we/Had beanfeasts with my father's firm/At huge and con-
voluted pubs/They used to set us down from brakes/In that half-
land of football clubs/Which London near the Forest makes.' At
a stroke he caught it all, the ultra-observant Edwardian child, the
boss's son, awkwardly mingling with his father's employees, who
were furniture-makers. The charabanc came into its own with
these large-scale works outings.

In her own childhood, the co-founder of the National Trust
Octavia Hill experienced several dramatic downturns beginning with her father's bankruptcy and removal from his family.
Her own misfortunes left her unusually sensitive to the likely
impact of the countryside on the very poorest city children.
On a wet July day in 1855, aged seventeen, the future housing
reformer and eventual co-founder of the National Trust accompanied twenty-five girls, aged between eight and seventeen, to
Romford. They were the toymakers that she taught in central
London, in Holborn, alongside their mothers, the women who
worked in the Ladies' Cooperative Guild workshop. They were
heading for Marshalls, the handsome rented home of a hospita-
ble Quaker friend of the Hill family, Daniel Harrison.

They travelled eastwards in a wagonette, a horse-drawn cart
with facing benches which, due to wet weather, had some loose
overhead protection rigged up for the journey. The following
year *Household Words*, Charles Dickens' magazine, published
Caroline Southwood Hill's description of the expedition, from
start to finish. (Her father, Dr Thomas Southwood Smith was
a friend and colleague of Dickens). Octavia's mother ran the
workshop. As she pointed out, few of the children had ever
visited the country before, let alone seen cornfields at harvest
time, rose covered cottages and gardens full of fresh cabbages
and runner beans or that strange structure, a windmill (the
construction of which was 'explained'). Once they reached the
grand elm avenue leading up to the house, the children fell
completely silent – a telling detail. They were given umbrellas
and overshoes and sent off to explore the grounds and outbuildings, the lake, the conservatories, the animals. The Harrisons

had twelve children of their own, of whom Mary, Octavia's friend, was the eldest, but for the visiting children, living many to a single room in grim conditions, this amount of space, and freedom, was enthralling, if stupefying.

After the visit, Octavia told Mary that the children 'have never ceased talking about it; the boat, the water, the garden, the flowers.' Another Harrison sister described Octavia herself that day, 'a little figure in a long skirt, seeming much older than her seventeen years, and followed by a troupe of poor and many of them ragged children.' She needed a retreat to the countryside for what would prove to be her own fragile equilibrium. Marshalls allowed her to recharge and she visited as frequently as she could, often painting the landscape or exploring Epping Forest.

Without Hill's personal experience, and observation, of the transformative power of places such as Epping Forest or Hampstead Heath, the National Trust might never have emerged, in 1895. The body was established principally out of her concern, and observation, that the urban poor needed places of importance and beauty preserved for their use and enjoyment, in perpetuity. In her youth, deploying teams of female rent-collectors as ersatz social workers on the low-rent housing schemes she began managing (with funds from John Ruskin), she also emphasised how decent conditions gave tenants a measure of self-respect, long before municipal provision, let alone the welfare state.[3]

An earlier and longer-term visitor to the Forest in 1837, was the profoundly troubled 'Northamptonshire peasant poet' John Clare. Thanks to the financial support of a small band of supporters, he had been admitted to Dr Matthew Allen's private asylum based at High Beech, a secure, but progressive, institution. Dr Allen set great store by the benefits of the natural setting to the disturbed patients' well-being, a theory given equal weight in modern psychiatry. They included 'pure air – sweet scenery' and he claimed that there was 'ample scope for walks, without annoyance and apparently without restraint.'

Yet Dr Allen was not quite the stainless professional he purported to be; in youth his occupations had included that of itinerant preacher, irregular apothecary and unlicensed vendor of soda water, his twists and turns taking him to Edinburgh and York, always supported in his difficulties by a steadfast brother, Oswald, until ever mounting debt and fecklessness sent him to jail, twice. Eventually, Matthew re-emerged on the outskirts of London, possessor of a medical degree, and the proprietor of progressive High Beech. Ostensibly at least he was the very model of Victorian self-improvement as set out by Samuel Smiles.

It's clear in retrospect that much of the forward thinking behind High Beech came from earlier, mostly Quaker-inspired advances in the treatment of the mentally ill in Yorkshire. What Allen would later present as his own innovations – the importance of fulfilling tasks and socialisation, separation of the most disturbed patients from the merely unwell, large, bright airy rooms and an emphasis on diet and exercise rather than purges and cures – had been tried, found successful and written about before, informing Allen's methods.

That doesn't diminish the fact that, for all his past and ongoing failings, Allen seemed to run a successful institution at High Beech, treating a range of male and female patients from oyster-dredgers and farmers to merchants and solicitors, and winning the praise of visiting inspectors for the care and compassion shown.[4] It's also to his credit that when the disturbed John Clare came to his attention (so disturbed that the poet had attacked Shylock at a recent performance of 'The Merchant of Venice', and believed himself to be a successful prize fighter), Allen saw the most immediate causes of the man's illness as extreme poverty and mental exhaustion. Allen wrote a letter to *The Times*, urging admirers of the poet to provide funds for an annuity, permitting the man to write and support his family without again becoming deranged by the anxieties caused by pennilessness. Once raised, however, these funds did not go toward an annuity, but directly to the costs of Clare's treatment at High Beech.

Clare responded well to the treatment at first, writing with great lucidity, taking walks in the forest, participating in group activities (patients at High Beech even produced their own newspaper). It did not, however, escape his attention that there was a degree of deliberate artifice to the institution, for all its leafy seclusion. As at the Quaker-led Retreat in York, the place was a prison designed not to look like one: iron bars, for example, were disguised to look like wood. In spite of Allen's insistence on socialisation and humane treatment, the building plans for High Beech reveal the presence of at least two isolated areas for the containment of 'noisy' patients, in line with contemporary norms of treatment.

Clare chafed especially under the allegedly discreet surveillance, complaining in a letter to Allen that he could have 'staid for years in the forest... but the greatest annoyance in such places as yours are the servants styled keepers who often assumed as much authority over me as if I was their prisoner and not likeing to quarrel I put up with it until I was weary of the place altogether.'

The trouble, no doubt, lay deeper than such irritations. Clare's fame as a poet had left him awkwardly poised between two worlds – the Northamptonshire peasantry and the London salons – neither of which welcomed him, nor he they, and whatever fragile balance he might have found was wrecked by heavy drinking. He felt painfully adrift from his family, writing plaintively of an encounter with a ploughboy who was 'just like my son Bill when he was that age... I was sorry I did not give him my last ha'penny... but perhaps I may see him again.'

Clare fled High Beech after four years, walking to Northampton over three long and difficult days, following directions given by the local gypsies. He composed a wintery sonnet evoking their miserable, squalid conditions and describing them as 'a quiet, pilfering, unprotected race.'

During the same period, Alfred Tennyson also spent time at Dr Allen's, either as a supporter (and thus a guest) or out-patient, painting the landscape in words as his mood took him, having 'nothing but that muddy pond in prospect.' He too spent time out walking in the forest, exploring the residual evidence of Iron Age sites and plodding on under the leafy canopy. Clare's biographer, Jonathan Bate, surmises that the two poets were almost certain to have crossed paths as they wandered around.

Unlike Clare, Tennyson and other members of his family were also tapped for cash by the ever enterprising Dr Allen, who had become particularly excited by a new machine for the engraving of wood. Early promises did not come to fruition, monies were demanded back, relationships were soured. His brother Oswald wrote Matthew out of his will, in recognition of the very considerable sums of money he'd expended on him over the years. In the grounds of the institution a subterranean folly was built a few years later, its fabric largely reconstituted stonework from Chelmsford Gaol. Perhaps it is wiser not to investigate further.[5]

The solitary wanderings of those enjoying therapeutic solitude were soon ruled out by the sheer volume of visitors to the Forest. The tin hut at High Beech where Edward Thomas was to live in such discomfort with the Artists' Brigade in autumn 1915 had been erected, so he believed, to accommodate Sunday School children going out to the forest for summer outings. It may have been one of the famous, but brief-lived, 'retreats' big enough, it was said, to serve tea to more than 3,000 children simultaneously. The grandest of them, the Riggs Retreat at High Beech, opened in 1881. Once the excursion trains ran from Stratford to Loughton, after the line opened in 1856, Epping Forest became easily accessible to all east Londoners who possessed the price of the fare.

For the poor these cheerful outings came, more often than not, loaded with an agenda, not always one immediately obvious. In 1856 Octavia Hill joined a trip organized by the Christian Socialists, headed by Charles Kingsley and F.D. Maurice and others. In an immense room decorated with beech branches, 80 tailors and their families sat down to tea at the Roebuck Inn, Woodford. She told Mary Harrison how the families came in 'vans' to 'spend the whole day, cricketing, swinging, riding, shooting with bows & arrows etc. After dinner Mr. Maurice and Mr. Cooper and others speak.'

In this energetic, even evangelical atmosphere, the tailors were distracted from other cheerful, time-wasting temptations such as funfairs and popular entertainments like donkey rides, barrel organs and fortune telling. Later on, the Socialist League (1884) in which William Morris played a key role, organized regular outings of affiliated socialist groups to his beloved Forest. An 1888 issue of the league magazine *The Commonweal* recorded the usual mix of entertainment, 'singing, revelry, songs in different languages, dancing and other games' together with stirring speeches by leading figures in the movement.

With the Epping Forest Act of 1878, the Corporation of London had promised to take care of its 'natural aspect' and everyone relaxed. Yet the essential contrivance of golf course design was less well suited to the natural landscape than it had seemed. The club proprietors and their designers, often former pros, were quick off the mark. Epping and Woodford, founded in 1890, offered nine holes, Wanstead – laid out on the site of the great mansion and its park – offered fourteen holes by 1893 and Chingford, luxuriantly titled Royal Epping Forest, ran to the full eighteen. But Theydon Bois (1897) was the image of a perfect sylvan golf course, an ersatz version of the ancient forest. As the club website puts it now, 'playing this traditional forest course through the changing seasons of the year is a delight to the senses and the soul.' The Victorians were as easily satisfied as we are by the apparent naturalism, although as Jonathan Meades pointed out in his 2013 television documentary *The Joy of Essex* it's essentially 'a sort of pretend landscape.'

Epping Forest in the 21st century has bigger problems. It is at a collision point between the overwhelming needs of visitors, their cars and preferred relaxations, and the sensitive management and conservation of a world class historic landscape and its ecology. As a reminder, you can walk into the Forest no more than five hundred yards from the end of the Central line at Epping and find yourself in a glade of trees, clear underfoot, mysteriously spaced and each trunk trim and grey, like a sleek damp seal. These are the ancient hornbeams of Epping Forest, still pollarded as in the past but only spared the axe in 1896 because of an impassioned newspaper article by William Morris, warning that thinning and incursions (such as those by golf courses) threatened to lay the ancient forest waste.

Those hornbeams remain an object lesson. The roads through the forest are clogged at the best of times, inoperable at the worst. The nearby motorway is an atrocious, insidious, pollutant. At the time of writing, the Kings Oak at High Beech, the location at which Queen Victoria presented Epping Forest to the City Corporation and, thus, the people, advertises itself with a website showing the building bathed in puce artificial lighting and a pair of gaudy pink lips, signalling its suitability for weddings, barmitzvahs and other events. Directly behind the pub languishes the derelict Speedway Track, self-seeded vegetation having long since obscured its outlines. Beyond, with a distant view out to the relentless M25, stretch tangled skeins of tracks and byways, from which you can find a way into the forest proper, past the Iron Age forts and off through the trees, before another road, another interruption.

The plain and ordinary Essex countryside, so near at hand, was an alternative escape valve for those struggling with the pressures of the city. In George Gissing's *The Nether World* (1889), set in the 1870s, the Clerkenwell artisan protagonists, Jane Snowdon, her grandfather Michael and their friend Sidney take the train out of Liverpool Street first going through 'miles of a city of the damned, such as thought never conceived before this age of ours.' After stopping at a grim series of stations came relief; 'the train… entered upon a land of level meadows, of hedges and trees, of crops and cattle.' At Chelmsford they were met by the 'stolid, good-natured' farmer, to drive them in the trap the five miles to Danbury. As Gissing describes the scene, one with 'no point of interest to distinguish it from any other bit of representative bit of Essex… one of those quiet corners of flat, homely England…' it is clear that he is writing about somewhere familiar.

In the novel, this journey into Essex is an annual week's holiday, perhaps it had been so for him too and certainly was for the Mechi family, the regular excursion that inspired small John Joseph, the most innovative farmer that Victorian Essex ever knew. Yet in Gissing's pages the palliative calm of the gentle landscape, the rural silence ('so deadly quiet that you could hear the flutter of a bird's wing or the rustle of a leaf') despite the distracting worries of their host, the farmer, 'farms lying barren, ill-will between proprietor and tenant… departure of the tillers of the soil to rot in towns that have no need of them' effectively evoke the reality of Essex in the middle of Queen Victoria's reign.

Between the options of a week on the farm or a week at the seaside came the attractions offered by resorts on the banks of the Thames. Purfleet had the Royal Hotel (still there, but its elegance long faded away) with views over the river and the chance to explore Botany Gardens (no longer there), its winding paths and grottoes cut into the disused chalk quarries. (Bram Stoker set Count Dracula there in his 1897 thriller.) In Dagenham, a fifty-five-acre lake, inadvertently formed when the seawall was breached, had turned into another fashionable waterside resort. It attracted fishermen but also people like Elizabeth Fry, the Quaker prison reformer and approved minister, who spent her summers in a willow-shaded cottage by the lake.

The coastal resorts had entered a kind of competitive frenzy, at first to catch middle class holiday-makers, and soon, the working classes who could claim paid holidays at last. Southend-on-Sea ran the first lap, mentioned by Jane Austen, and soon had a large resident population as well as waves of seasonal visitors arriving by water. The pier at Walton-on-the-Naze, rebuilt in 1869 and extended, to an astonishing 800 metres in the late 1890s, had a subtle curve to accommodate all the steamers. Clacton-on-Sea grew from a pair of villages into a fully-fledged seaside resort within a couple of decades. A large hotel was built in 1872 and the pier opened in 1873. Then came the Prom, the Pier Pavilion and, to crown it all in the 1930s, a scenic railway. Visitors still arrived by sea; the

Laguna Belle (previously the *Southend Belle*) delivered passengers to the end of Clacton pier from where they would make their way up to their lodgings. The sequential development of Walton, Clacton and, finally, Frinton was all due to an entrepreneurial engineer, Peter Schuyler Bruff whose almost ninety-year-long life included building his own railway line and viaduct (at Chappell, on the Stour Valley line). Bruff's wish to build a pier at Frinton was scuppered by the more cautious developer who succeeded him as well as the often bruising experience of mass tourism in the more commercial resorts in his portfolio.

The railways were in competition with coastal steamers and the entrepreneurial Riggs who had set up those massive holiday retreats in Epping Forest now turned their attentions to Dovercourt, Clacton and Southend. In the summer of 1888, Frederick Charrington, an ex-brewer turned temperance activist, owner of the Osea Island retreat, arranged an exceptionally ambitious day trip out of London. He took 1,700 working men and women by two chartered trains to Clacton. On arrival they were led in procession to the pier by a Brass Band and then encouraged to 'engage in the various amusements usually afforded at seasides' – apparently stopping just short of swimming but indulging in decorous paddling in that unfamiliar element, seawater, according to the report in the *East London Observer*. There was cricket in the afternoon and more music. But they paid for these pleasures; at six o'clock they were corralled for hymns, prayers and three short improving addresses, one from Charrington, before taking the train back into London.

The atmosphere was very different in Frinton, a resort smugly barricaded behind 'no charabanc' notices and prohibiting outdoor washing lines, public houses and other devilish distractions, such as that unbuilt pier. In the mid-1930s a recherché modernist villa development by the South Coast Development Company was proposed, shock therapy for the self-satisfied town, and including a svelte hotel designed by Oliver Hill. He was consultant architect for the 200-acre Frinton Park Estate where,

after a damascene conversion to modernism due to a visit to the
Stockholm Exhibition of 1930, he aimed to attract 'the cream of
our younger designers in the contemporary style'.[6] There would
be hundreds of houses, three churches, a circular shopping mall
and, above all an elegant sliver of a building, wrapping the coastline, his hotel. The chosen architects, most of whom insisted on
building in concrete, had hardly submitted their designs before
Hill resigned, the company collapsed and a modest, watered-
down version of the scheme was built, consisting of a few white
rendered villas with flat roofs, sun balconies and verandahs.
Around then, the Frinton Summer Theatre began life. Now the
oldest repertory theatre in the country, running a summer programme of seven productions in seven weeks, it flourishes on a
wing, a prayer and much good will, recently marking its eightieth anniversary.

The Holidays With Pay Act (1938) put a feral cat among
the hotel and boarding house pigeons of the east coast: those
well-upholstered landladies referred to by James Agate as 'bur-
nished doves'. The proprietors of the pastel-painted guesthouses
and other holiday accommodation mounted a strenuous campaign against the South
African-born showman
Billy Butlin's plan to set up
in Clacton, closely following on his initial holiday
camp in Skegness, arguing
that it would lower the tone
of the place. (He wouldn't
have dared touch Frinton.)

Warners, at Dovercourt
near Harwich, was the first
holiday camp in Essex.
It accommodated up to
800 visitors and marked
a brief business partner-
ship between Capt. Harry

*'Most of the sun'. A very British sales pitch from this
Warner's advertisement*

Warner and Butlin. Opened by the mayor of Dovercourt, the site had been purchased only sixteen weeks earlier in January 1937. In the 1980s it would become the site of Maplin's Holiday Camp, in the sit-com series *Hi-de-Hi!*, prolonging its life until 1990. Nostalgia is a valuable currency in Essex.

Apart from the colour and the haircuts and the length of the skirts, there's little difference between postcards and photographs from the Dovercourt site in the 1930s and the 1970s: the Palm Court lounge and bar looks the same, as do the boating lake and the hired bicycles being pedalled sedately along the tailored avenues and between the flower beds. The communal 'holiday village' experience may have gone out of fashion in Britain, but in fact the attractions on offer at Essex's first holiday camp in 1937 look very similar to those provided at many a modern family-oriented camping or chalet site in today's France and Italy: a swimming pool, kids' club and games room, nightly music and dancing and a pedal boat or two.

Essex, and indeed Britain as a whole, had little chance to embrace any of this when the rise of Hitler saw Dovercourt repurposed for things less frivolous. From December 1938, the holiday camp was to be a reception centre for the 10,000 Jewish children brought to Britain from Germany by the Refugee Children's Movement, an exodus driven by the terrible night in November, which became known as Kristallnacht after the breaking of glass and the daubing of walls wherever Jews were thought to be, by roaming Nazi thugs. The message had been definitively delivered overnight – no Jew was safe in Germany or, with the Anschluss, Austria.

From the half-hour special programme broadcast by the BBC, entitled 'Children In Flight', you might have thought the children in question were on a mid-winter exchange trip. In January 1939, teenage Lothar Baruch, a fluent English-speaker, talked happily of runs to the beach and card games, hot chocolate and cinema trips, almost as if penning a postcard home. But Lothar Baruch would never go back and many of these children would never see their parents again. Despite his carefully upbeat tone, Lothar let slip one telling detail – 'Now it is very cold and we cannot stay in our house' – hinting at the extremely inadequate accommodation arrangements, exacerbated by bad weather and overcrowding.

With permanent stays in mind, the R.C.M. put the educational needs of the Harwich Kindertransport in the hands of Anna Essinger, a German-born educator of Jewish origin, who embraced Quaker values during a lengthy stay in the USA. Her school for troubled children in rural Germany had fallen foul of the authorities, after she obeyed the rule to hoist a swastika flag above the building but while doing so, pointedly removed the children from it. Essinger had relocated her charges to Bunce Court, near Faversham, and she took a few teachers and older pupils from the Kent school to assist in her efforts at Harwich.

Initially the holiday camp, while experiencing typical East Anglian December weather, was caught up in a whirlwind of publicity and high-profile visits. A consignment of gum boots was donated by Marks and Spencer's. The Mayor of Harwich appeared with the town band in tow, to welcome the refugee children. J.S. Homes, National Liberal M.P. for Harwich, put in an appearance, and the Chief Rabbi planted a symbolic tree. The awful truth of Kristallnacht and the forced flight of the children was obscured and distorted in a welter of facile newspaper reports about the newcomers' beauty, health and promise, soft soap to quell the still-raging controversies about shipping them to Britain in the first place.

Like the Basque children who had come to Britain after Guernica, the harsh immediate realities were at odds with the high principles of those who welcomed them. According to R.C.M. policy, the children were to be fostered. Some families travelled to Harwich to take a child home with them. In 2017 Patricia Losey, aged 86, wrote movingly in *The Guardian* about the journey taken by her gentile parents and a couple of teachers from her school, coming back late one night with thirteen-year old Ursula, who became her friend, trained as a nurse, had her own family, and, at the time Patricia was writing, was still alive in Australia.

Older children, especially boys, were the least likely to find a home, and understandably disoriented and resentful, became a handful for those trying to keep them occupied and contained within the out-of-season holiday camp. One party of lads made a foray to the Harwich red light district; fights occasionally broke out between Viennese and Berlin contingents. But like many, young Lothar Baruch – who became Leslie Brent – fared well: though he told the BBC his ambition was to become a cook, he ended his career as a Professor of Immunology at the University of London.[7]

Butlin's at Clacton-on-Sea had an even briefer pre-war start, opening in 1939, its capacity 2,500 visitors (only half the size of Butlin's Filey), providing a rest for parents (from their children), for women (from their kitchens and housewifely duties) and a change of pace and scene for all the family. Billy Butlin commandeered a special train service from London, so that every Member of Parliament who had voted for the Holidays With Pay Act could come and experience for themselves the delights of the affordable working class break.

With the outbreak of hostilities the brand-new site was requisitioned, the 10 foot by 10 foot chalets, made of chicken wire frames infilled with concrete and painted in pastel hues, were now swabbed an unfetching barrage-balloon grey, and the sun-trap dining room windows blacked out, as the camp was given over to the internment of German civilians, and then for various military purposes.

Despite the Radio Butlin loudspeakers – positioned at the end of each row of 20 chalets – having been used to announce the declaration of war and to urge service personnel to cut short their holidays and rejoin their units, this development seems to have taken Mr Butlin himself by surprise. He received a visit from the Admiralty at the start of September 1939 and was asked how soon he could clear the camp for military use. A week after the declaration of war, disgruntled Butlin's customers were having their end-of-season bookings refunded. All the same, like many a businessman, Billy – or Sir William Butlin as he became in 1964 – had a good war, selling various holiday camps to the Ministry of Defence and then buying them back for a fraction of the price, often with improvements, in peace-time.

When the Clacton camp reopened, brightly repainted, Billy Butlin's background as a fairground showman came to the fore; his was the first independent business to advertise at railway stations, selling his holiday camp as 'a resort within a resort' and (a neat pun) 'holidays with play'. In Clacton, the bound-aries between the town and the camp remained transparent, the large boating lake there for all to see what a good time was being had.[8]

Further good times being had on a grand scale in the Dining Hall

Butlin's laid on non-stop amusement, indoors and out, com-petitive or not, in good weather and bad, from mini-golf to div-ing for crockery in the swimming pool. In between, there were four substantial meals. Everything was paid in advance and par-ents had their (labelled) children taken off their hands each day. In the Viennese Ballroom, with its fairy castle features, 'celebrity Sundays' were held and stars from film, television and the new world of pop music, were imported for the evening, some just starting their careers. Cliff Richard's first professional engage-ment was here and soon Rock and Twist ballrooms were added for the younger campers. Holidaymakers were encouraged to write postcards on a Monday, to say 'guess who I saw'. For those with ambitions to leap the fence and see more of Essex while there, the 1951 *Butlin's Holiday Book* pointed out that 'the camp at Clacton is served by two bus companies, which carry sightseers to the delightful Essex villages and small towns round about, Brightlingsea, Frinton, St Osyth Priory, Harwich and Dovercourt.'

The 1949-50 book featured beauty tips from novelist Ursula Bloom and recipes from the first celebrity chef, Philip Harben

Similar excursions were available if your fancy turned to spending a summer holiday, out of term-time, at the brave new world of the University of Essex. In 1975 it had decided to offer the campus as a base for tourism and made an awkward promotional film to tell people so. The university was eager to tell the world that the dust was settling after the long and fractious years of student insurgency. In the film an unlikely collection of 'tourists', mostly conservatively dressed middle-aged women with tight perms but pepped up with a family or two (and even a stylish girl from somewhere abroad) converge, by train from London or by ferry from Europe. They pick up brochures from the Tourist Office at Harwich quayside or in their chaperoned railway carriage and are soon seen drifting across the New Brutalist plazas or settling into their compact quarters high in the residential towers. There is tennis (for the younger visitors) or the option of a beer in the sun, and then they are whisked off to the local attractions, first Colchester and then beyond, in a coach – maybe hired from the same company that served the campers at Butlin's.[9]

A visit to Butlin's in the 1960s offered options for moral guidance as well as cultural coach tours. The crime writer, broadcaster and prolific *Daily Express* columnist Nancy Spain, by now working anywhere she could (given her spending habits) edited Butlin's *Beaver Annual* (the Beaver Club was for younger campers) and also gave Birth Control lectures to girls who might be careless and carefree while on holiday.

Meanwhile, the Redcoats, their status somewhere between staff and holiday-makers, were 'yours to command' and they had their own uncertain reputations as I learned when two of us applied to join the staff one summer. At seventeen we were rejected as being too young; to be a Redcoat required maturity and, I guess, wider experience than we had, even though my schoolfriend was heading for drama school. Others more successful in the Redcoat selection process would go on to have stellar careers as entertainers, including Jimmy Tarbuck, Des O'Connor and Ted Rogers.

To keep in step, camp facilities were modernized in the 1960s and self-catering bungalows added to reflect changing patterns of leisure. (Caravan parks were by then offering sharp competition, being far cheaper and much less dragooned). New attractions were added, at one extreme performances of opera and ballet at the Gaiety Theatre, at the other glitter, chrome and neon setting the scene for snappier dancing. But Butlinland, as the Rank Organisation renamed the camp after buying it in 1972 from Billy's son Bobby, could not compete. Access to cheap foreign holidays in the dependable sun, so convenient from Southend and Stansted airports, would prove too tempting. In 1983 it finally closed for good, throwing many out of work. For those who were happy to remain close to home, caravan parks remained while for those who wanted to swim and sunbathe without the inconvenience of sand and salt water, there was always the option of the lido, often closer at hand. Whipps Cross Lido could accommodate a crowd of up to two thousand.

As John Betjeman wrote in the 1950s, 'Southend is a cheaper Brighton. Clacton a cheaper Worthing and Dovercourt a cheaper Bournemouth.' Propinquity is all for, so he pointed out, there were over a million Londoners living in Essex. Southend had sold itself at time of the 1951 Festival of Britain as the 'peer of resorts' and 'London's own seaside resort' joining forces with Westcliff, Leigh, Thorpe Bay and Shoeburyness to offer 'bumper Festival programmes.' All that sand, and the donkeys, were to inspire Frank Stuart, variously described as a theatrical mask maker and an engineer. Immediately post-war, he built three life-sized mechanical elephants, powered by 8 horsepower engines and covered by a special toughened paper hide. He patented his creation. On the elephant backs were 'howdahs' and in July 1950, 'Jumbo' first stepped out on the lanes near Thaxted, his home, with a party of children atop. The elephants toured seaside resorts around the country and, seemingly the world, but ultimately the creatures proved flimsy and too expensive to repair.[10]

Jumbo giving a ride to some children at Thaxted, where it had been made

It is easier to get to Southend by conventional means on the road or by rail and the resort, so accessible, still has special ties to London. Annually in the summer, the London Taxidrivers' Fund for Underprivileged Children takes special needs children to the seaside. In 2017, to mark the eightieth anniversary of the charity, one hundred decorated black cabs – their drivers donating a whole day, as every year – left a supermarket car park in Chingford, with more than three hundred children on board, heading for Southend.

Raymond Levy, licensed cab driver, self-described 'PR/ Entertainment Officer' of the fund, told the *East London and West Essex Guardian* the objectives; 'we want to get the children out of their environment, away from their school, their home-life and their problems just for the day.' The charity lays on a lunch at the Cliffs Pavilion, an afternoon at Adventure Island, the Southend amusement park, and back to the pavilion for a disco and a competition to find the best decorated taxi. Many drivers of these classic London vehicles live in Essex, although Hertfordshire, according to their association, runs it close.

In the 1960s, the Barking-based Bragg family headed out from Gallows Corner following, to quote their son, 'a tar-macadam trail to the Promised Land.' Billy Bragg's song, 'A13, Trunk Road to the Sea' was an anthem for its time. Reaching Southend, they passed the handsome domed 1901 Kursaal (the world's first amusement park, later a zoo and later still a music venue, hosting frenzied nights of Black Sabbath and Queen), on down the Golden Mile and the pier, reputedly the longest in the world at one-and-a-third miles long, and kept pressing on. Nothing distracted them, off to take up their habitual spot on the beach at Shoeburyness and, from there, to set out at low tide to walk almost to Holland, as it seemed. Many years on, apart from some obligatorily retained Grade II listed features, the Kursaal is little more than a shell, holding a faint memory of its former glories, living too long and too late to provide even a mordant coda to Bragg's song.[11]

To walk along the stretch of coast from the furthest tip at Shoeburyness, through the buffed-up demilitarized garrison, now a little island of retro-elegance, past the massive, inscruta-ble concrete Battery, dating from 1898, and then a mile or two of family beaches, breakwaters at intervals, is adequate prepara-tion for the energising bluster of Southend proper, a fair slice of coastal Essex on holiday. Those sandy Shoeburyness wastes that the Braggs walked are, given the right kind of weather, pulsing with distant windsurfers, while nearer at hand, the tidal pool offers a friendly space for timid swimmers and paddlers. The shore is bounded by two sets of new beach huts, determinedly different from the candy coloured traditional versions. These have monopitch sedum-planted roofs and primary coloured doors with over-sized numbers, while the side walls are made of sandwiched layers of pebbles and sand. Some changes, but much stays the same around here.

Once you are by the water, you can't look at Essex without a nod to its serious sailing fraternity. Arnold Bennett arrived in Thorpe-le-Soken in 1912, drawn to the water. He kept his beloved Dutch yacht at Brightlingsea. Although his ambitions went much further than the Blackwater or the Colne, since Bennett was an avid cross Channel sailor, he soon found himself confined to dry land, and on the written page, for the war years. The Walton Backwaters become the Mozewater in his 1916 novel, *The Lion's Share*. Not far away, Arthur Ransome's *Secret Water*, one of that writer's series of Swallows and Amazons children's stories, is set on Hamford Water, behind Walton-on-the-Naze. The book was ornamented by the illustration of an accurate map and now modern children can go out seal watching in their wake.

For the wealthy, those with big, deep-draughted yachts (like Bennett) rather than titchy dinghies, sailed by disciplined crews instead of amateurs, Burnham-on-Crouch was the destination of choice. The clubhouse that the well-heeled sailors built themselves, and occupied from 1931 onwards, was a

The Royal Corinthian Yacht Club, in cake

glittering, translucent palace. Largely constructed from steel and glass, its end walls rendered white, the Royal Corinthian Yacht Club evoked a progressive spirit more usually to be found in mainland Europe at this date. Joseph Emberton had translated Le Corbusier's *Vers une Architecture* into English in 1927 and afterwards designed the smartest new department store in London, Simpsons of Piccadilly. At Burnham, the verandahs and balconies cascade down onto the harbour; a clean, fresh image for what was, quintessentially, a clean, fresh pastime.

The club was to be the only English building included in the 1932 *International Style* exhibition, held at New York's newest exhibition space, the Museum of Modern Art in Manhattan. Its young and absurdly arrogant co-curator Philip Johnson wrote to Emberton thanking him for sending photographs but took the opportunity to point out 'some things about the building which do not please me completely, such as the extraordinarily bad circular staircase which you were probably forced to use' and the unsatisfactory arrangement of the slanted windows in the stairwell.[12] Did Emberton, in his forties, realise that this rude pup was just twenty-five years old and although at Harvard, not even a student of architecture? Johnson, who would soon express marked Fascist sympathies, continued to spout his bile against things English in the catalogue, pointing out that 'the large glass area is particularly suitable in a dull, foggy climate'. Long Grade I listed and still cutting something of a dash, the yacht club has the last laugh since, at the time of writing, Johnson's flawed postmodern swansong in New York, the AT&T headquarters, known due to its broken pediment as the Chippendale building, faces substantial alterations.

As in Frinton-on-Sea, 1930s white modernism by the sea was glorious under glassy blue skies, but tended when exposed to a long winter of easterlies to deteriorate fast and require constant maintenance. For later generations, Norman Foster's Stansted airport (at least from the exterior, thankfully unaltered) is better suited to conjuring up the excitement of travel, even if it is a journey by budget airline to somewhere not quite where it claims to be. Recent series of TOWIE, as it begins to flag and slip in the ratings (or until the next juicy scandal erupts) have been filmed in Malaga, Tenerife and Barcelona, to which there are direct flights from both Stansted and Southend airports.

But holidays follow the convenience and the pleasure of the holiday-maker. In a commission for the National Maritime Museum, the photographer Martin Parr, a consummate recorder of the ordinary scene, spent August 2017 catching aspects of *The Great British Seaside* – confining himself to Essex. He found a cheerful and diverse reality. Sikhs are tucking into a picnic, knots of giggling, celebratory Hindus are down at the waters' edge to mark the last day of Shiva, while Muslim mothers and children stick to the promenade. He catches static sun-bathers, active exercisers old and young, paddlers but scarcely a swimmer. He finds them in a landscape of breakwaters and beach huts and, just once, Clacton pier appears in the distance. Parr is out with them for those days, passing neither comment nor judgement, observing a range of simple outdoor pleasures at Clacton, Shoeburyness, Frinton and Southend, at Walton and Leigh, whatever the weather. The mood is gentle, his sightings fond.

For all the apparent seemliness, the county still has a few naturist colonies, discreetly hidden in woodland in various locations, though the glory days of the nudist holiday camp in the 1920s and 30s are gone, let alone the bohemianism evoked in H. G. Wells' fictional artists' holiday village in *Days of the Comet* (1906). 'Bone Cliff', apparently remote on the Essex coast, some miles from 'Sharphambury', consisted of recondi-tioned railway carriages, 'little improvised homes, gaily painted and with broad verandas and supplementary lean-tos added.' Mixed bathing and 'careless living' were accepted, far from 'the dull rigidities of the decorous resorts.'

Mersea Island, where Margery Allingham and her family spent holidays 'trying the glass' (of the Ouija board) and chat-ting to spirits such as Joseph Pullen, a smuggler with lurid tales to tell, (the basis for her first, teenaged, novel, *Blackerchief Dick*,

1921) now offers its mostly unvarnished coast as a place not just to sail but to walk, eat fresh seafood, or take the kids crabbing. Simple, but sophisticated tastes are indicated by signs asking people not to pick the samphire and the availability of very drinkable white wines from the vineyard in East Mersea (one of a growing number in Essex). One wine luxuriates in the name

Mehalah, the name also graces a Mersea restaurant – both seeming to tease the Rev. Sabine Baring-Gould into a furious retort from his grave.

Mehalah's A (more upbeat) story of the salt-marshes

It is all a far cry from the decidedly frowsy Frinton of my childhood. In that prim resort landscape of clean sandy beaches, bordered by rows of other people's (enviable) beach huts, backed by immaculately well-kept public lawns and a popular golf course, the remorseless erosion of the coastline was masked by gentility and mown grass. Nowadays, beach huts in desirable resorts can change hands for astonishing sums and the fretwork, timber and delightfully *ad hoc* nature of the originals is in some locations mocked by pastiche versions, in saccharine lilac and pale blue, pink and cream.

Arnold Bennett considered Frinton an 'excellent imitation of the suburbs of London and cleaner' and berated himself for his kneejerk disdain for the place, so far from his own ideas of how to live freely, which included playing tennis in bare feet with H. G. Wells although his discontented French wife Marguerite preferred to play golf with her shoes on. As always, there is more than one way to approach Essex, two sides of the same coin, as indeed, there are different views of the county from either side of the River Stour, that lazy river dividing Essex from Suffolk.

The author, at Frinton, in 1957

10   FILMS NOT FORDS

Picturing Essex

Visitors who saw John Constable's 'Hay-wain' hung so prominently at the 1857 Art Treasures exhibition in Manchester were, with justification, confused about the location it depicted. Just back from France (where it had nearly been bought for the nation), this evocation of all things rural and southern, so the exhibition guide said, was of a location in Sussex, the river shown being 'the Avon's greatest tributary'. But there are five rivers named Avon in England and this was nowhere near any of them. Constable had in fact painted the scene on the River Stour, of which there are two – neither in Sussex. Easily a hundred miles north, the river in question, the one the painter knew so well, marks the border between Essex and Suffolk.

But travellers in Britain, searching for picturesque, or romantic scenery found little in eastern England and knew even less about it. Those who followed in the footsteps of nature poets and landscape watercolourists headed for the Lake District, the Wye Valley and North Wales. Essex apparently had little to offer them – no pitchy lakes, deep sided valleys or craggy hilltops. It was in fights over such places – Lakes and Peaks –

so the short-form version of history tells us, that the National Trust cut its teeth, defending the wilderness from the railways. In fact, Robert Hunter, who with Octavia Hill and the Rev. Hardwicke Rawnsley was one of the three founders of the organization, had earlier set up the Commons Preservation Society (CPS) in order to secure Epping Forest for the nation. Years later the National Trust itself would take responsibility for vulnerable Hatfield Forest as well as Eastbury Manor, Barking, a building as romantic as any Tudor manor house in the county, menaced by the rapid eastward spread of London.

Yet when J.M.W. Turner travelled east he did not linger. An album of light pencil sketches promisingly titled 'Essex' proves to be a disappointment; he glanced fleetingly at Southend, Foulness and Purfleet but hardly bothered with Colchester. Only Constable had taken much trouble over Essex, even though he was more often over the border in Suffolk. Artists from the Low Countries had no such difficulties on their own territory. As Turner wrote, Rembrandt etched a scene showing merely 'the meanest piece of Common' and three backlit trees, restrained so that 'his bursts of light and darkness… be *felt*.'[1]

Constable's stormy view of Hadleigh Castle and the North Sea churning beyond it conveyed something of that feeling on a far wider stage. When he first sketched the castle in 1814, there was upheaval on almost every continent and Britain was thoroughly implicated in most of it. The nation was handing back distant territories to the Dutch after their seizure in the Napoleonic wars, and both countries were moving towards banning the slave trade. The Emperor Napoleon had abdicated, giving the allies hope of victory (dashed in the short term by his return from Elba) while in North America, British troops torched the White House.

By the time Constable painted the same view, now consolidated in thick oil impasto, in 1829, France had long been open again to visitors, and the principal European conflict – that of a newly-energised Russia going after the territories of an ailing Ottoman Empire – seemed very remote. The clouds and waves of Constable's clifftop vision appear prescient: the tiny human figure and the dominance of the sky, the water and above all the weather over what ought to have been a monument to human power and permanence (had it not been stripped for its materials by Richard Rich, the 1st Lord Rich, in the middle of the 16th century) remind us of the frailty of humans against the elements and the quirks of history. By the time Constable, now a recent widower himself, painted Hadleigh, even the rapacious Rich dynasty had fizzled out half a century earlier.

When another local artist was picturing the Essex landscape almost a century earlier, well inland from there, he changed it around in the convention of the time, shifting a church tower into view there, adding a turn in the road there, but leaving the essentials intact. Thomas Gainsborough painted the young Mr. and Mrs. Andrews (Robert Andrews, his near contemporary, had been his fellow student at Sudbury Grammar School) sitting outdoors, on the fringes of their well-tended farmland, at Bulmer, high on the Essex side of the river.

The mother of Frances Andrews, née Carter, was from a Huguenot family in the cloth business, the Jamineaus, she came from the next village, Ballingdon, and was, along with her husband, also the subject of a Gainsborough portrait.

The Andrews' marriage had been a carefully planned alignment of property and wealth: Frances was not yet twenty. The doll-like pair (based on manne-

The difference in stature between Mr and Mrs Carter, painted in a parkland setting c. 1747-8, may be due to Gainsborough's use of studio mannequins

quins and painted in the studio) sit under an oak which still survives, against a backdrop of farmland.

Just a few hundred yards east, on almost the same contour line, is Ballingdon Hall, a handsome, beefy, 16th-century timber-framed house that stood quite close to Frances' home. In 1972, a crowd of around 10,000 came to watch (paying a fee of 10p a head, towards the upkeep of the local church) as the house was rolled uphill, in an operation that would have tested the engineering skills of the ancient Egyptians, because the owners wanted to remove themselves from the spreading industrial estate on the southern edge of Sudbury. Gainsborough's nipping and tucking, his alterations of the familiar Stour Valley landscape, was a similar adjustment, even if in just one dimension. The area seems to attract it, somehow: in a curious move at the time of the 1832 Reform Bill, Ballingdon and neighbouring Bulmer, though both on the Essex side of the river, were reassigned for obscure bureaucratic reasons to Suffolk.

The only stretch of classic landscape for which Essex is widely known extends further east along the Stour. Dedham Vale became,

Ballingdon Hall... being hauled uphill

immutably, 'Constable Country' in the 1890s once Thomas Cook & Co. entered into an agreement with the Great Eastern Railway to provide introductory tours of the area. Soon visitors could buy photographic postcards in Dedham, where the artist had attended the Grammar School, and then stand on the very spot at Flatford where, they believed, he had set up his easel. In Suffolk they were looking out over the Essex water meadows. Easier still, by the turn of the century they could visit the 'Hay-wain' hanging on the walls of the National Gallery in London. Preserved there intact, the reality of that bucolic landscape was already threatened.

In time, another mill owner's son became the resident artist in Dedham. By the 1950s Sir Alfred Munnings had risen to be the President of the Royal Academy. From that august pulpit the arch-reactionary sounded off, to the delight of some, the enragement of others, against Picasso and, soon, his fellow countryman Henry Moore. Munnings, whose fluency in oils was never matched by his way with words or even less with ideas, had been the courtier of the racetrack and the society hunt circuit. If he hit upon a satisfactory composition, he repeated it endlessly. I know this to my cost since one of my earliest jobs involved an attempt to list his subjects, a preparatory stage towards a possible monograph and catalogue of his life and work which was to be written by a suitable expert from an auction house. I was defeated, equally by confusion and boredom, though impressed by his ability to conjure up sweating horse flanks or upper-class features at will and in prodigious quantities to repetitive effect.

The resolute conservatism of Munnings' approach to painting was still regarded as exemplary in some 1950s art schools, and with the confidence of age and his presidential status, he launched a typically choleric outburst on Henry Moore's 'Family Group' (1949-50) destined for a school in Stevenage New Town. 'Distorted figures and knobs instead of heads get a man talked about these foolish days. Anyone can do round balls for heads. Few can chisel the features of a face.' Taste should be determined, Munnings proclaimed, by 'the man in the street', poetry should rhyme, schools should be small and their teachers not 'urbanised'. [2]

On the matter of Picasso, meanwhile, Munnings appeared to have overstepped the mark. At a speech to the Royal College of Art in 1949, the fulminating painter claimed to have had a conversation whilst on a walk with Winston Churchill, during which the wartime leader had asked, 'Alfred, if you met that Picasso walking down the street, would you join with me in kicking his something something?' Churchill, who'd been present at the speech, wrote Munnings a letter, denying that he had ever walked anywhere with him, much less said anything of the sort about Picasso.

New art, new towns, modern sculpture and modern mores were not for Munnings. He had already aired his mounting fury with the world around him, particularly in the arts, via an unforgiveable outburst of *schadenfreude* over the disaster that overtook Cedric Morris and Arthur Lett-Haines at their East Anglian School of Painting, set up in Dedham in 1937. They had attracted some sixty students, one of whom was Lucian Freud, drawn there by the freedom of the teaching, the diametric opposite of the stultified academic English practice still enshrined on the walls of the Royal Academy. On the night of 26 July, 1939 the school burned to the ground and Munnings was seen driving to and fro in Dedham in his mustard yellow car, shouting uncontrollably and crowing about the disaster, the Mr. Toad of modern art.

Cedric Morris and his partner had presented a sitting target to the reactionary and homophobic Munnings, but they didn't let him win the day. The school was re-founded at Benton End, in Suffolk, and prospered in idiosyncratic fashion for many decades.[3] Morris also became a noted horticulturalist, the nation's specialist iris grower. In the 21st century his paintings are increasingly admired, and valued, while Munnings is praised in a backhanded fashion, largely for his virtuoso technique and his recording of bloodstock and war.

After his death in 1959, Munnings' widow, Lady Violet, turned their Georgian residence, Castle Hill, into a distinctly creepy museum. Taken there as a child I remember the three chairs lined up along a wall in the entrance hall; on the first two sat stuffed Pekinese dogs (one of which had been awarded the Freedom of the City of London) while the third turned out to be alive, at which I threw a rare tantrum. After her day, the house-museum was sanitized and took on the appearance of a bland middle-market furniture showroom.

Munnings would no doubt have enjoyed, either directly or vicariously, the next adversarial chapter in Dedham's history. In the early 1960s a furious campaign erupted against a proposed development that would double the combined population of Dedham, East Bergholt and Stratford St Mary, to provide 'overspill' housing. The Dedham Vale Society, founded 1938, fielded a joint defence force, led by the vicar, the Rev. 'Johnnie' Johnston, and the Dedham architect (and founder Chairman of the Society), Raymond Erith. He was no provincial figure, despite describing himself as a 'market town architect', since he was carrying out the onerous commission to rebuild and repair Nos. 10, 11 and 12 Downing Street (after serious war damage) for the Ministry of Works. The Rev. Johnston was an equally worldly figure: before entering the church he had been a journalist working for an American news agency. In Ipswich with a gang of his fellow hacks on the track of the latest royal scandal, he alone had spotted Wallis Simpson arriving with her lawyer, Sir Norman Birkett, only to learn, minutes later, that Mrs. Simpson had been granted her divorce. Johnston commandeered a telephone at the local dairy and rang New York, gaining a world exclusive.

Erith, a thoughtful architect with a playful streak, referred to himself, like his hero John Soane, as a 'progressive classicist'.[4] The house he designed in Dedham for his parents-in-law after a fire, the Great House, combines the essentials of a 'white brick' double-fronted Georgian townhouse with maverick touches, such as the irregular scale and placing of the street front windows, leaving the middle bay all but blank above the front door. As the various threats to build in Dedham Vale came to a head in 1965, the Society mounted an effective opposition and the final scheme was rejected outright.

In 1970 Dedham Vale was designated an Area of Outstanding Natural Beauty (AONB), some years after the introduction of this level of landscape protection in England and Wales, and the village could breathe a little easier. With subsequent extensions the AONB (one of 40) now covers 90 square kilometres. But the pressures continue to mount while a proposed Stour Valley Visitor Centre, equally strongly opposed, was rejected in 2013 after years of persistence. It was an ill-starred brainchild of the Bunting family, abandoning pioneering tomato growing for intrusive tourism in a highly protected natural landscape. These direct descendants of the lily-importer Isaac, whose own business instincts had never failed him, remained safely within the nurseryman tradition for some two hundred years, only to see their debt-laden business going into administration.

Raymond Erith died young in 1973 but in 1980, the new bishop of the affluent Roman Catholic diocese of Brentwood, Thomas McMahon, decided to commission a new cathedral. Quinlan Terry, Erith's architectural partner since 1969, was a far more orthodox classical revivalist than he had been, a somewhat puritan figure in manner and beliefs, and a surprising choice to design the cathedral for the Catholic diocese, taking in the entire 'historic county' of Essex. In the event, Terry covered the territory by bringing together under one roof a combination of 'the early Italian Renaissance fused with the English Baroque of Wren.'[5] Brentwood is a pleasant market town easily reached off the M25, and the cohabitation of the Roman Catholic diocese with TOWIE is merely one more instance of those strange contradictions and odd bedfellows to which Essex is so cheerfully privy.

Architecturally charming, Great Bardfield was a prosperous working village in north-west Essex, 'pretty without being picturesque.' It would become inextricably linked with a loose cohort of artists whose subject matter was what Alexandra Harris in *Romantic Moderns* (2010) neatly describes as a version of England, 'seen from below stairs with a crisp, practical aesthetic' and whose style of life verged on bohemian.

It began in the mid-1920s, when two students at the Royal College of Art, Eric Ravilious and Edward Bawden, took a train to Dunmow, hired bicycles and started looking for a cottage or rooms for rent. According to Tirzah Garwood, (Ravilious' former student and soon his wife) they had even considered living in Thaxted town hall, that 'deserted-looking building in the middle of the road'. The three-storied, double-jettied 14th-century Guildhall had not yet emerged in its pale glory of limed oak, let alone as the cover image on the 1954 edition of Nikolaus Pevsner's *Buildings of England* volume. Instead, they settled upon a 'prim Georgian house' in nearby Great Bardfield.

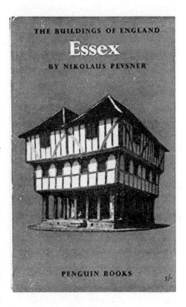

To get there from London, they needed to take a bus from King's Cross, a journey of three and three-quarter hours, with stops and diversions (almost twice the current journey time of the Eurostar from St Pancras to Brussels). It quickly became clear why this part of Essex had retained its unspoiled rustic character. In 1932, after Bawden's marriage to the potter Charlotte Epton, his father bought them the freehold of Brick House as a wedding present. They continued to share the house, with difficulty, with a Mrs Kinnear who 'had kept up a butcher's shop in Romford' and had several children and an itinerant partner. These were hardly the traditional villagers envisaged by the middle-class artists from London, to whose number was now added John Aldridge, a self-taught painter who arrived in 1933. He bought Place House and stayed there for the rest of his life.

Ravilious, the best known of this loose (and always expanding) group of artists, was soon discontented. The landscape was not to his taste; he complained of the 'unpleasant colour of the Essex earth and... the vivid green of grass.' His muted palette was best suited by the chalky soils of Sussex, the close-cropped olive-green downs and the huddles of beech trees cresting the high ground in winter. What he chose to depict was the erosion of the rural setting by construction, the litter of discarded farm imple-ments and even fly-tipped household detritus, all of which he carefully recorded to fine effect. (Ironically, Ravilious is probably most widely known for his elegant designs for Wedgwood china, pared-down Georgian in flavor, in which there is no sign of the abandoned hardware of the working countryside). He confessed, frankly, that he personally hadn't found much pleasure in the local scenery, although its undemanding contours suited walking and cricket – both of which he enjoyed. His impressions during his brief stay in the area, moving from Great Bardfield to Castle Hedingham in 1934, were of uncouth local people and what he saw as a flat, crudely toned, landscape.

In 1942, by then a war artist, Ravilious was reported miss-ing over Iceland. His version of Essex reflected the uncertain 1930s, but his preferred landscape was somewhere more clearly defined, the rolling downlands or cliffs of southern England. His widow Tirzah died in March 1951.

Edward Bawden too had been a war artist, serving in France and then the Middle East. On his return in peacetime, Bawden became the focal figure in the group, and the preparations for the 1951 Festival of Britain were in many ways a joint project shared between various Great Bardfield figures.

Already, several Great Bardfield artists had been rewardingly distracted by Kenneth Clark's admirable 'Recording Britain' project, which ran from 1940 until 1943. It was a domestic ver-sion of the official war artist programme, without necessitating contact with the actual theatre of war. As the fabric of the coun-try seemed at ever greater physical risk, whether from invasion, bombing or just the desultory damage meted out when large houses were requisitioned and treated carelessly, Clark's object was to let the artists catch their own version of the here and now, whatever or wherever it might be. So, for example, elderly Walter Bayes, who had once been a member of the Camden Town group, painted twenty-three views of Essex, mostly interiors and largely in towns, ranging from a tattoo parlour in Colchester where the client was a young soldier about to leave for wartime service, to a ball in the Shire Hall, Chelmsford.[6]

More conventionally Kenneth Rowntree (who had moved to Great Bardfield in 1941) chose fine old buildings – windmills, watermills, Georgian townhouses and vernacular cottages – but often caught moments, especially in chapels and churches, that conveyed the everyday and provisional, an enamel water jug or some old doors reused as partitions, perhaps offering a hint of wartime making-do. He concentrated on favourite spots around Thaxted and Dunmow such as Tilty church and the Black Chapel, North End, while his 'Livermore Tombs', a watercolour of the grassy churchyard at Barnston, captures loss on several planes. With leafless trees in the background, four identical gravestones relate the human tragedy of the four Livermore sisters, all lost to their parents in their teens, while the church graveyard itself is unknowingly a memorial to a vanishing way of life.

These domestic 'war artists' chose their topics according to their own preferences, picking up invaluable aspects of social context, quirky or traditional detail as well as conventional architectural quality. A 21st-century Essex explorer can do worse than to follow in their footsteps.

Postwar, change was afoot, even deep in the countryside. Edward Bawden's title in the King Penguin series, *Life in an English Village* (1949) was focused on the village he knew best, inevitably Great Bardfield, and was given grit with a sharp foreword from the publisher Noel Carrington, who was admirably blunt about the need for rapid improvement in the quality of life and society for its resident population, rather than distractions such as fussing about the erosion of the picturesque surroundings. 'The large village is a better unit of social life than the small hamlet' and as Bawden's range of illustrations showed included 'not only a good general store, but a baker who will also put your joint in the oven… a cobbler who can make your straps as well as mend your shoes, a tailor who can alter a suit for the next child, and above all, a handyman builder or plumber.' A village of that size could support a school with several classes and a range of ages for 'the new practice of sending children by car from one village to another cannot be very economic or sound.' Bawden's sixteen lithographs were, to some extent chosen, like Bayes', to show the real range of activities and skills in and around the village, the busy lives of local people and the first signs of the new Welfare State. The child welfare clinic reflects Carrington's forthright text which greeted the demise of forelock tugging feudalism and the likelihood that 'there will not be so much boredom, nor so much rheumatism from damp floors' from now on.

Bawden was deeply rooted in Essex, born in Braintree, he died in Saffron Walden. The long years in between he had spent in Great Bardfield. At home he was an inveterate collector of everything from jelly moulds to brass rubbings, the Bawdens' house a labyrinthine cave of quirky possessions while his immediate location provided him with limitless subjects, found 'simply by looking in a new direction down his own village street.'[7] Back in the village after wartime service, Bawden found the artistic community in the village 'an emotional storm centre' as marriages crumbled and couples rowed, or swapped partners. Though hardly on a par with the shenanigans of the Bloomsbury circle, the sexual tensions and competitive atmosphere were uncongenial to him. Perhaps Bawden concentrated on the quotidian as a way of drowning out the emotional noise around him.

In the late 1940s he painted several large-scale murals, compilations around themes, forming a kind of graphic collage borrowing different regional elements such as building materials or windows. One was for the ocean liner, the SS *Oronsay* on the topic of 'English Country Pubs' and another for the Lion and Unicorn Pavilion at the Festival of Britain. The latter covered the height and width of the entire end wall, its theme 'Country Life in Britain'. For the sharp-eyed, identifiable Essex features cropped up all over the place. It was what he knew, and liked, best. The 1951 Festival of Britain, although focused on its South Bank site with highlights in the Royal Festival Hall, the Dome of Discovery and the Skylon, and with subsidiary locations elsewhere in London, particularly Battersea Park and Poplar, was a national postwar endeavor, aiming to lift the mood, engage the country in forward gear and, to the best of its organisers' abilities, show off British strengths to anyone looking.

Great Bardfield and its resident artists and artisans were to be considerable beneficiaries of the Festival of Britain. Fred Mizen, long straw thatcher and corn dolly maker supreme had made a guest appearance in Bawden's village book, standing

In Bawden's sketch of The Bell, John Aldridge leans at the bar with his pipe, talking to straw thatcher Fred Mizen – who stands under a corn dolly bell made by himself – while the landlord pulls a pint... presumably not for the local bobby

at the bar in the Bell, with his signature eyepatch, underneath one of his own creations, a corn bell. The following year British Pathé featured him, still hard at his craft after forty-eight years, the commentator intoning – 'he just works till he stops, it's an old country tradition' – pointing out that he had been commissioned to make the seven-foot high monumental lion and unicorn for the eponymous Festival pavilion.[8] Varnish gave these creations a longer life but sadly, years later, they were eaten by mice in storage. When not turning straw to gold, Mizen was the Bawdens' jobbing gardener.

In fact, it was disingenuous in the extreme to choose Great Bardfield as one of the Festival's 'typical' villages. By then it might as well have been standing on the actual South Bank site, so entwined was it with the organisation. However, to appear even-

Fred Mizen with his Festival creations

handed, the journalist and broadcaster James Fyfe Robertson described the key criteria in *Picture Post* thus: '[chosen villages] must all be reasonably near each other, beautiful and typical in setting and style, and with a community spirit lively enough and organised enough.' In short, not typical at all.

In the House, Tom Driberg, cheerleading for Essex as often, pleaded with the political father of the Festival, Herbert Morrison, that some Essex villages might share the limelight with Trowell, an inconspicuous Midlands industrial village marked out for its 'have a go' attitude. Driberg suggested Coggeshall, but Great Bardfield, Finchingfield and Thaxted were the preferred candidates of the Essex Rural Community Council. As they well knew, all three were full of escapees from the art, theatre and literature worlds, open to the unconventional, and certainly more amenable to the visiting public than many sulkier, more enclosed, neighbouring villages.

Finchingfield 'did' theatre. Their drama group, the Field Players, under the 'farmer-producer' G. Stuart Whatley, produced a 'dialect comedy' (shades of Bensusan's *The Furriner*). Thaxted, with recent memories of Gustav Holst and Conrad Noel's ventures into folk music, took on music. The magnificent clear-glazed Perpendicular Gothic parish church swelled with the sound of madrigals and other music from the twenty-person village orchestra and choir. In Thaxted, that musical tradition continues, now an annual three-week summer music festival, quite conservative in its programmes these days. The focus of musical life has moved to a comprehensive school outside Saffron Walden, where Saffron Hall opened in 2013, one of the finest new concert halls anywhere in the country. The donor was a local businessman, who, as one journalist put it, 'with rare grace, preferred to stay anonymous'.

Once the villages had been identified, the wheels of the Festival publicity machine were engaged. *Picture Post*, which had flown the flag for state driven planning and welfare for postwar Britain, had lurched to the right. The issue of 6 January 1951, featured 'national parochialism' with a heavy side-serving of cloying whimsy. Although centred on London, the Festival 'begins at home' – and so the focus was upon 'neighbourhood activities' as in these three (atypical) Essex villages where 'the audience can walk among the players, and the players will be village people going about their daily work, or continuing in the normal recreation.' Wheel-wrighting, hurdle-making, handloom weaving, thatching and smithing were all featured as well as actual harvesting and the crafts as practiced by the local Women's Institute. Journalists bathed in easy cliché. Great Bardfield 'nestles snugly in a crumpled patchwork quilt of corn-yellow and poppy-red fields', set against a distant prospect of London, thirty miles away, 'where the sky is a tell-tale smokey grey.' Edwardian social realist fiction lived on in hackneyed postwar newspeak.

The artists, all of whose work was figurative, were encouraged by the positive response to the open studio initiative during the Festival fortnight. During the rest of the 1950s Edward Bawden, John Aldridge and the printmaker Michael Rothenstein held intermittent summer openings. Open House events (which included their houses, alongside the studios, where hand-printed wallpaper and other domestic artefacts could be seen *in situ*) continued from the Queen's Coronation year until the end of the decade. People came to the village in droves for mainstream art, their parked cars cluttering the roadsides – a growing, but still entirely under-estimated, rural blight.

Oddly, it took the opening of the Fry Gallery in Saffron Walden in 1985 (in the mid-Victorian gallery built to show off the collection of a benevolent Quaker family, the Gibsons) to give the artists of Great Bardfield, by then becoming known as the North West Essex Artists, the publicity boost they'd hoped for, but not had in the postwar Festival era. Their work, so far removed from 1960s and 70s international abstraction, now seemed to strike a chord, accessible and charming as it was. The artists were gone, but exhibitions, based around growing holdings of their work and promoted with an energetic publishing programme, made them familiar, their graphics on cards and tea towels, their output as well as their open private lives examined in a flurry of books.

There is still, entirely based on volunteer effort, a flourishing industry around the group, while Richard Bawden, Edward's son, choses subjects ('Clutter', 'Mistley Towers' or 'Richard's Press') that indicate his own continued interest in the domestic and the local as subject matter. Another artist who calls up Great Bardfield connections, but shorn of any parochialism, is Grayson Perry. For a while in his teens he alleviated the tensions at home (a caravan outside the village, where the family lived temporarily while his step-father was building an ugly, over-large house) by getting involved in punk in Chelmsford and going to the Radio Caroline Roadshow in Braintree. For all that, there is an element of real Arts and Crafts era skill underlying

Perry's work, whether in ceramics, tapestry or on paper, despite his endearing urge to rock the boat under every conceivable heading. Those rich cargoes of expletives may hark back to his Essex punk days, while the efflorescence of detail and colour and reference all illuminate the erudite cross-dresser on a Harley-Davidson.

Beyond Great Bardfield an interwoven circle of writers, photographers and historians spun out into north-west Essex. In Norman Scarfe's *Shell Guide to Essex* some of the most remarkable of the superb, texturally dense photographs, almost photogravure in quality, were taken by Edwin Smith in the 1950s and 1960s. He revelled in texture or pattern, picking up the almost archaic stone zig-zag markings on the massive pillars at Waltham Abbey and the dazzling pyrotechnics of chequered flint and stone on the gatehouse at St Osyth's Priory. Smith and his wife, the writer and painter Olive Cook, lived in a cottage near Saffron Walden and were two of Scarfe's four dedicatees, along with Wivenhoe-based illustrator Dicky Chopping and painter Denis Wirth-Miller, described as his 'Essex friends who are always opening my eyes.' Chopping – who designed the classic James Bond dust-jackets published by Jonathan Cape in the 1950s and 60s – and Wirth-Miller were the first couple to celebrate a civil partnership in Colchester in 2005.

Within five years, both of these talented Essex figures had died, but their involvement in the fertile, and sometimes quite hostile pre- and postwar arts circles around Dedham Vale came more recently under the spotlight on a BBC television programme. In 2016 the author and designer Jon Lys Turner had approached makers of the art-detective series 'Fake or Fortune' with a painting of a man in a black cravat, which he had inherited from Wirth-Miller.

The painting's back story was that Wirth-Miller and Chopping had retrieved this work of art from Cedric Morris' fire-ravaged East Anglian School of Painting, and that it was a very early example by Wirth-Miller's contemporary at the school, Lucian

Photographs by Edwin Smith. Weather-boarded houses and cockle-shed
at Leigh-on-Sea/Saffron Walden Library

Freud. An adolescent clash had turned into a lifelong feud
between the two painters: Freud's name for his adversary was
'Denis Worst Miller' and he spent decades denying that he'd created 'The Man In A Black Cravat' (on occasion saying that he had
started it, but that it had been finished by another hand), possibly in order to prevent Wirth-Miller from selling and profiting
from it. The BBC's forensic investigation revealed it was indeed
an early work by Freud alone although the details of the dispute
might suggest diversionary tactics to cover up the master's (and
maybe his dealers'?) blushes over a clumsy juvenile work.

After the death of Edwin Smith in 1971, his widow Olive
Cook wrote evocatively about the traditional farmhouses
and buildings of Essex, using her late husband's photographs
against a text which drew heavily on inventories, both the
proud accounts of yeoman farmers in their new found early
17th-century prosperity but also the sad property lists made
by desperate tenants, auctioning their possessions in extremis
as they fell victim to the long years of Victorian agricultural
depression. Until then farmhouses had gently swelled in social
stature, nudging into gentry territory. So various bedrooms
might be listed as the 'Red Room', the 'Blue Room' or the 'Grey

Room' while parlours became 'drawing rooms' and the breakfast room and the morning room were distinct from the dining
room. Olive Cook's eye for telling domestic details was just as
acute as her husband's had been behind the camera. A bankrupt tenant farmer in Arkesden had a revealing mix of old and
new items of furniture to sell off at Hobs Aerie in 1887. An
oak table and a Davenport writing desk, an immense dinner
service, leather-seated dining chairs, Brussels carpets and rugs,
watercolours and prints, a stuffed magpie and gull under glass
domes, all combined to paint a poignant picture of family comfort, even luxury, before the recent sudden fall. Throughout
north-west Essex, farmhouses had emptied into late Victorian
auction houses, their catalogues vivid evidence of aspiration,
taste or, sometimes, vulgarity. On occasion, as in Hole Farm,
Little Sampford, (being sold in the 1840s) another picture
emerges, that of a traditional interior, with its ladderback and
elbow chairs, 18th-century 'flap' tables, clocks and newly fashionable sideboards instead of dressers. Upstairs, the bedrooms
were still 'chambers' and two out of three boasted four poster
beds. Cook dedicated *English Cottages and Farmhouses* (1982)
to Norman Scarfe and his lifelong partner Paul Fincham,
'defenders of our heritage and dear friends'. They were a virtuous circle at a time when the traditional was frequently under
siege, often from ignorance and misunderstanding.

Other ways of looking around Britain, seeking out the last
sights and sounds of the traditional, were driven by television.
In 1979 the BBC made a three-part series titled 'The Front
Garden' presented by Candida Lycett-Green (John Betjeman's
daughter). Among the romantic cottage gardens, mixing flowers
and vegetables in the old-fashioned way, Essex came into its
own, offering strong contrast. After a digression to admire
the rigidly controlled and fancily arranged winner of the best
kept garden competition at Becontree, where the husband of
the winning youngish couple was fiercely proud of his bright
green, close-cut grass, director Eddie Mirzoeff well remembers
their expedition on to Jaywick Sands. There, an extraordinarily

elaborate 'garden' of shells and little models took up all the space in front and beside a nicely kept small house. It was a kind of a tiny folly, a highly personal and creative exercise in modelling, with no plants in sight. Recently sold, the new owners from East Ham, a couple with two dogs, had other ideas for it – not for flowers, but as a dog run. Without a moment's pause, and no doubt encouraged by the presence of a television camera, they set about destroying the sweetly naïve construction, plaster and sea shells flying around under the onslaught of mallet and hammer. As the work progressed Mirzoeff noticed, and captured on film, a ring of aghast neighbours standing close by, horrified by the wanton destruction of something they must have grown fond of. Despite the wealth of images of Jaywick then and now, only the YouTube footage exists to memorialise that particular, quirky little creation.

Film making has taken a lazy circle on the estuarial banks of the Thames. The redundant West Thurrock church, St. Clement's, over which the Procter and Gamble detergent factory looms, gained international recognition through its scene-stealing role as the key location in 'Four Weddings and a Funeral'. It stands less than ten miles east of the proposed new film and tv studio facility to be built, with American funding, just outside Dagenham. Costing around £100 million, it promises 12 state-of-the-art sound stages and 96,000 square feet of production offices, alongside vast cinema screens and events facilities and an extensive media technology complex for teaching and training. If not just another estuarial mirage, then the development is undoubtedly good news for Dagenham. 'Films instead of Fords' to paraphrase the words of Barking and Dagenham Council leader, Darren Rodwell, might be just the right vehicle for creating jobs and opportunities in a hard-hit part of 'historic Essex'.

Stories don't always wrap up neatly as neatly as they do in the movies, of course, as the experience of neighbouring borough Thurrock proves. In 1990 it was announced that Universal Studios were on the point of deciding between Rainham Marsh and a site in northern France for their new European film studios and theme park. Then, as now, there was much excitement and expectation, matched by the levels of disappointment when the decision went to a patch of land right next to Disneyland Paris.

The tale had an uplifting sequel, though: ten years later the RSPB bought the long-disused firing range from the Ministry of Defence and began to create a large wetland site on the estuary. It opened in 2006 complete with visitor centre. The quiet pleasures of bird-watching and walking alongside the evident satisfaction of volunteering have brought Rainham Marsh triumphantly back into the public domain, rich in wild-life all year round.

With the exception of Walthamstow Studios, churning out silent films between 1916 and 1930, the county has, up until now had only glancing brushes with what's known in Los Angeles as 'the business.' With Gainsborough and Elstree studios to the north, and Ealing and Pinewood to the west, the east has until now been overlooked, perhaps due to the many deficiencies of the A13.

The county's landscapes, as well as minor (and thus rentable) stately homes and picturesque villages in Essex tend to feature on the big and small screens masquerading as somewhere else, or nowhere in particular. Just as Tilbury has obligingly doubled up as Venice for an Indiana Jones blockbuster and Amsterdam for the 2017 romance 'Tulip Fever', so Hedingham Castle has pretended to be in Prague and Stansted Airport became a snowbound Denver Stapleton when the Hertfordshire-based director of 'The Shining', Stanley Kubrick, developed a strong aversion to flying. Stranger still, when Republican congressional candidate Dr Nick Stella put out an advert in 2018, warning voters of the poverty and decay that would ensue in America's towns and cities if they voted Democrat, he chose (long outdated) pictures of Jaywick Sands.

As previously described, the loneliness, the peril and the menace of Tollesbury's coastal marshes were put to good use for a television adaptation of *Great Expectations*, while the 2012 film of Susan Hill's ghost story, *The Woman In Black*, was shot on and around Osea island. Hill, quite deliberately, never said where her fictional settlement of Crythin Gifford was meant to be, indeed, she even suggested North Wales or Cheshire with one stray reference in the text, but it seems almost as if Essex picked itself for the part.

The gentle BBC sit-com, 'The Detectorists' featured a pair of hobbyist metal detectors, of whom many can be seen out on the plough on a moderately kind winter's day. Viewers were told that the series was set in Danebury (Danbury), Essex. MacKenzie Crook, the writer and co-lead, with Toby Jones, was most insistent on this, and offered constant location reminders as if there might be some doubt. Their club leader's self-published magnum opus, its run of forty-five copies launched from an all-purpose village Scout hut, is titled *Common Buttons of North West Essex* so how could it be otherwise? And yet, in fact, the series is filmed near Framlingham, in north Suffolk, apparently because the cast and crew fancied being further from the capital and in rather deeper countryside than the geography of Essex provides.

11   BUFFALO BILL IN ILFORD

Stories of Essex

There's always been something uncharted and insoluble about Essex. Joseph Conrad's *Heart of Darkness* begins, not in the Congo, but with its narrator Marlow describing his diabolical journey to a trio of men sitting peaceably on a yacht, moored where the Thames meets the sea around Canvey Island. Conrad knew this estuary well, and had spent time sailing there in his friend's yawl, the *Nellie*. In spite of the clubbable atmosphere on deck, the tension he paints between the lowering city in the distance and the placid waters of the estuary, provides an air of menace presaging what is to unfold in the centre of Africa.

Conrad, born in Polish-ruled Ukraine as Jósef Teodor Konrad Korzionowski, but now with an anglicized name and British citizenship, bought a house ('a brand-new twin villa') in the village of Stanford-le-Hope in 1896, although he and his wife quickly moved out from their 'damned Jerry-built rabbit hutch' into a medieval timber-framed farmhouse, probably more congenial to a displaced minor aristocrat. By the time he was writing *Heart of Darkness* they had moved to Kent, but the estuarial imagery had been deeply imprinted on his sailor's retina and provided a luminous prelude to his dark story.

Against a middle ground of the 'tanned sails' of Maldon barges, and a backdrop of sea and sky 'welded together without a joint', the yawl drifts with the tide. The mist on the marshes seems to be 'radiant fabric, hung from the wooded rises inland.' The Thames sea-reach is marked by a Chapman Lighthouse, a jaunty 'tripod' (actually seven legged) with what looks like a log cabin on top. As he was writing, it had already stood for fifty years

To nautical men like Conrad, the Chapman Light signalled the beginning and the end of long journeys an apt symbol for the opening of a novel

and would do so for fifty more, guarding vessels from the mudflats, an engineered folly with a purpose.

As the book opens and dusk arrives, Conrad's seafaring storyteller looks out over the far shore, at the brilliant Chapman Light, the illuminations from constantly moving vessels and beyond, out west, towards 'the monstrous town… marked ominously on the sky, a brooding gloom in sunshine, a lurid glare under the stars.' That reading of 1890s east London, a seeping inkblot on the horizon, tainted Essex too, and it recurs *ad nauseam* in the fiction of that period.

Not surprisingly, in the early 20th century people were eager to hear or tell other stories. The same railways that drove development out east were importing some surprising distractions.

In 1903 and 1904 Buffalo Bill brought his astonishing travelling Wild West entertainment to Essex. As the subtitle of David Dunford's recent book on this episode points out, it was *The First Reality Show in Essex* since the participants, including some hundreds of cowboys and Indians, as well as cavalrymen and their mounts, were the genuine article. Three special trains brought the vast affair, performers, staff, horses and elaborate props to Leyton and it played on a September evening to an audience of 14,000 people. Next stop was Southend, then Colchester. The following year William Cody was back in Essex, this time taking in Chelmsford and then Ilford. Over those two visits, many thousand people witnessed the phenomenal production and while it may have sounded like confused ramblings to their families, when decades later old people claimed to have seen Buffalo Bill in Ilford or a group of American Indians walking around Colchester, they were telling the truth.[1]

Soon the pressured, fast expanding, old market towns and villages of outer London, still in Essex, were moved to grab onto their own past, as if it was a lifeboat hurtling by on the flood. In 1929, Walthamstow gained a town charter, and Barking followed. Both these proud, new boroughs held pageants, as if to claw back their tapestry of history, embellished and simplified to

Justice, Barking-style, at the 1931 pageant

everyone's satisfaction, against a reality of unstoppable development, suburban housing racing out of the capital along the trunk roads and railway stations like iron filings towards a magnet.

The Barking pageant ran to a dozen performances in October 1931, stretching its enormous cast to their limits. An imaginative script and exuberant costuming played fast and loose with scant shreds of its history, such as the Romans at Uphall Camp and the foundation of Barking Abbey, 666 AD, the immense monastic establishment that had been wiped clean away in the Dissolution. The pageant master was Frank Lascelles, whose reputation had been made when he masterminded the British Empire Exhibition pageant at Wembley in July 1924; on the proceeds he built himself a brand-new medieval-style manor house in the Cotswolds. As Lascelles' own taste suggests, story-telling was the point, not veracity. In Essex the subtext was an urgent search for a shared sense of history, to give social traction to the enormous incoming population: 9,000 of the 26,000 houses making up the LCC's Becontree Estate were within Barking's boundaries.

Poster advertising the 1931 pageant

In 1932 Lascelles was back again, to mount a more broad-brush account. The seven episodes of the Pageant of Essex, held in Ilford, told of Boadicea (in four scenes), followed by the legend of the seven kings, a corruption of the Saxon Seofeca's people, the Seofecingas, which became Sevekyngges and then morphed into a spurious tale of seven lords, or kings, who paused to let their horses drink from a stream in Hainault

Forest and left the name behind them. Moving on, the pageant picked up events around late summer 1532 (two scenes) including Henry VIII at New Hall outside Chelmsford, 'complaining about his current wife, Katherine', Queen Elizabeth I at Tilbury Fort c. 1588 hearing the news that the Spanish fleet had been defeated and the Siege of Colchester 1648 – which, being perhaps the most intense of these dramatic episodes, ran to four scenes. The Fairlop Fair c. 1780s (two scenes) included Dick Turpin and folklore associated with that ancient gathering and, finally, the 'Celebrations in Epping Forest on its Dedication to the Public by Queen Victoria'. Four thousand people took part – attendances at pageants were always estimated in (high) round numbers – and the profit of £880 went, very honourably, to the King George Hospital Fund.[2]

Agatha Christie did not set out to be an historian but she was confident capturing the atmospheres and period details that would be fascinating to generations of later readers. Her first detective story, *The Mysterious Affair at Styles* (1920) is set in 'flat Essex country... green and peaceful' in a country house in 1916. Tableaux and recitations by the hostess (shades of Daisy Warwick at Easton Lodge?) were laid on to entertain the guests before the fatalities began to mount up. Christie's final title, *Curtain* (1975, although written much earlier) returns to the same place, where a wheelchair-bound Hercule Poirot is back at Styles, by then reduced from its former grandeur to a shabby hotel.

Her liking for rural settings in which multiple mysterious deaths take place led one critic to invent a generic village, Mayhem Parva, for the purpose. It could very well have been the affluent, actual, Coggeshall, once grown rich on the medieval wool trade. This comfortable locale stole headlines in the 1980s by fielding no less than three high profile murder cases, along with other tragedies. Well worthy of Christie's imagination, the series of seemingly unconnected episodes begins with witnesses reporting a quarrels between the village GP, Dr Robert Jones and his wife Diane, followed by her disappearance and the eventual discovery of her battered body near Ipswich. After 60 hours of questioning, her husband was released without charge, and the case remains unsolved.

Soon after this, Patsy Bull was found shot in the family antiques warehouse, initially presumed to have been the victim of thieves. But her husband Wilfred was the killer, having aimed his shotgun at her as she confronted him over his infidelities. He subsequently had his prison sentence extended for seeking to offload a consignment of rhino horn worth around £2 million, a matter which the High Court subsequently deemed not to be a crime. Wilfred Bull died not long after his release from prison, and never returned to Coggeshall.

Meanwhile, in the same village and decade, a clay pigeon shooter turned his gun on his wife and then himself, and just down the road, a restaurateur died from his injuries, seven weeks after setting himself on fire in a bid to stop his wife from leaving him.

Then from Tolleshunt D'Arcy, the village where Margery Allingham lived and wrote many mysteries featuring dapper sleuth Albert Campion, there came another bleak example of fact outperforming fiction. The sinister Bamber case was a family saga that unfolded out on the marshy fringes – a scenario involving inheritance and dark envy fit for the pen of the Rev. Sabine Baring-Gould. Eventually Jeremy Bamber was convicted of the killings of his adoptive parents, his sister 'Bambi', a model (upon whom Bamber laid the blame for five deaths) and her two small children. He continues to protest his innocence and in 2018, lawyers acting for Bamber sent a folder of evidence to the Crown Prosecution Service, possibly raising some doubts over a piece of evidence critical at the trial, a rifle silencer. [3]

The Judge had ordered the jury to pay careful attention to this silencer, instructing them that 'it could, on its own, lead them to believe that Jeremy Bamber had been the killer.' However, if there's any truth in the 2018 findings, other strands of important evidence were overlooked. A week before the trial, forensic examiners had sent Essex Police a letter, saying that the results of tests would show that blood traces on the silencer could have come from Bamber's sister – whose real name was Sheila – or a relative named Robert Boutflour, who was a regular visitor to the family farm and a frequent user of the guns kept there. At the trial, however, the jury was told that the only blood trace was Sheila's. Seventeen minutes after retiring to deliberate, they returned a majority (10-2) guilty verdict.

As Bamber turns to science, others in the marshy peninsulas of the internet, if not Essex, seek mystical explanations for the spate of killings and suicides that afflicted this small area, noting the confluence of ley lines and the persecutions pursued in the 17th century by the self-titled Witchfinder-General, Matthew Hopkins in the locality. Based in Manningtree from 1644, the son of a Suffolk minister, Hopkins became preoccupied, even obsessed, by the high number of supposed witches in the waterside town. As he and his assistant began their searches, they rounded up many more women accused of witchcraft and the black arts across Essex and into East Anglia, and became a catalyst for the wider panic which eventually caught up some 250 women in horror and apparent retribution. In his own relatively brief tenure as Witchfinder, lasting from 1645 until his death and burial in Mistley in 1647, Hopkins interrogated women 'suspects' in Colchester Castle before sending thirty-six 'witches' to be tried at the Essex Assizes in Chelmsford, nineteen of whom were executed, and many more of whom soon died in prison. Nobody knows where Hopkins' fanaticism came from, but the profit motive entered into the picture, since each town he cleansed of devilish business, by torture, ducking and other means, paid him well for his services. He certainly died rich.

None of this should besmirch the sociable psychic nights regularly held at village halls and pubs around Essex, even those whose star performers occasionally claim to be in touch with the unhappily departed souls of Coggeshall and Tolleshunt D'Arcy. But in many parts of the county, no doubt driven by an ageing demographic, there's a growing appetite for more solid, evidence-based, journeys into the past, a changing relationship between Essex people and their history.

After the carnivalesque Festival of Britain and the pageants of the Twenties and Thirties, the past was no longer being presented in a participatory, let alone imaginative fashion. With so much bomb damage, seemingly untouched settings and surviving buildings now had added value – and were reliably authentic. Families had cars too, and they often wanted to go for a drive and do a spot of sight-seeing. Publications from the Automobile Association, Shell and the *Reader's Digest*, as well as the handy little Festival-era *About Britain Guides* were all part of a publishing phenomenon, volumes of different weight and editorial ambition helping the public to choose the village, church or country house to visit. History was everywhere if you knew where to look.

Immediately after the war, the Ministry of Works and the Treasury had been faced with an enormous crop of unwieldy country houses and mansions, those requisitioned by the military, but which could no longer support a lifestyle based around phalanxes of servants. The authorities had to take action and nowhere troubled and confounded them more than the major Jacobean 'prodigy house' in Essex, Audley End near Saffron Walden. Having been bought by Charles II in 1666, it was the nearest equivalent to a royal palace that Essex could offer. After an inspection for the Office of Works in the 1690s Christopher Wren was left distinctly unimpressed; he found the lead roof failing, the timber decayed and 'the Fabric weake, built after an ill manner rather Gay than substantial.' No wonder that the Crown hurriedly returned it to the Earls of Suffolk in 1701. In the mid-18th century the house was extensively remodelled since it was understood that King George III would be visiting. He never came.

Requisitioned from the aged seventh Lord Braybrooke in 1941, Audley End passed an ostensibly quiet war, the discreet headquarters of the Polish SOE, as described in Chapter Seven. After the peer's death and those of his sons, both killed on active service, the estate had passed in 1943, now encumbered with double death duties, to an unprepared and understandably unwilling cousin, Henry Neville. James Lees-Milne of the National Trust became involved, hoping that the house might be acquired through their new Country Houses Scheme in 1944.[4] Lees-Milne reported that the ninth Lord Braybrooke was 'embarrassed by his inheritance. At his wits' end what to do with Audley End.' His trustees were in charge but he had his own views, considering an adult education establishment unsuitable since Audley End 'should be occupied by persons who will be susceptible to the influence of their surroundings.' Then Braybrooke had an inspired idea. Why not make it into a royal palace again, and offer it to the Duke of Windsor or one of the young Princesses?

Even Lees-Milne, rarely averse to the lure of blue blood, was sceptical. 'Royalty are peculiar people and they never seem to adopt other people's apparently flawless ideals.' The notion of the disgraced Duke and Duchess of Windsor ensconced in this down-at-heel palace, with little to relieve the gloom, would have been the perfect satirical coda to its saga, and theirs.

Despite that diversionary tactic, the Treasury pressed on and purchased Audley End via the Ministry of Works for £30,000 'to adapt and use the house for the requirements of the Ministry of Education.' A last-minute flurry of interest came from Cambridge University and then Magdalene College, of which the Braybrookes were hereditary Visitors, but it was all too late.

Braybrooke thanked the National Trust for their help but, relieved and reasonably well remunerated, he handed it over to the government while the family had cannily retained the six thousand-acre estate, only to be saddled with another set of difficulties on his death in 2015. The encrusted laws of aristocratic inheritance deemed Braybrooke's many daughters ineligible to inherit the title – a theme explored in an episode of *Downton Abbey* at the time and an anomaly only patched up as Establishment minds concentrated on the legal problems that the impending birth of the Duke and Duchess of Cambridge's first child might bring, if he happened to be a she. The Braybrooke daughters missed the boat and the title passed to a fourth cousin, described by the *Daily Mail*, with a scintilla of mingled distaste and delight, as an internet entrepreneur who lived over a Battersea hair salon. The immense estate, meanwhile, was inherited by a Devon-based art historian, the grand-daughter of the seventh Earl. Neither beneficiary had to worry about the house.

Ever since the 1940s Audley End has been continuously open to the public, initially attracting eager queues, fading into a memorably dull destination for a family outing around 1960 and currently run by the (now charitable) English Heritage with what looks like reluctance. Struggling to sell the impressive mansion to a public with dwindling interest in great piles – unless seen on television in the service of a good script or as the backdrop to an episode of *Antiques Roadshow* – they describe it as 'a decadent Jacobean mansion house'. Of course, full decadence, or a glimpse of the dodgy Duke and Duchess of Windsor, might have pulled in the crowds but in 2018, visitors were being encouraged to take a trip to the coal bunkers or try to meet 'the staff' in the Victorian Service Wing. Maybe Lees-Milne, for all his snobbery, had a point when he despaired of the 'tasteless Ministry of Works'.

Nonetheless, Audley End graces the Monopoly board in the Essex edition of the game. In the 2001 version it is priced at £100, against £120 for Layer Marney Tower and a more princely £260 for two great piles rescued thanks to energetic campaigns, Chelmsford City Council's pride (now), Hylands House and estate (all but derelict in the 1970s) or the fire-gutted Copped Hall, Epping (its repair a volunteer project since 1995). The historic houses of Essex take their place around the board alongside shopping centres and car dealerships, but Colchester Castle is king, at £350.

Happily, in the face of the lacklustre curatorial efforts at Audley End, taste for 'heritage' is heading in the opposite direction, and recognizing this, local authorities such as Tendring District Coun-

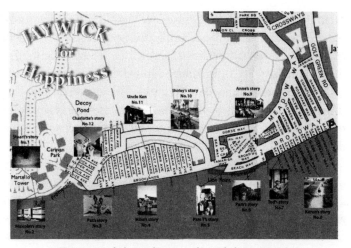

Heritage meets fresh air and exercise in this novel scheme at Jaywick

cil are aiming to attract new audiences and levels of 'engagement' that might have seemed absurdly optimistic a few years ago.[5] At Jaywick Sands, visitors are encouraged to take a two-mile circular route around the site, while an associated app links home movies and photos of families on holiday at 'Jaywick Sands in its heyday.' The material is accessible online, on smart phone or on the spot.

Elsewhere, at Monopoly-topping Colchester Castle, a generation of visitors well used to walking round with a screen in their hands can tap on the app to see the rooms they're in brought to life, or observe the hunting and fighting tableaux on the Roman-era Colchester Vase like bystanders, while 'son et lumière' spectacles projected onto the castle's east wall engage new audiences with the museum professional's version of installation art.

Chelmsford Museum is undergoing another refurbishment in which the enormously popular Victorian stuffed birds and animals from an earlier state-of-the-art local museum have been reprieved (but not the minority taste minerals collection). Here history is more generously interpreted. On a given day you may find the local bee-keepers demonstrating a glass hive to kids in the corner beside the model of the Marconi and Hoffman factories that helped the Luftwaffe bomb their town centre. They are justly proud of their Grayson Perry pot, bought in 2004, and titled 'The Chelmsford Sissies', illustrating 'a fictional transvestite festival' based around the 'true tale' of Sir Thomas Sissye, a royalist who was forced to parade through Chelmsford wearing women's dress. The cover of the pot, transfer printed with new housing estates, is a car nose-dived into the lid. The visitors are left to thread their way between this melée of fact-based fiction.

You could say that Essex lends itself to the inspired spoof. An online 'local newspaper', seeking to serve an area where almost nothing beyond the trivial or the absurd ever happened, began to make waves in the early 2000s. Jason Hazeley describes himself and his three school friends from Chelmsford as running 'on a constant diet of silliness'.[6] They put out eight pages on a web domain bought for £25 (inspired by Charlie Brooker's 'TV Go Home') and called it the 'Framley Examiner'. The format was based on that of the 'Essex Chronicle', warts, software and all, and where Jason Hazeley had worked for a time. In late 2001 each of them emailed a handful of friends and by the end of that day, Hazeley remembers, they were getting their own (anonymous) work recommended back to them by others. A fortnight later they had received two serious book offers. Having opted for Penguin, whose conscientious printers had to be assured that the four misaligned plates on the cover were examples of their slavish attention to detail and entirely deliberate, they irreverently bisected the penguin on the spine, the first such heresy in the history of that sacred imprint. Online content consisted of both stories and classified ads (the aim was to cram 100 onto the first page). Examples of the latter include a boxed display 'Parrot Cage with Ceefax' and further down 'Goblin Teasmade. Also Goblin kettle, Goblin hat and goblin shoes. I am a goblin and I am selling my goblin things.' The material was idiotic and random, drawn from everywhere, 'an enormous pile of local newspapers we had collected'. Jumbled place names, Fracton and Clinton, vie with all-but recognizable people, such as 'Taunton Mishap, whose trademark journalistic style is to miss the point of the story'. At one point, the actual 'Chronic Essicle' – as they nickname the paper that so inspired them – prepared a piece on the 'local boys done good' until the editor spotted that his own office had been used to represent that of the 'Framley Examiner' and he summarily spiked it. As Hazeley says, there's no unkindness meant, even though Framley is definitively the Chelmsford that they had known in the 1980s, a grim town. Now it has changed so much 'comparisons are largely meaningless.' They have never stopped writing the Examiner but do so very intermittently these days after Hazeley and Joel Morris embarked on the Ladybird Books for Grown-ups (including such delights as *The Story of Brexit*) while the various enterprises of faux-tv-academic Philomena Cunk (with Diane Morgan and Brooker) are further inspired effusions of meaningful nonsense. Essex gets a hit in Cunk's musings on British history, for as she says, 'Romans put their capital in Colchester where nobody would want to come and get it.'

Alas, Douglas Adams, who grew up in Brentwood, found the inspiration for his *Hitchhikers' Guide To The Galaxy* whilst lying drunk in a field in Innsbruck. He did, however, find the answer to 'life, the universe and everything' at St. Peter's church, Bradwell-on-Sea – at least that's what Tim Fox, warden of the adjacent Othona retreat believes. In Adams' trilogy, a supercomputer crunches away at this 'question' for aeons until finally delivering the cryptic answer of '42'. The windows of the ancient chapel at Bradwell, where Adams was a frequent visitor, apparently contain exactly 42 panes of glass. Coincidence? Adams himself claimed he just picked an ordinary, mundane number at random.

More conventionally, memories are being stirred across the county. Oral history consists of stories like yours and mine, or those of someone you know. To share a place and a story or two is to connect. The volunteers at the Haven, met earlier here, with their experience and knowledge of the plotlands, are a case in point. The explosion in local history groups in Essex, volunteers who gather, winter and summer, to learn and exchange information, recollections and knowledge is phenomenal. Is this a resurgence in confidence, a validation of a renewed sense of place, a recognition of things thought unimportant until recently – or a bit of all three? It must certainly be aided by the digital revolution: research that might once have involved lengthy correspondence and trips into the deepest and dustiest of archives can now be done on the bus, on a smartphone. Where once our history was absorbed on trips round stately homes and museums, a small fee grants the historically curious access to millions of online records and sources without moving from the sofa, while many a local history group has set up a website, few better than that run on Canvey Island, freely available to all who click on the link. Across the county, countless charitable trusts have sprung up within the last thirty or so years, driven by energetic volunteer groups and formidable individuals. They range from Alan Cox's ambitious twenty-year long programme at Copped Hall and its estate, the continual restoration and research work around great Edwardian gardens such as Easton Lodge or Warley Place (once planted by leading horticulturalist Ellen Willmott and her countless gardeners) and the many sites run by one of the most impressive county wildlife trusts in Britain, often protecting sites which have emerged from the post-industrial landscape. Others worry away at desultory owners (public or private) of key buildings. Colchester's notable silhouette, the imperial-looking Grade II-listed water tower known as Jumbo, but officially called the Balkerne Tower, is an example of the latter. With the Heritage Lottery Fund in their sights, the enthusiasts press on, hoping to preserve, protect and promote it even in the face of continual setbacks. And just as the story of Essex industry sketched earlier indissolubly melds agriculture, engineering and technology together, so the story of Essex people is one of linkages between individuals, their skills and sense of place coming together, arguing for a new, self-driven, validity.

To quote Tim Burrows, the author and indefatigable champion of the county– who got married at the end of Southend's unfeasibly long pier – we have to 'pull at the threads of received notions of what Essex is'. In doing that we are obliged to challenge our own preconceptions, as well as those of others. There are many variants of Essex. The landscape that spooks some is the landscape that enthrals others, the architecture that repelled or, at least, disappointed, is now the architecture of choice for an entire generation. Histories long overlooked are reread, or retold, and forgotten episodes (and people) come back to mind, for better or worse. And there are always new stories, new tellers, new listeners, new artistic endeavours.

Michael Landy constructed a full-scale model of his parent's house, 62 Kingswood Road, Ilford in the Duveen Galleries at Tate Britain in 2004, in authentic materials and minutely reproducing every inch of its actual condition. The late Victorian house had been their home for thirty years, and for his father, drastically disabled after an accident at work, a prison. The replica house stood for six months before being demolished and the materials reused, many claimed back by his father John, such as down pipes and p.v.c. windows. Landy had already disposed of all his material possessions in 2001, in a piece he titled 'Break Down', doing so in full view of the passing public. He worked behind the immense plate glass shop windows of the former C&A store at Marble Arch before taking the resulting 5.85 tons of waste to an Essex landfill site. It was likely to have been Mucking, of course, where these pages began.

I am a writer; more often than not about architecture. In the summer of 2016, I was commissioned by the *Architectural Review* to write an essay on 'A House for Essex', to argue its virtues since it was in the running for an international competition. The now dissolved practice FAT (Fashion Architecture and Taste) had been commissioned by Alain de Botton's Living Architecture to design a 'home' for Julie May Cope, Grayson Perry's fictional Essex Girl, a house which would then be available as a short-term holiday let. It was heavily publicised, ending up with a Channel 4 documentary and generating such abnormally high levels of demand that the lets are decided by lottery.

On a gently grey day in mid-June I set out in an easterly

direction with the Essex-born architect Charles Holland, a former partner in FAT. We left the parking garage beneath the Barbican, a raw underside of Brutalism, to head out on the A12 towards Wrabness. Pulling in for petrol somewhere featureless around Marks Tey, (*echt* mid Essex) the car failed to start again – here in the very county which claims the highest percentage of motor engineers in its workforce (the long shadow of Ford, perhaps). Charles' classic BMW being of a certain age, I sat quietly as hope drained away of either reaching our destination in time to see and talk to the housekeeper, or of meeting my tight deadline. He dried plug after plug (and afterwards admitted to a measure of panic, at the time well disguised by eerie calm). Somewhere around plug twenty, one sparked to life and we were back on the road.

Telling the tale of this most unusual commission, Holland was initially given the tricky task of finding a site, quartering the county but always with 'Essex as a given'. Eventually, somewhere emerged: the impossibly perfect Wrabness with its railway station, views out over the Stour estuary towards Felixstowe and an elevated site, just a hundred yards or so from a riverside stretch of the Essex Way. And the next door neighbour

Grayson Perry's A House For Essex

turned out to be a woman with an architectural background who had no problem with the whole slightly dotty project.

The curious brief required fictional Julie, through her real-life representative Grayson Perry, to be evoked and even encapsulated in the house. Ideas came fast and furious from Perry, but also from Holland – for who but a drab spoilsport would not enjoy being asked to design a decorative fairytale casket, or as I wrote in my *Architectural Review* piece, 'a cottage for Rapunzel, illustrated by Arthur Rackham'?

Julie is a woman of Perry's class and generation, 'caught between tough reality and the dream gifts of social and intellectual mobility.' She is from a New Town (Basildon) and attends, as a mature student, a New University (Essex). She is 'born' on Canvey Island (during the floods) and 'dies' in a road accident with a takeaway delivery scooter. Her life had turned around; she might have left Essex for good (plenty of people do), but instead she set to, benefitting from her own intelligence and attitude.

The house is a Russian doll in architectural form, layer upon layer of interleaved symbolism (and copper roofs) and, inside, a gallery celebrating this Essex Girl with a difference. It is, quite literally, a fabulous little building, drenched in light, colour, stolen views and, always, those stories. It is of no particular style or moment, but full of references and inferences. The exterior ceramic cladding (pargetting had been considered too) includes the motif of the ubiquitous seaxe. Like Perry, whose own identity is an amalgam, a clever accommodation with Claire, his cross-dressing 'other half', Julie Cope took a journey out of one Essex into another, towards a wider, more generous world. The more I think about Julie Cope, the more she emerges as a figurative Essex.

When I had fully explored the house, flooded with light despite its seemingly impermeable exterior carapace, we left Julie and

The safety pin and the seaxe... Even the tiles tell Julie's story

her 'grave', a nearby slab in a knee-high pasture of ox-eye daisies and campion, and headed for Harwich. There, where Trinity House still keeps operational headquarters in a world without lighthouses, and where the Hook-Harwich ferries still ply their routes to Europe, is an exceptionally attractive small port town. Once it provided the first impression of England for thousands of nervous arrivals, including mail-order bride Princess Charlotte of Mecklenburg coming to meet King George III in 1761 and mid-20th-century *emigré* children, those lucky enough to have escaped death at the hands of the Nazis. We visited an old friend of mine, bravely converting a double height industrial building into her new house and workspace, and then headed to Frinton to measure up a beach hut for some small improvements for Charles' client, a local nurse.

Frinton suits that kind of soft, woolly, weather. My last visit had been blighted by a plague of ladybirds, like micro-grape-shot, only escaped by sticking close to the shore line and the sea breeze. With the millennium the town broke the rules and opened a pub, grappling with modern life in its particular way. In 2014 Clacton (with Frinton) was the only parliamentary constituency to elect a UKIP MP, when the hatchet-jawed former Conservative, Douglas Carswell, successfully fought a bye-election and then held onto his seat in 2015. A one-man swingometer, he turned Independent and decided not to stand at the subsequent election. Out west, beyond the endearing thatched public conveniences, and the enduring trim and evergreen Tennis and Golf Clubs, is the other Essex, that inexorable landscape of saltmarsh, reeds, mudflats and water.

So, plugs sparking in harmony now, we set off again. And on the way we talked some more about the contradictions and complexities of Essex, so misunderstood, so rewarding.

Less than ten days later, slightly more than half of those who voted in the Referendum would opt for Brexit – especially in the east of England. In Essex, where the welcome for strangers has long been so generous, where the sense of person and place is so particular, the conversation can and must go on.

END NOTES

Introduction

1 Hilda Grieve's *The Great Tide: the story of the 1953 flood disaster in Essex* (1959) is a magnificent hour-by-hour chronicle of the tragedy, set against the history of this vulnerable location and framed by what followed. See also Ken Worpole's essay: https://www.newstatesman.com/writers/314044

2 A useful survey is given in Essex Record Office publication 118, J. R. Smith, *Pilgrims & Adventurers; Essex (England) and the making of the United States of America* (1992).

3 This owes much to the welcoming words customarily offered by the former Lord Lieutenant of Essex, Lord Petre to applicants for UK citizenship who are also gaining, 'in a less official sense', citizenship of the county of Essex. 'In this part of the world there is a tradition of welcoming migrants from overseas… who have contributed immeasurably to the cultural fabric and prosperity of our society.' I am very grateful to Lord Petre for a copy of his text.

4 Nick Bartos, 'Writing Mucking: Lives in Land', *Current Archaeology*, January 10th 2016. https://www.archaeology.co.uk/articles/features/writing-mucking-lives-in-land.htm

Chapter 1

1 I am quoting from the 1971 edition of Defoe's *Tour*, abridged and edited by Pat Rogers, published in the Penguin English Library series.

2 A fine essay by Martha Vandrei in *History Today* (18th September 2018, https://www.historytoday.com/miscellanies/queen-boudica-life-legend) outlines the sparse factual background as well as exploring the enduring appeal of the Boadicea myth.

3 Detail of the 1898 feast are given in a footnote within Sylvanus Thompson's *Life of William Thomson, Baron Kelvin of Largs*.

4 See http://www.rochforddistricthistory.org.uk/page/hms_beagle_at_paglesham?path=0p146p70p

5 Illustrated article by Essex historian Andrew Summers https://www.newhamrecorder.co.uk/news/heritage/woolwich-the-town-on-both-sides-of-the-thames-1-4009530

6 *Printed Maps of Essex from 1576*, by Peter Walker (Friends of Historic Essex, 2016) provides an exhaustive, and beautifully illustrated, account of cartography in the county.

7 *Map of a Nation: a Biography of the Ordnance Survey* (2011) by Rachel Hewitt is a delightful account of the entire, epic development of the OS.

8 *My House of Sky: the Life of J. A. Baker* by Hetty Saunders (2018) draws to great effect upon recently revealed material about Baker's life, now lodged in the University of Essex, and includes his marked-up maps.

9 The quote is included in Oliver Rackham's fascinating section on moats in his classic account *The History of the Countryside* (1986)

10 The late John Hunter, though trained as an architect, turned to environmental planning and joined Essex County Council in 1971 to help set up strategies for a landscape ravaged by Dutch Elm Disease. His wise book *The Essex Landscape* (1999) was the fruit of his close familiarity with the county.

11 The correspondence of Ida John (Nettleship) is a remarkable record, published as *The Good Bohemian: the letters of Ida John* (2017) edited by Rebecca John and Michael Holroyd. Part IV covers her 18 months spent at Matching Green 1903-1905.

12 I have drawn from Matthew Hollis' moving biography of the last years of Edward Thomas' life, *Now All Roads Lead to France* (2011).

13 Ian Dury duly cemented the false trail when he titled his 1981 album 'Lord Upminster'.

14 Ian Nairn thanked Essex County Council in *Outrage* (1955) for 'keeping its share of the green belt truly green (apart from wholesale incursions by the LCC).' Further material on Cranham can be found within the vaults of the Hidden London website: http://hidden-london.com/gazetteer/cranham

Chapter 2

1 These details are contained in one of two invaluable anthologies of material from family papers held in the Essex Record Office, as compiled with a light touch by A.F. Brown, *English History from Essex sources 1750-1900*, (ERO publications, no. 18, 1952).

2 Details from Leonore Davidoff and Catherine Hall, *Family Fortunes: Men and Women of the English Middle-class, 1750 – 1850* (revised edition 2002). Taking two regions, one urban, Birmingham, one rural, around Colchester, the authors provide, in the latter, a rich source of social information on Essex, particularly on women's lives.

3 A.F.J. Brown as above.

4 Susie Harries's *Nikolaus Pevsner: The Life* (2011) points out that neither were in good health in 1952. Yet as they cruised, the caravan swinging behind their borrowed Ford Prefect, post-war Essex even offered Pevsner modernist delights in the surprising shape of the 'cantilevered concrete platforms' at Loughton station and the 'thrilling… industrial structures' at Coryton oil refinery, where he singled out the abstract beauty of the

'Air-lift Thermo-Fin Catalytic Cracking Unit'. As Harries suggests, this is surely a first such mention in architectural history.

5 All quotes from Hansard, 1951: https://5. parliament.uk/Commons/1951-04-16/ debates/6e3d0f0a-4bb4-4198-b100-84914e30c0d8/TransportRuralEssex

6 Details gleaned from Simon Bradley's encyclopaedic *The Railways: Nation, Network and People* (2015).

7 Robert Beaumont, *The Railway King: A biography of George Hudson, railway pioneer and fraudster*, (2016).

8 Thames News, ITV, 15th September 1981 (viewable, as part of the Thames News archive, on YouTube).

9 Information on the 1826 Borough of Maldon poll, the 1836 South Essex poll, a list of Shenfield residents from Kelly's Directory of Essex, 1895 and a trove of detail on local court cases was found on www.history-house.co.uk

10 Studied in detail in Joe Moran's thoughtful piece: https://joemoran.net/academic-articles/housing-memory-and-everyday-life-in-contemporary-britain/

11 https://www.theguardian.com/books/2018/oct/06/michael-morpurgo-bradwell-sea-essex-village-home]

12 John Hunter, *The Essex Landscape: a Study of its Form and History* (1999).

13 https://www.indymedia.org.uk/en/regions/london/2004/03/287260.html

Chapter 3

1 Fiona MacCarthy, *William Morris: A Life for our Time* (1994).

2 Described as 'a remarkable survival' in Chingford. The volume of the *Buildings of England* that covers such areas of historic Essex is *London: East* (2005), edited by Bridget Cherry and Charles O'Brien.

3 The SPAB file, held in the Society's archive, is a window onto the Gorman 'case', including contemporary news coverage and correspondence.

4 Details of the procession are given in an (undated but c. 1986) brochure to Layer Marney Tower.

5 https://www.theguardian.com/books/2018/jul/21/made-in-stisted-andrew-motion

6 https://www.nationaltrust.org.uk/flatford/features/willy-lotts-house-at-flatford

7 John Updike describes his house and its neighbours (as he remembered them from the 1960s) in *Architectural Digest*, June 1, 1990.

8 The story, from both sides of the Atlantic, is well illustrated in Braintree Museum.

9 'Obituary: Cecil Hewett', A. Gibson and D. Andrews, *The Independent*, 30th September 1998.

10 *The Brickmaker's Tale* (2014) is Peter Minter's proud account of his family firm.

11 The extraordinary riches of the activities pursued by the Essex Field Club are now digitised and can be accessed via www.essex-fieldclub.org.uk

12 The Crittall family, and their work-force, come to life in their revolutionary Unit Construction site in this short film: https://www.britishpathe.com/video/building-of-homes-for-heroes/query/Braintree

Chapter 4

1 https://www.bbc.co.uk/news/uk-england-essex-39203795

When the reward for information was doubled (to £100,000) new information came to light. But at the time of writing, the case remains unsolved, despite his widow's strong suspicion that he had been stalked long before the killing.

2 'The Only Way Is Essex: the worst address in England?' William Langley, *The Daily Telegraph*, 17th October 2010

3 The resplendent and growing 'showman' section of Chelmsford Crematorium demonstrates the vitality of this community within Essex, where a dozen permanent local authority sites are provided for gypsies and travellers. Their history, from the encampments in Epping Forest or on wide village greens, such as that at Matching Green – where Augustus John drew them – up to the present, with uneasy recent memories of the stand-off at Dale Farm which unhelpfully demonised the travellers, is woven through the county.

4 https://www.theguardian.com/books/2020/oct/02/how-i-learned-to-love-being-an-essex-girl-sarah-perry

5 Stephen Daniels' monograph, *Humphry Repton: Landscape Gardening and the Geography of Georgian England* (1999) is the authoritative account, alongside Repton's own *Memoirs*, edited by Ann Gore and George Carter (2005).

6 John Claudius Loudon, *Landscape Gardening and Landscape Architecture of the Late Humphry Repton* (1840).

7 William was such a bounder that he has the honour of being the focus of a website entirely dedicated to his doings: www.wickedwilliam.com

8 https://www.nationaltrust.org.uk/hat-field-forest/features/a-most-generous-gift

9 Woodford remains a rare survival of continuing common grazing rights within Epping Forest. Interrupted by the mass cull due to the BSE emergency in 1996, the cattle returned in 2001, albeit on a limited scale.

10 Details of Locke are largely taken from the *Oxford Dictionary of National Biography* (ODNB) and the pamphlet 'Locke Unlocked'

available in High Laver church.

11 For almost all the material on Norman Lewis in Essex, I have depended on Julian Evans' exemplary biography, *Semi Invisible Man: the life of Norman Lewis* (2009) while Lewis' own views are in his essay: https://granta.com/essex/

Chapter 5

1 https://somesuchstories.co/story/essex-island-london

2 I discuss all this in my essay 'Plotlands to New Towns' in *Radical Essex* (2018).

3 Perhaps paradoxically, there is now an extensive plant near Stansted dedicated to the preparation and assembly of materials for prefabricated house building.

4 John Tusa, 'Living in Modernism', C20, Issue 3, 2014

5 David McKie and I wrote our *Ian Nairn: Words in Place* (2013) to trace this unlikely journey and celebrate the great writer. More to be found there.

6 https://www.theguardian.com/global/2012/oct/11/leo-kersley-obituary-letters

7 See my short piece, 'Geoffrey goes to Basildon', in *New Town Utopia* (2018), ed. Christopher Ian Smith. We reproduce four pages of Jellicoe's doodles.

Chapter 6

1 Ken Worpole has written widely on the topic of alternative communities in Essex. *New Jerusalem: the Good City and the Good Society* (2015) puts them into a wider framework.

2 Included by A.C. Edwards in *English History from Essex Sources 1550 – 1750* (ERO publications no. 17, 1952)

3 The Braintree Museum has a section on this and Smith (ER0) cited above, includes interesting material about Essex families.

4 See Nellie Shaw's *Whiteway: a Colony in the Cotswolds* (1935) which gives a glimpse of the previous venture and its pitfalls.

5 For more on the Peculiar People, see Ken Worpole's essays: https://thenewenglishlandscape.wordpress.com/2016/01/08/the-peculiar-people-of-essex/

6 Included in *Memories of Revolution: Russian Women Remember* (1993) edited by Anna Horsbrugh-Porter.

7 http://www.essexrecordofficeblog.co.uk/page/8/

8 See *Campaigning for the Vote: Kate Pary Frye's Suffrage Diary*, edited by Elizabeth Crawford (2013).

9 Much of the following is drawn from Margaret Blunden's biography, *The Countess of Warwick* (1967).

10 The photographs are reproduced handsomely in Robin Whalley, *The Great Edwardian Gardens of Harold Peto* (2007).

11 See *Oil Paintings in Public Ownership in Essex* (2006); also online on ArtUK.

12 http://www.foxearth.org.uk/holst.html

13 http://blackmorehistory.blogspot.com/2008/08/vaughan-williams-and-essex.html

14 http://www.essexrecordofficeblog.co.uk/document-of-the-month-december-2015-byrds-song/

15 https://www.britishpathe.com/video/labour-partys-chequers-1

16 The words of James Bettley, editor of (revised) *Buildings of England; Essex* (2005).

Chapter 7

1 'Archaeologists find 1,400-year-old tomb of Anglo-Saxon king', Rebecca Allison, *The Guardian*, 6 February 2004; 'Inside "British version of Tutankhamun's tomb" discovered between a pub and an Aldi', Jon Sharman, *The Independent*, 9 May 2019.

2 'The Prittlewell (Essex) burial: a comparison with other Anglo-Saxon graves', Leslie Webster. *Proceedings of the 60th Sachsensymposion, 19-23 September 2009, Maastricht.*

3 A good local account of memories of the real characters behind the fiction is in http://www.merseamuseum.org.uk/mmres-details.php?tot=1&pid=COR2_017&typ=ID&wds=&hit=1

4 From Quarter Sessions records, ERO no 17 (cited above).

5 'Wilko Johnson: Things I Have Learned About Canvey Island', interview with Zoe Howe, *The Quietus*, May 1, 2012.

6 Personal communication, email 01/05/2018.

7 Full account in James Bettley (ed., revised) *Buildings of England; Essex* (2005).

8 'The Heroic Style in "The Battle of Maldon"'. Edward B. Irving, Jr. *Studies in Philology*, Vol. 58, No. 3 (July, 1961); 'Maldon and Mythopoesis', John D. Niles, *Old English Poetry* (2002), ed. by R.M. Liuzza; 'The Battle of Maldon: A Heroic Poem', George Clark, *Speculum*, Vol. 43, No. 1 (January, 1968).

9 See the ODNB entry for Angell.

10 Ironically these were to be the Debden estate, the location for Young and Willmott's contentious study of displaced East Londoners.

11 Among a welter of books on the subject, Sir William Addison's *Portrait of Epping Forest* (1977) is a useful, well informed, source.

12 Arnold Bennett's 'Journals' published in various editions from 1954 onwards, are an entertaining, fluent, guide to his life in and around Essex in these years.

13 There is a display devoted to the Zeppelin incident in the Essex Police Museum, Chelmsford. In addition the ERO blog has the following http://www.essexrecordoffice-blog.co.uk/zeppelins-over-essex/

14 I wrote an LRB blog about the episode: https://www.lrb.co.uk/blog/2016/02/11/gillian-darley/los-ninos-de-guernica/ Afterwards, Harriet Ward (Colin Ward's widow) kindly sent me a video and other material.

15 I have been happily dependent on Julia Jones's *The Adventures of Margery Allingham*, the revised 2009 edition of her 1991 biography. In addition comes Allingham's own *The Oaken Heart* (1941) which is, as Ronald Blythe writes in his introduction, an 'astonishing book' in which she missed nothing 'the uncomfortable throwing together of people… the drab days, the dreadful "cheerfulness", the suppression of fear, the weariness and the sheer goodness of folk.'

16 Much of this, and more, is recounted in Ian Valentine's *Station 43: Audley End House and SOE's Polish Section* (2004). Aleksandr Tarnawski's story – and that of his less fortunate *Cichociemni* comrades – was told in *The Guardian* article by Julian Borger, 'Honouring "silent and unseen fighters" who led Polish resistance' (10 June 2016).

17 http://www.adls.org.uk/t1/node/512

18 Well covered in the section 'Warfare and Defence', in James Bettley, ed. *Buildings of England; Essex* (2005).

19 Prince Roy of Sealand made it into the Royal Obituaries section of the *Daily Telegraph* on 11 October 2012. Those who can't face a choppy sea-crossing may visit the principality in cyberspace: https://www.sealandgov.org

20 In 2014, the exhibition 'Something Fierce' curated by Jules Lubbock told the architectural story and more can be discovered online at https://www.essex.ac.uk/news/2017/02/23/something-fierce-adds-bite-to-exhibition-at-royal-academy

21 'Obituary: Sir Albert Sloman', *Daily Telegraph*, 5 August 2012.

22 From *The Red Atlas: How the Soviet Union Secretly Mapped the World* (2017) by John Davies and Alexander J. Kent.

Chapter 8

1 'The History of Maldon Salt, The Stuff You Already Put On Everything', Nick Paumgarten, 31 March 2017, www.bonappetit.com

2 See for Collinson (and others mentioned here) *Rooted in Essex*, a gazetteer of people connected to historic gardens in Essex, edited by Twigs Way for the Essex Gardens Trust (2006). For Collinson and Petre, see Andrea Wulf, *Brother Gardeners* (2008).

3 For Ray and Derham, see their respective ODNB entries. For Derham's experiments at Upminster, see http://www.upminster.com/history/people/willian-derham.htm

4 Account in Norman Scarfe's edition and translation of *A Frenchman's Year in Suffolk, 1784: François de la Rochefoucauld* (1988).

5 Based on an excellent lecture given by John Miners for the Essex History Group at Essex Record Office in 2017. Miners is involved in the (currently precarious) Halstead Heritage Museum, guardian of much of the Courtauld company's history in the area.

6 http://cat.essex.ac.uk/reports/EAS-report-0030.pdf

7 This conservation work echoed the efforts of the County Council in other historic towns around Essex to encourage respect for the massing and forms, if not the construction or detail, of traditional work. It was codified in the *Essex Design Guide* (1973) and, at best, produced some compact 20th-century domestic architecture.

8 https://www.suffrage-pioneers.net/the-list/katharine-mina-courtauld/

9 Vanners, one of the three survivors, now has a small factory in Basildon, so textiles are back in Essex.

10 The recent trial of the Stansted 15, protesters accused (and convicted) of endangering public safety by chaining themselves to a Boeing 767 taking deportees back to their countries of origin, was a sobering moment.

11 See Roy Brigden, *Victorian Farms* (1986) and Mechi's ODNB entry.

12 See entry on Bunting in *Rooted in Essex* (note 94 above). I am grateful to Ailsa Wildig who pointed me to the attached essay, via Paula Sewell http://karn.lib.kagoshima-u.ac.jp/bitstream/123456789/14723/2/AA11895463_v26_1_p127-150_Sakasegawa.pdf

13 See the excellent section in Chelmsford Museum covering Crompton, Marconi and Hoffman. Also Marconi's entry in ODNB and *Chelmsford – Birthplace of Radio* by Janet Olivia Lee (2001), a pictorial souvenir produced by Chelmsford Borough Council to mark the centenary of the first transatlantic wireless transmission.

14 See *Silver by the Ton: A History of Ilford Limited 1879- 1979* by R. J. Hercock and G. A. Jones.

15 Remembered by John Howard Norfolk, as follows. https://www.francisfrith.com/uk/debden/bank-of-england-printing-works-at-debden_memory-266271 Also http://www.bbc.co.uk/legacies/myths_legends/england/essex/user_3_article_1.shtml

16 The Spitalfields Life blog, written by 'The Gentle Author', featured Holt in a piece

published on 8 November 2018, http://spit-alfieldslife.com/2018/11/08/rod-holt-design-er-set-builder-modelmaker/

Chapter 9

1 The story is told in full here http://www.defunctspeedway.co.uk/High%20Beech.htm

2 For more, see *Full Circle: the Rise, Fall and Rise of Horse Racing in Chelmsford* (2017) by David Dunford.

3 See more on this in my biography *Octavia Hill: Social Reformer and Founder of the National Trust* (2010 revised edition).

4 Many writers have engaged with Epping Forest recently. Adam Foulds put Dr Allen's institution, and his literary patients, at the centre of his novel, *The Quickening Maze* (2009). For a more factual view of Allen's career, institution and dealings with John Clare and others, see Iain Sinclair's essay 'The Edge of the Orison: In The Traces of John Clare's "Journey Out of Essex"' (http://www.vam.ac.uk/content/articles/m/contemporary-prose-on-essex-the-edge-of-the-orison-in-the-traces-of-john-clares-journey-out-of-essex-by-iain-sin-clair/) and 'Matthew Allen, MD (Aberdeen) 1783-1845' by Margaret C. Barnett in *Medical History*, 9 (1965).

5 See the description in Barbara Jones, *Follies and Grottoes* (1964).

6 See Alan Powers, *Oliver Hill: Architect and Lover of Life, 1887-1968* (1989).

7 I have had helpful conversations with Katherine Ferry, author of *The Nation's Host: Butlin's and the Story of the British Seaside* (2016).

8 The film is, in its own, quite unintentional way, a treat. Viewable here: https://player.bfi.org.uk/free/film/ watch-holidays-at-Essex-1975-online

9 *The Refuge and the Fortress: Britain and the Flight from Tyranny*, Jeremy Seabrook (2009); *One Small Suitcase*, Barry Turner (2003).

10 More on Frank Stuart, and the creators of other mechanical fauna at: http://cybernet-iczoo.com/walking-machines/1949-50-me-chanical-elephant-frank-stuart-scottish-g-b/

11 You can read more in Billy Bragg's *The Progressive Patriot* (2006).

12 'Faint Praise', Catherine Croft, *C20*. Issue 2, 2015.

Chapter 10

1 Turner's sketchbooks are viewable online on the Tate website.

2 This is covered in the second volume of Sir Alfred Munnings' three-volume autobiography, *The Final Burst*. A Tate exhibition of British artists influenced by Picasso in 2012, and the auction of some of Munnings's private correspondence in 2016 provided handy pegs for various journalists to dust off the tale of Munnings, Picasso and Churchill, including Claire Voon on www.hyperallergic.com, Sarah Cascone on news.artnet.com and Arifa Akbar in *The Independent*.

3 An exhibition of Cedric Morris' work as an artist and plantman was held at the Garden Museum in London, ccompanied by Andrew Lamberth's catalogue (2018) Also, Richard Morphet's Foreword and Diana Grace's Introduction to *Benton End Remembered: Cedric Morris, Arthur Lett-Haines and the East Anglian School of Painting and Drawing* (2002) give a flavour of the two establishments.

4 The description is James Bettley's in *Buildings of England: Essex*.

5 English examples from the 'Recording Britain' project in the V & A Museum can be searched online.

6 The blog below also offers a pdf of the book: https:// inexpensiveprogress.com/post/.../life-in-an-english-village-discovered-a-pdf

7 This clip shows Mizen, eyepatch in place, at work in 1950. The Mizen family remain thatchers in the eastern counties. https://www.britishpathe.com/video/corn-dollies/query/traditions

Chapter 11

1 See David Dunford, *Buffalo Bill's Wild West: The First Reality Show In Essex* (2018).

2 The Barking Pageant is described in the London Borough of Barking and Dagenham 'Local Studies Information Sheet' No. 8. The following link provides more detail on his creation for Ilford. http://www.historicalpageants.ac.uk/pageants/1064/

3 'Scientist's Report Casts Doubt on Jeremy Bamber's Trial Evidence', Eric Allison and Simon Hattenstone, *The Guardian*, 21 September 2018.

4 I am indebted to Ben Cowell, of the Historic Houses Association, for a copy of his notes prepared for a lecture, throwing light (and humour) on this protracted saga.

5 A day-long conference organized by Tendring District Council, 'Resorting to the Coast: Valuing the Past to Shape the Future', was held in April 2018 at Walton-on-the-Naze. As well as a strong programme of talks, the lunch-time History Fair gave space for nine voluntary local societies to demonstrate their work. It was invigorating and surprising.

6 I am grateful to Jason Hazeley, whose emails (December 2018) offered an entertaining description of the zany publication's genesis.

IMAGES

Linda Foster 1953: © Alamy, Ltd.

Frederick Whitbread & Co, Eastbury Manor: by kind permission of London Borough of Barking and Dagenham Archives.

Boadicea Haranguing The Britons: from *A History of England In Three Volumes*, by David Hume, Tobias Smollett, E. Farr and E.H. Nolan (James Virtue, London 1860), artist unknown.

Colchester Oyster Feast: *Henry Laver, Colchester Oyster Fishery: Its Antiquity and Position, Method of Working, and the Quality and Safety of its Product: Colne Fishery Board, Colchester (1916)*. Creative Commons, from the University of Washington Freshwater and Marine Image Bank.

St Botolph's Priory: ©John Wakefield, via www.flickr.com

Detail from tapestry: Grayson Perry 'In its Familiarity, Golden', 2015 (detail); Tapestry 290 x 343 cm 114 1/8 x 135 1/8 in © Grayson Perry. Courtesy the artist, Paragon | Contemporary Editions Ltd and Victoria Miro, London/Venice.

Beaulieu Palace: 'Beaulieu Palace, built by Henry VIII, now New Hall School, Chelmsford', 2008 Creative Commons, identified as own work by user amaibron.

Queen Elizabeth II Bridge: © Matthew Slade (via www.flickr.com).

Chipping Ongar airfield: 387th Bomb Group B-26 Marauders parked at Chipping Ongar. 1944 USAAF photograph. Posted to www.flickr.com by D. Sheley, Fulton, MO.

Early London Stansted sign, 1967 © PA Images.

North Weald airfield market – photograph courtesy of Saunders Markets, www.saundersmarkets.co.uk.

Chestnut Green, Wanstead – Creative Commons, identified as own work 24 August 2006, by user: Standard.

Queen Elizabeth's Hunting Lodge – before: reproduced by kind permission of The View Epping Forest Collection, City of London (LDQED.2017.31)

Queen Elizabeth's Hunting Lodge – after: author's photograph.

Layer Marney Tower: photograph by Alfred Capel Cure, 1857. Metropolitan Museum of Art, No 265814. Creative Commons.

Church Langley Water Tower: by kind permission of Ian Jones, www.m11watertower.org.uk

'Jumbo' water tower, Colchester: Creative Commons, identified as own work, by user: The Wub.

High Easter water tower: author's photograph.

Yeoman cottage: from *English Villages and Hamlets*, H. Pakington, Batsford 1934.

Colchester Earthquake: postcard, c.1884 –private collection.

Sketch of Crittall by Alfred Munnings; first house at Silver End: both from *Fifty Years of Work and Play*, by F.H. Crittall, Constable, 1924.

Silver End house – author's photograph.

Essex Joke Book cover: from *The Essex Joke Book* by Nicholas Knights published by Virgin Books. Reproduced by permission of The Random House Group Ltd. ©2012.

TOWIE tours advert: from the (now-defunct) www.towietours.co.uk

Sir Thomas Smith's tomb: author's photograph

Before and after paintings: from *Fragments*, Humphry Repton 1816.

Finchingfield: postcard, private collection.

Bata Workers: reproduced by kind permission of the Bata Heritage Centre.

Bata Statue: author's own.

Gibberd statue: © Simon Farr via www.flickr.com

Ongar: drawing by Peter Shepheard in *The Greater London Plan*, Patrick Abercrombie, 1944.

The Haven brochure: produced by Basildon Development Corporation c. 1986

Discotheque poster: hand-drawn by Vince Clarke's brother. Reproduced in *Stripped: The Depeche Mode Story* by Jonathan Miller, Omnibus Press, 2003.

'The Witch': Lithograph by Joseph E. Baker 1892. U.S. Library of Congress. Creative Commons.

Daisy, Countess of Warwick, 1881: Creative Commons.

Hadleigh Farm Hay-carriers photograph: reproduced by kind permission of the Salvation Army Heritage Centre.

Hadleigh Farm goats, reproduced by kind permission of the Salvation Army.

Part of William Byrd's motet 'Ne irascaris Domine' in a sixteenth century music book from the Petre collection (D/DP Z6/1), reproduced by kind permission of the Essex Record Office.

Suffragettes demonstrating at a bye-election, 1908. Kern, Keegan, 'General' [Flora Drummond], Gye, Bray, Flatman, Joachim'. From the Women's Library Collection, London School of Economics, TWL.2009.01.41 (https://www.flickr.com/photos/lselibrary/35043626543)

Daisy, Countess of Warwick with Margaret Bondfield and Mary Quayle, 1926: reproduced by kind permission of TUC Library Collection, London Metropolitan University.

Prittlewell Grave sketch: by Faith Vardy, ©Museum of London Archaeology (MOLA).

Mersea boats and letter box: ©Frances Kent.

Canvey Dutch cottage: Creative Commons, identified as own work by user: oneblackline.

Lea Bridge Bungalows, postcard - author's own

Labworth Café: photograph published in *Architect and Building News*, 16th February, 1933.

Canvey flooded: © Susan Sergeant.

St Peter on the Wall, Dengie: Creative Commons, identified as own work by user: Colm O'Laoi, July 2012.

Byrhtnoth sculpture, Maldon: sculpture by John Doubleday, author's photograph.

Jaywick Martello Tower: reproduced by kind permission of Essex Record Office.

Epping Forest Welcomes The Queen: reproduced by kind permission of The View Epping Forest

Collection, City of London.

Trench digging in Epping: ©Imperial War Museum Photography Archives, photographer unknown, image no. Q23554.

L33 Zeppelin: Creative Commons: Official Record of the Great War, H.D. Girdwood (India Office, 1921).

U boat Surrender, Harwich: ©Imperial War Museum Photography Archives, photographer Horace Nicholls, image no Q20162.

Springfield – bayonet charge, reporting, signs on the green: 'Everyday Life In An Essex Village,' August 1941, Ministry of Information. Creative Commons: Imperial War Museum.

Red Atlas: image reproduced by kind permission of John Davies and Alexander J. Kent www.redatlasbook.com

'A brace of poynters': from the *Chelmsford Chronicle*, Friday 26th March 1784; reproduced by kind permission of David Newman, Goldhanger Past website: www.churchside1.plus.com

Salt-panning statutes: from *The Statutes At Large, of England and of Great Britain: From Magna Carta to the Union of the Kingdom of Great Britain and Ireland*; reproduced by kind permission of David Newman, Goldhanger Past website: www.churchside1.plus.com

Salt extraction at Maldon photographs: reproduced by kind permission of The Maldon Salt Company.

Historia Plantarum: by John Ray, 1704. Creative Commons: Wellcome Images. Photo No. L0070056. https://wellcomecollection.org/works/kcmt22s5

Courtaulds Advertisement and Courtaulds Rules: from *A History of Courtaulds*, C.H. Ward-Jackson, Curwen Press, 1941.

Joseph Mechi: reproduced by kind permission of the Museum of English Rural Life

Marconi transmitter: from *The Story of 25 Years: 1910-1935*, W.J. Makin (George Newsnes, London 1935)

Nellie Melba: from November 1920 issue of *The Wireless Age*.

Marconi advertisement: reproduced by kind permission of www.aviationancestry.co.uk

Bank of England printworks sketches: by Feliks Topolski, reproduced by kind permission of Teresa Topolski and the Feliks Topolski Estate, and with thanks to the Bank of England Museum.

Rod Holt: image reproduced by kind permission of The Gentle Author, www.spitalfieldslife.com

Ceremony at DP World: image courtesy of DP World London Gateway.

Gendarmes in Essex: ©Tony Sale Photography.

Tour de Essex sign: author's photograph.

B. Leach bicycles: image reproduced by kind permission of Vestry House Museum, Walthamstow.

Trio of cyclists: Creative Commons, date estimated 1919, photographer unknown.

Billy Galloway crash: © The John Chaplin Speedway Archive.

Cheetah at Walthamstow, © Illustrated London News Group.

Charabanc outings: both reproduced by kind permission of Vestry House Museum, Walthamstow

Warner's advertisement: Creative Commons, via www.flickr.com, user: Harwich & Dovercourt.

Butlin's Dining Room, postcard - private collection.

Butlin's Book 1949-50: edited by Lyle Blair, designed and produced by Adprint Exclusively for Butlins Limited, 1949.

Jumbo at Thaxted: ©Alamy, Ltd.

Royal Corinthian Yacht Club cake: author's photograph.

Mehalah's Restaurant: ©Mehalah's Restaurant, East Mersea, Colchester CO5 8TQ.

The author at Frinton: author's photograph

Portrait of Mr and Mrs Carter of Bullingdon House, Bulmer, Essex, by Thomas Gainsborough, c. 1747-8: Tate Britain. Accession No. T12609. Bequeathed by Simon Sainsbury 2006. Accessioned 2008.http://www.guardian.co.uk/arts/gallery/2007/oct/29/art?picture=331099273 Guardian re Sainsbury bequest.

Ballingdon Hall moving: reproduced by kind permission of Historic England/Sudbury Museum Trust.

Thaxted Guildhall: from *Buildings of England: Essex*, by Nikolaus Pevsner, Penguin Books, 1954.

Sketch of 'The Bell', Great Bardfield: by Edward Bawden, in *Life In An English Village*, by Edward Bawden, and Noel Carrington. Penguin Harmondsworth, 1949.

Fred Mizen with Lion and Unicorn: reproduced by kind permission of the Museum of Rural Life.

Cockle sheds at Leigh-on-Sea and Saffron Walden Library: photographs by Edwin Smith, reproduced by kind permission of RIBA.

Chapman Lighthouse: postcard image, date unknown, reproduced by kind permission of Mike Millichamp, Lighthouse Compendium, www.mycetes.co.uk

Barking Pageant images reproduced by kind permission of London Borough of Barking and Dagenham Archives.

Jaywick map created and co-ordinated by Arterial Cultural CIC, supported by the Heritage Lottery Fund.

A House for Essex, Wrabness: designed by Grayson Perry and FAT Architecture; exterior image reproduced by kind permission of Vagrantpunk, via www.flickr.com

Tiles on A House for Essex, Wrabness: © Jack Hobhouse, www.jackhobhouse.com

Front endpapers: Saxton's Map of Essex; by permission of British Library, London, UK; © British Library Board. All Rights Reserved/Bridgeman Images

Back endpapers: Detail from tapestry: Grayson Perry; 'In its Familiarity, Golden,' 2015 (detail); Tapestry 290 x 343 cm 114 1/8 x 135 1/8 in © Grayson Perry. Courtesy the artist, Paragon | Contemporary Editions Ltd and Victoria Miro, London/Venice

INDEX

READING AROUND ESSEX

An Extremely Selective List

Many more titles are referred to, either in the text or endnotes; I'll leave readers to ferret them out. There has also been a recent tidal wave of estuarial literature and nature writing, touching on the Thames and Epping Forest in particular, and comprising far too many titles to list. There are numerous blogs to consider as well, especially: New English Landscape (https://thenewenglishlandscape.wordpress.com), Somesuch Stories (https://somesuchstories.co) and Caught By The River (https://www.caughtbytheriver.net).

Local history interests, meanwhile, are catered to at the Essex Record Office (http://www.essexrecordofficeblog.co.uk), while Essex Belongs To Us (https://essexbelongstous.org) makes an excellent calling-point for everyone interested in reading and writing about the county.

[A] denotes academic, [B] less so or not at all.

Abercrombie, Patrick, *Greater London Plan 1944* (London, HMSO 1945) [A]

Allingham, Marjorie, (foreword by Ronald Blythe, introduction by Julia Jones), *The Oaken Heart* (Gold Duck, Pleshey, 2011) [B]

Artists at the Fry: Art & Design in the North West Essex Collection, essays by Olive Cook and Andrew Lambirth (Fry Art Gallery, Saffron Walden, 2012) [B]

Bawden, Edward, *Life in an English Village* (16 lithographs), essay by Noel Carrington (King Penguin, London, 1949)

Bennett, Arnold, *The Journals of Arnold Bennett* (Penguin, London 1954 edn.), entries through 1913 -20 are intermittently relevant to his time living in Essex. [B]

Bettley, James and Pevsner, Nikolaus, *The Buildings of England; Essex*, (Yale University Press, London and New Haven 2007) [A]

Bragg, Billy, *The Progressive Patriot* (Transworld, London, 2006) [B]

Cherry, Bridget, O'Brien, Charles and Pevsner, Nikolaus, *The Buildings of England London 5: East* (Yale University Press, London and New Haven, 2005). This volume covers 'historic Essex', parts of the county that fell within the boundaries of the Greater London Council after its formation in 1965.

Davidoff, Leonore & Hall, Catherine, *Family Fortunes: Men and Women of the English Middle Class 1780-1850* (Routledge, London 2002) [A]

Defoe, Daniel, *A Tour through the Whole Island of Great Britain*, Volume 1 (1724) (Penguin, London, 1971 [A/B]

Engel, Matthew, *Engel's England*, (Chapter 35) (Profile, London 2014) [B]

Grieve, Hilda, *The Great Tide: the story of the 1953 flood disaster in Essex* (Essex Record Office Publications, Chelmsford, 1959) [A/B]

Haining, Peter, *The Great English Earthquake* (Robert Hale, London, 1976), verbatim reports from surviving children of the time [B]

Hardy, Denis and Ward, Colin, *Arcadia for All: the Legacy of a Makeshift Landscape* (Mansell, London, 1984) [A/B]

Hunter, John, *The Essex Landscape: a Study of its Form and History* (Essex Record Office Publications, Chelmsford, 1999) [A]

Jones, Julia, *The Adventures of Marjorie Allingham* (Golden Duck, Pleshey 2000) [B]

McKie, David, *McKie's Gazetteer* includes sections in East of England devoted to Foulness, Frinton and Walton, Jaywick (Atlantic Books, London 2008) [B]

New Town Utopia, edited by Christopher Ian Smith (kick-starter campaign, 2018) [B]

Oil Paintings in Public Ownership in Essex, Sonia Roe, Editor, Julia Abel Smith, Essex Coordinator (Public Catalogue Foundation, London, 2006) [A]

Perry, Sarah, *The Essex Serpent* (Serpents Tail, London, 2016), a novel for those who can't quite face the full Mehalah on a kindle [B]

Phippen, Roy, *M25 Travelling Clockwise* (Pallas Athene, London 2005) [B]

Radical Essex, various contributors (Focal Point Gallery, Southend, Essex, 2018) [A/B]

Ransome, Arthur, *Secret Water* (1939), Swallows and Amazons go east (Penguin, London) [B]

Saunders, Hetty, *My House of Sky: the life and work of J. A. Baker,* introduction Robert Macfarlane (Little Toller Books, Toller Fratrum 2017) [B]

Scarfe, Norman, *The Shell Guide to Essex* (Faber, London 1968) the most seductive of the county guides available, particularly due to the photographs [A/B]

The Complete Works of J. A. Baker, introduction by Mark Cocker, ed. John Fanshawe (Collins, London, 2010) [A/B]

The Framley Examiner, 'assembled' by Robin Halstead, Jason Hazeley, Alex and Joel Morris (Penguin, London, 2002) [B]

Walker, Deanna, *Basildon Plotlands: the Londoners' Rural Retreat* (Phillimore, Chichester, 2001) [B]

Warner, Sylvia Townsend, *The True Heart* (Virago, London,

1978), one of her several novels set in Essex and the 'undiscoverable' marshes, which she'd begun exploring in 1922 [B]

Worpole, Ken and Orton, Jason (photographer), *350 miles, An Essex Journey* (ExDRA, Chelmsford, 2005) [B]

As above, *The New English Landscape* (Field Station, London, 2013) [B]

ACKNOWLEDGEMENTS

A book woven from so many threads, as this has been, leaves an author owing many debts. I hope that I have acknowledged the important ones, but apologise in advance should anyone have slipped my memory.

I start with my walking friends. As we have walked, we have talked and I have tried to listen hard, since between them they represent enormous reserves of wit and wisdom. A lot of this book emerged while tramping hedges or sea walls, following the old tracks or riversides. So, for that, my thanks to Ken Worpole and Jason Orton, to Alister Warman, Ailsa Wildig, Ralph Metson, Otto Saumarez-Smith, Domo Baal, Bill Knight and Stephanie Williams and, closer to home, to Michael and Susannah Horowitz. For two memorable estuarial boat trips, I owe thanks to Clare Bentley and John Coombe-Tennant and Liz and the late Bernard Towns. For invaluable, more sedentary conversations thanks to Christine Townley, Lord Petre, Julia Jones, Julia Abel-Smith and, indirectly at least, to James Bettley, whose 'Pevsner' of Essex was the topic of my essay-review in the *London Review of Books* that started all this off, ten years later. For offering close focus critical advice in the early stages of the book, special thanks to Elizabeth Seward, Caroline Boyd Harte, David McKie and Veronica Horwell and they all stayed supportive throughout. For willingly accepting a miscellany of Essex-themed blogs which helped nail down, or even spark off, some topics, thanks to Thomas Jones, editor of the *LRB* blog. For friendship and encouragement, Clare Pawley, Philippa Lewis, Andrew Saint. And then for all kinds of help, advertent and inadvertent as the case may be, Ben Cowell, Eva Salomon, Malcolm Noble, Hayley Dixon, John Grindrod, Hannah and Susan Sergeant, Maggie Goodall, Kathryn Ferry, Richard Max, Tim Burrows, Clarrie Wallis, Jean Seaton, Lynne Woolfson, Eddie Mirzoeff, Jason Hazeley, Margaret Willes, Travis Elborough and Charles Holland. I owe the magnificent cover design to James Nunn while publisher Ben Yarde-Buller is due my gratitude for his continuing faith in the project (albeit one that he originally suggested!) and my editor Matthew Baylis for his unfailing good humour, positive editorial input and all-round support over the months. Finally, I owe thanks and much gratitude to the exceptional Essex Record Office (past and present) the lecture programme organised by the Essex History Group, the Vestry House Museum, Walthamstow and countless local history groups across the county, many of whom boast their own, excellent websites. More latterly, the trying events of 2020 obliged many to holiday close to home, in the course of which helpful road tests of various aspects of Essex came my way, courtesy of Elena Henson and Nicholas Rutland, Diana Fortescue and Guy de Jonquieres.